52nd Annual Meeting of the Association for Computational Linguistics (ACL 2014)

Student Research Workshop

Baltimore, Maryland, USA
22 – 27 June 2014

ISBN: 978-1-63439-192-4

Printed from e-media with permission by:

Curran Associates, Inc.
57 Morehouse Lane
Red Hook, NY 12571

proceedings.com

Some format issues inherent in the e-media version may also appear in this print version.

Printed by Curran Associates, Inc. (2014)

Association for Computational Linguistics
209 N. Eighth Street
Stroudsburg, Pennsylvania 18360

Phone: 1-570-476-8006
Fax: 1-570-476-0860

acl@aclweb.org

Additional copies of this publication are available from:

Curran Associates, Inc.
57 Morehouse Lane
Red Hook, NY 12571 USA
Phone: 845-758-0400
Fax: 845-758-2634
Email: curran@proceedings.com
Web: www.proceedings.com

Introduction

Welcome to the ACL 2014 Student Research Workshop.

Following the previous years' ACL Student Research Workshops, this year we have two different kinds of papers: research papers and thesis proposals. Thesis proposals are intended for advanced students who have decided on a thesis topic and wish to get feedback on their proposal and broader ideas for their continuing work, while research papers can describe completed work or work in progress with preliminary results.

We received 7 thesis proposals and 19 research papers this year. Out of these, we accepted 5 thesis proposals and 8 research papers leading to an acceptance rate of 71% for thesis proposals and 42% for research papers. This year's workshop also offered pre-submission mentoring for student authors wishing to improve the presentation of their papers prior to submission of the paper for the reviewing process. 6 students participated in this pre-submission mentoring program this year.

The SRW offers multiple avenues for the student authors to receive feedback at the conference.

This year's workshop features three sessions of student paper presentations. All the papers will be presented at the main conference poster session, giving the opportunity for students to interact and present their work to a large and diverse audience. We also have a separate oral presentation session for thesis proposal papers on the first day of the main conference. The third session is another oral presentation venue where student authors of the research papers briefly advertise their posters. This year, 15 students whose papers were accepted to the ACL main conference were chosen to also present their work at and be partially funded by SRW. These students' posters are also advertised during the poster highlight session.

In addition to oral presentation and poster sessions, each SRW paper and the 15 papers sponsored by the SRW is assigned a dedicated mentor. The mentor is an experienced researcher from academia or industry who will prepare in-depth comments and questions in advance for the presentation or poster session and will provide feedback to the student author.

Thanks to our funding sources, this year's SRW covers registration expenses and provides travel and lodging support to all student authors of the SRW papers. We gratefully acknowledge the support from the NSF, Google, Yahoo! and Baidu. In addition to the SRW papers, the NSF supports travel and registration for another 15 student authors of ACL main conference papers.

We are very grateful to our program committee members who gave constructive and detailed reviews for each of the student papers. Some of our PC members also participated in the pre-submission mentoring program and immensely helped student authors with writing and presentation of their papers. We also thank researchers who agreed to mentor and provide expert feedback on the student papers. We thank our faculty advisers Bill Byrne and Jordan Boyd-Graber for their guidance. We also thank the ACL 2014 organizing committee – Daniel Marcu, Kristina Toutanova, Hua Wu, Alexander Koller, Miyao Yusuke, David Yarowsky and Priscilla Rassmussen for their constant support and suggestions. Finally, we thank all students for their submissions and participation in the SRW.

Organizers:

Ekaterina Kochmar, University of Cambridge (UK)
Annie Louis, University of Edinburgh (UK)
Svitlana Volkova, Johns Hopkins University (USA)

Faculty Advisors:

Jordan Boyd-Graber, University of Maryland (USA)
Bill Byrne, University of Cambridge (UK)

Program Committee:

Gabor Angeli, Stanford University (USA)
Yoav Artzi, University of Washington (USA)
Chris Biemann, TU Darmstadt (Germany)
Arianna Bisazza, University of Trento (Italy)
Ted Briscoe, University of Cambridge (UK)
Shu Cai, University of Southern California (USA)
Asli Ceyilkamaz, Microsoft Research (USA)
Ilia Chetviorkin, Lomonosov Moscow State University (Russia)
Monojit Choudhury, Microsoft Research (India)
Trevor Cohn, University of Sheffield (UK)
Hal Daumé III, University of Maryland (USA)
Leon Derczynski, University of Sheffield (UK)
Aciel Eshky, University of Edinburgh (UK)
Kilian Evang, University of Groningen (Netherlands)
Annemarie Friedrich, Saarland University (Germany)
Thomas François, Université catholique de Louvain (Belgium)
Michael Gamon, Microsoft Research (USA)
Juri Ganitkevitch, Johns Hopkins University (USA)
Qin Gao, Microsoft Research (USA)
Liane Guillou, University of Edinburgh (UK)
Eva Hasler, University of Edinburgh (UK)
John Henderson, The MITRE Corporation (USA)
Ruihong Huang, University of Utah (USA)
Amjad Abu Jbara, University of Michigan, Ann Arbor (USA)
Beata Klebanov-Biegman, Educational Testing Service (USA)
Varada Kolhatkar, University of Toronto (Canada)
Jonathan Kummerfeld, University of California, Berkeley (USA)
Angeliki Lazaridou, University of Trento (Italy)
Angeliki Metallinou, University of Southern California (USA)
Mitch Marcus, University of Pennsylvania (USA)
Thomas Meyer, Google (Switzerland)
Meg Mitchell, Microsoft Research (USA)
Alessandro Moschitti, University of Trento (Italy)

Courtney Napoles, Johns Hopkins University (USA)
Patrick Pantel, Microsoft Research (USA)
Rashmi Prasad, University of Wisconsin, Milwaukee (USA)
Owen Rambow, University of Columbia (USA)
Roi Reichart, Technion - Israel Institute of Technology (Israel)
Philip Resnik, University of Maryland (USA)
Kairit Sirts, Tallinn University of Technology (Estonia)
Joel Tetreault, Yahoo! Labs (USA)
Ivan Titov, University of Amsterdam (Netherlands)
Eva Maria Vecchi, University of Cambridge (UK)
Stephan Vogel, Carnegie Mellon University (USA)
Jason Williams, Microsoft Research (USA)
Travis Wolfe, Johns Hopkins University (USA)
Bishan Yang, Cornell University (USA)
Xuchen Yao, Johns Hopkins University (USA)
Torsten Zesch, University of Duisburg, Essen (Germany)

Table of Contents

Bayesian Kernel Methods for Natural Language Processing
Daniel Beck 1

Extracting Temporal and Causal Relations between Events
Paramita Mirza 10

Towards a discourse relation-aware approach for Chinese-English machine translation
Frances Yung 18

Analyzing Positions and Topics in Political Discussions of the German Bundestag
Cäcilia Zirn 26

A Mapping-Based Approach for General Formal Human Computer Interaction Using Natural Language
Vincent Letard, Sophie Rosset and Gabriel Illouz 34

An Exploration of Embeddings for Generalized Phrases
Wenpeng Yin and Hinrich Schütze 41

Learning Grammar with Explicit Annotations for Subordinating Conjunctions
Dongchen Li, Xiantao Zhang and Xihong Wu 48

Going beyond sentences when applying tree kernels
Dmitry Ilvovsky 56

Multi-document summarization using distortion-rate ratio
Ulukbek Attokurov and Ulug Bayazit 64

Disambiguating prepositional phrase attachment sites with sense information captured in contextualized distributional data
Clayton Greenberg 71

Open Information Extraction for Spanish Language based on Syntactic Constraints
Alisa Zhila and Alexander Gelbukh 78

Improving Text Normalization via Unsupervised Model and Discriminative Reranking
Chen Li and Yang Liu 86

Semi-Automatic Development of KurdNet, The Kurdish WordNet
Purya Aliabadi 94

Conference Program

Monday, June 23, 2014

SRW Thesis Proposal Presentations

13:20–13:45 *Bayesian Kernel Methods for Natural Language Processing*
Daniel Beck

13:45–14:10 *Extracting Temporal and Causal Relations between Events*
Paramita Mirza

14:10–14:35 *Towards a discourse relation-aware approach for Chinese-English machine translation*
Frances Yung

14:35–15:00 *Analyzing Positions and Topics in Political Discussions of the German Bundestag*
Cäcilia Zirn

Poster Highlights

18:05–18:50 SRW Research Papers

A Mapping-Based Approach for General Formal Human Computer Interaction Using Natural Language
Vincent Letard, Sophie Rosset and Gabriel Illouz

An Exploration of Embeddings for Generalized Phrases
Wenpeng Yin and Hinrich Schütze

Learning Grammar with Explicit Annotations for Subordinating Conjunctions
Dongchen Li, Xiantao Zhang and Xihong Wu

Going beyond sentences when applying tree kernels
Dmitry Ilvovsky

Multi-document summarization using distortion-rate ratio
Ulukbek Attokurov and Ulug Bayazit

Disambiguating prepositional phrase attachment sites with sense information captured in contextualized distributional data
Clayton Greenberg

Open Information Extraction for Spanish Language based on Syntactic Constraints
Alisa Zhila and Alexander Gelbukh

Improving Text Normalization via Unsupervised Model and Discriminative Reranking
Chen Li and Yang Liu

Poster Highlights

18:05–18:50 Main Conference Papers Sponsored by SRW

Poster Session

18:50–21:30 SRW Thesis Proposal and Research Papers

Poster Session

18:50–21:30 Main Conference Papers Sponsored by SRW

Bayesian Kernel Methods for Natural Language Processing

Daniel Beck
Department of Computer Science
University of Sheffield
Sheffield, United Kingdom
debeck1@sheffield.ac.uk

Abstract

Kernel methods are heavily used in Natural Language Processing (NLP). Frequentist approaches like Support Vector Machines are the state-of-the-art in many tasks. However, these approaches lack efficient procedures for model selection, which hinders the usage of more advanced kernels. In this work, we propose the use of a Bayesian approach for kernel methods, Gaussian Processes, which allow easy model fitting even for complex kernel combinations. Our goal is to employ this approach to improve results in a number of regression and classification tasks in NLP.

1 Introduction

In the last years, kernel methods have been successfully employed in many Natural Language Processing tasks. These methods allow the building of non-parametric models which make less assumptions about the underlying pattern in the data. Another advantage of kernels is that they can be defined in arbitrary structures like strings or trees, which greatly reduce the need for careful feature engineering in these structures.

The properties cited above make kernel methods ideal for problems where we do not have much prior knowledge about how the data behaves. This is a common setting in NLP, where they have been mostly applied in the form of Support Vector Machines (SVMs). Systems based on SVMs have been the state-of-the-art in classification tasks like Text Categorization (Lodhi et al., 2002), Sentiment Analysis (Johansson and Moschitti, 2013; Pérez-Rosas and Mihalcea, 2013) and Question Classification (Moschitti, 2006; Croce et al., 2011). Recently, they were also employed in regression settings like Machine Translation Quality Estimation (Specia and Farzindar, 2010; Bojar et al., 2013) and structured prediction (Chang et al., 2013).

SVMs are a frequentist method: they aim to find an approximation to the exact latent function that explains the data. This is in contrast to Bayesian settings, which define a prior distribution on this function and perform inference by marginalizing over all its possible values. Although there is some discussion about which approach is better (Murphy, 2012, Sec. 6.6.4), Bayesian methods offer many useful theoretical properties. In fact, they have been used before in NLP, especially in grammar induction (Cohn et al., 2010) and word segmentation (Goldwater et al., 2009). However, only very recently kernel methods have been applied in NLP using the Bayesian approach.

Gaussian Processes (GPs) are the Bayesian counterpart of kernel methods and are widely considered the state-of-the-art for inference on functions (Hensman et al., 2013). They have a number of advantages which are very useful in NLP:

- Kernels in general can be combined and parameterized in many ways. This parameterization lead to the problem of model selection, which is difficult in frequentist approaches (mainly based on cross validation). The Bayesian formulation of GPs let them deal with model selection in a much more more efficient and elegant way: by maximizing the likelihood on the training data. This opens the door for the use of heavily parameterized kernel combinations, like multi-task kernels for example.

- Being a probabilistic framework, they are able to naturally encode uncertainty in the predictions, which can be propagated if the task is part of a larger system pipeline.

Besides these properties, GPs have also been applied sucessfully in many Machine Learning

Proceedings of the ACL 2014 Student Research Workshop, pages 1–9,
Baltimore, Maryland USA, June 22-27 2014.

tasks. Examples include Robotics (Ko et al., 2007), Bioinformatics (Chu et al., 2005; Polajnar et al., 2011), Geolocation (Schwaighofer et al., 2004) and Computer Vision (Sinz et al., 2004; Riihimäki et al., 2013). In NLP, GPs have been used only very recently and focused on regression tasks (Cohn and Specia, 2013; Preotiuc-Pietro and Cohn, 2013). In this work, we propose to combine GPs with recent kernel developments to advance the state-of-the-art in a number of NLP tasks.

2 Gaussian Processes

In this Section, we follow closely the definition of Rasmussen and Williams (2006). Consider a machine learning setting, where we have a dataset $\mathcal{X} = \{(\mathbf{x}_1, y_1), (\mathbf{x}_2, y_2), \ldots, (\mathbf{x}_n, y_n)\}$ and our goal is to infer the underlying function $f(\mathbf{x})$ that best explains the data. A GP model assumes a prior stochastic process over this function:

$$f(\mathbf{x}) \sim \mathcal{GP}(\mu(\mathbf{x}), k(\mathbf{x}, \mathbf{x}')), \tag{1}$$

where $\mu(\mathbf{x})$ is the *mean* function, which is usually the $\mathbf{0}$ constant, and $k(\mathbf{x}, \mathbf{x}')$ is the kernel or *covariance* function. In this sense, they are analogous to Gaussian distributions, which are also defined in terms of a mean and a variance values, or in the case of multivariate Gaussians, a mean vector and a covariance matrix. In fact, a GP can be interpreted as an infinite-dimensional multivariate Gaussian distribution.

The full model uses Bayes' rule to define a posterior over f, combining the GP prior with the data likelihood:

$$p(f|\mathbf{X}, \mathbf{y}) = \frac{p(\mathbf{y}|\mathbf{X}, f)p(f)}{p(\mathbf{y}|\mathbf{X})}, \tag{2}$$

where $\mathbf{X}$ and $\mathbf{y}$ are the training inputs and outputs, respectively. The posterior is then used to predict the label for an unseen input $\mathbf{x}_*$ by marginalizing over all possible latent functions:

$$p(y_*|\mathbf{x}_*, \mathbf{X}, \mathbf{y}) = \int_f p(y_*|\mathbf{x}_*, \mathbf{X}, f)p(f|\mathbf{X}, \mathbf{y})df. \tag{3}$$

where y_* is the predicted output. The choice of the likelihood distribution depends if the task is regression, classification or other prediction setting.

2.1 GP Regression

In a regression setting, we assume that the output values are equal to noisy latent function evaluations, i.e., $y_i = f(\mathbf{x_i}) + \eta$, where $\eta \sim \mathcal{N}(0, \sigma_n^2)$ is the added white noise. We also usually assume a Gaussian likelihood, because this able us to solve the integral in Equation 3 analytically. Substituting the likelihood and the prior in both Equations 2 and 3 and manipulating the result, we compute the posterior also as a Gaussian distribution:

$$y_* \sim \mathcal{N}(\mathbf{k}_*(\mathbf{K} + \sigma_n\mathbf{I})^{-1}\mathbf{y}^T, \\ k(\mathbf{x}_*, \mathbf{x}_*) - \mathbf{k}_*^T(\mathbf{K} + \sigma_n\mathbf{I})^{-1}\mathbf{k}_*). \tag{4}$$

where $\mathbf{K}$ is the Gram matrix corresponding to the training inputs and $\mathbf{k}_* = [\langle\mathbf{x}_1, \mathbf{x}_*\rangle, \langle\mathbf{x}_2, \mathbf{x}_*\rangle, \ldots, \langle\mathbf{x}_n, \mathbf{x}_*\rangle]$ is the vector of kernel evaluations between the test input and each training input.

2.2 GP Classification

Consider binary classification using -1 and $+1$ as labels[1]. The model in this case use the actual, noiseless latent function evaluations $\mathbf{f}$ and "squash" them through the $[-1, +1]$ interval to obtain the outputs. The posterior over the outputs is then defined as:

$$p(y_* = +1|\mathbf{x}_*, \mathbf{X}, \mathbf{y}) = \\ \int_{f_*} \sigma(f_*)p(f_*|\mathbf{x}_*, \mathbf{X}, \mathbf{y})df_*, \tag{5}$$

where $\sigma(f_*)$ is a squashing function. Two common choices are the logistic function and the probit function. The distribution over the latent values f_* is obtained by integrating out the latent function:

$$p(f_*|\mathbf{x}_*, \mathbf{X}, \mathbf{y}) = \int_f p(f_*|\mathbf{x}_*, \mathbf{X}, f)p(f|\mathbf{X}, \mathbf{y})df. \tag{6}$$

Because the likelihood is not Gaussian, the resulting posterior integral is not analytically available anymore. The most common solution to this problem is to approximate the posterior $p(f|\mathbf{X}, \mathbf{y})$ with a Gaussian $q(f|\mathbf{X}, \mathbf{y})$. Two such approximation algorithms are the Laplace approximation (Williams and Barber, 1998) and the Expectation Propagation (Minka, 2001). Another option is to use Markov Chain Monte Carlo sampling methods on the true posterior (Neal, 1998).

2.3 Hyperparameter Optimization

The GP prior used in the models described above usually have a number of hyperparameters. The

[1] Extensions to multi-class settings are possible.

most important ones are the kernel ones but they can also include others like the white noise variance σ_n^2 used in regression. A key property of GPs is their ability to easily fit these hyperparameters to the data by maximizing the marginal likelihood:

$$p(\mathbf{y}|\mathbf{X}, \boldsymbol{\theta}) = \int_f p(\mathbf{y}|\mathbf{X}, \boldsymbol{\theta}, f)p(f), \tag{7}$$

where $\boldsymbol{\theta}$ represents the full set of hyperparameters (which was suppressed from all conditionals until now for brevity). Optimization involves deriving the gradients of the marginal log likelihood w.r.t. the hyperparameters and then employ a gradient ascent procedure. Gradients can be found analitically for regression and by approximations for classification, using methods similar to the ones used for prediction.

2.4 Sparse Approximations for GPs

SVMs are naturally sparse models which use only a subset of data points to make predictions. This results in important speed-ups which is one of the reasons for their success. On the other hand, canonical GPs are not sparse, making use of all data points. This results in a training complexity of $O(n^3)$ (due to the Gram matrix inversion) and $O(n)$ for predictions.

Sparse GPs tackle this problem by approximating the Gram matrix using only a subset of m *inducing inputs*. Without loss of generalization, consider these m inputs as the first ones in the training data and $(n - m)$ the remaining ones. Then we can partition the Gram matrix in the following way (Rasmussen and Williams, 2006, Sec. 8.1):

$$\mathbf{K} = \begin{bmatrix} \mathbf{K}_{mm} & \mathbf{K}_{m(n-m)} \\ \mathbf{K}_{(n-m)m} & \mathbf{K}_{(n-m)(n-m)} \end{bmatrix},$$

where each block corresponds to a matrix of kernel evaluations between two sets of inputs. For brevity, we will refer $\mathbf{K}_{m(n-m)}$ as $\mathbf{K}_{mn}$ and its transpose as $\mathbf{K}_{nm}$. The block structure of $\mathbf{K}$ forms the base of the so-called Nyström approximation:

$$\tilde{\mathbf{K}} = \mathbf{K}_{nm}\mathbf{K}_{mm}^{-1}\mathbf{K}_{mn}, \tag{8}$$

which result in the following predictive posterior:

$$\begin{aligned} y_* \sim \mathcal{N}(&\mathbf{k}_{m*}^T\tilde{\mathbf{G}}^{-1}\mathbf{K}_{mn}\mathbf{y}, \\ &k(\mathbf{x}_*, \mathbf{x}_*) - \mathbf{k}_{m*}^T\mathbf{K}_{mm}^{-1}\mathbf{k}_{m*} + \\ &\sigma_n^2\mathbf{k}_{m*}^T\tilde{\mathbf{G}}^{-1}\mathbf{k}_{m*}), \end{aligned} \tag{9}$$

where $\tilde{\mathbf{G}} = \sigma_n^2\mathbf{K}_{mm} + \mathbf{K}_{mn}\mathbf{K}_{nm}$ and $\mathbf{k}_{m*}$ is the vector of kernel evaluations between test input $\mathbf{x}_*$ and the m inducing inputs. The resulting complexities for training and prediction are $O(m^2n)$ and $O(m)$, respectively.

The remaining question is how to choose the inducing inputs. Seeger et al. (2003) use an iterative method that starts with some random data points and adds new ones based on a greedy procedure, in an active learning fashion. Snelson and Ghahramani (2006) use a different approach: it defines a fixed m a priori and use *pseudo-inputs* which can be optimized as regular hyperparameters. Later, Titsias (2009) also used pseudo-inputs but perform optimization using a variational method instead. Recently, Hensman et al. (2013) modified this method to allow Stochastic Variational Inference (Hoffman et al., 2013), which reduces the training complexity to $O(m^3)$.

3 Kernels

The core of a GP model is the kernel function. A kernel $k(\mathbf{x}, \mathbf{x}')$ is a symmetric and positive semi-definite function which returns a similarity score between two inputs in some feature space (Shawe-Taylor and Cristianini, 2004). Probably the most used kernel in general is the Radial Basis Function (RBF) kernel, which is defined over two real-valued vectors. Our focus in this work is on two different types of kernels which can be applied for NLP settings and allow richer parameterizations.

3.1 Kernels for Discrete Structures

In NLP, discrete structures like strings or trees are common in training data. To apply a vectorial kernel like the RBF, one can always extract real-valued features from these structures. However, kernels can be defined directly on these structures, potentially reducing the need for feature engineering. The string and tree kernels we define here are based on the theory of Convolution kernels of Haussler (1999), which calculate the similarity between two structures based on the number of substructures they have in common. Other approaches include random walk kernels (Gärtner et al., 2003; Vishwanathan et al., 2010) and Fisher kernels (Jaakkola et al., 2000).

3.1.1 String Kernels

Consider a function $\phi_s(\mathbf{x})$ that counts the number of times a substring s appears in $\mathbf{x}$. A string kernel is defined as:

$$k(x, x') = \sum_{s \in \Sigma^*} w_s \phi_s(x) \phi_s(x'), \quad (10)$$

where w_s is a non-negative weight for substring s and Σ^* is the set of all possible strings over the symbol alphabet Σ.

Usually in NLP, each word is considered a symbol, although some previous work also considered characters as symbols (Lodhi et al., 2002). If we restrict s to be only single words we end up having a *bag-of-words* (BOW) representation. Allowing longer substrings lead us to the Word Sequence Kernels of Cancedda et al. (2003), which also allow gaps between words.

One extension of these kernels is to allow soft matching between substrings. This is done by defining a similarity matrix $\mathbf{S}$, which encode symbol similarities. This matrix can be defined by external resources, like WordNet, or be inferred from data using Latent Semantic Analysis (Deerwester et al., 1990) for example.

3.1.2 Tree Kernels

Collins and Duffy (2001) first introduced Tree Kernels, which measure the similarity between two trees by counting the number of fragments they share, in a very similar way to string kernels. Consider two trees T_1 and T_2. We define the set of nodes in these two trees as N_1 and N_2 respectively. Consider also $\mathcal{F}$ the full set of possible tree fragments (similar to Σ^* in the case of strings). We define $I_i(n)$ as an indicator function that returns 1 if fragment $f_i \in \mathcal{F}$ has root n and 0 otherwise. A Tree Kernel can then be defined as:

$$k(T_1, T_2) = \sum_{n_1 \in N_1} \sum_{n_2 \in N_2} \Delta(n_1, n_2),$$

where:

$$\Delta(n_1, n_2) = \sum_{i=1}^{|\mathcal{F}|} \lambda^{\text{size}(i)} I_i(n_1) I_i(n_2).$$

Here, $0 < \lambda < 1$ is a decay factor that penalizes contributions from larger fragments cf. smaller ones.

Again, we can put restrictions on the type of tree fragment considered for comparison. Collins and Duffy (2001) defined Subtree kernels, which considered only subtrees as fragments, and Subset Tree Kernels (SSTK), where fragments can have non-terminals as leaves. Later, Moschitti (2006) introduced the Partial Tree Kernels (PTK), by allowing fragments with partial rule expansions.

Tree kernels were used in a variety of tasks, including Relation Extraction (Bloehdorn and Moschitti, 2007; Plank and Moschitti, 2013), Question Classification (Moschitti, 2006; Croce et al., 2011) and Quality Estimation (Hardmeier, 2011; Hardmeier et al., 2012). Furthermore, soft matching approaches were also used by Bloehdorn and Moschitti (2007) and Croce et al. (2011).

3.2 Multi-task Kernels

Kernels can also be extended to deal with settings where we want to predict a vector of values (Álvarez et al., 2012). These settings are useful in multi-task and domain adaptation problems. Kernels for vector-valued functions are known as *coregionalization* kernels in the literature. Here we are going to refer them as multi-task kernels.

One of the simplest ways to define a kernel for a multi-task setting is the Intrinsic Coregionalization Model (ICM):

$$\mathbf{K}(\mathbf{x}, \mathbf{x}') = \mathbf{B} \otimes k(\mathbf{x}, \mathbf{x}').$$

where $\otimes$ denotes the Kronecker product and $\mathbf{B}$ is the coregionalization matrix, encoding task covariances. We also denote the resulting kernel function as $\mathbf{K}(\mathbf{x}, \mathbf{x}')$ to stress out that its result is now a matrix instead of a scalar.

Cohn and Specia (2013) used the ICM to model annotator bias in Quality Estimation datasets. They parameterize $\mathbf{B}$ in a number of different ways and get significant improvements over single-task baselines, especially in post-editing time prediction. They also point out that the well known EasyAdapt method (Daumé III, 2007) for domain adaptation can be modeled by the ICM using $\mathbf{B} = \mathbf{1} + \mathbf{I}$, i.e., a coregionalization matrix with its diagonal elements equal to 2 and remaining elements equal to 1.

An extension of the ICM is the Linear Model of Coregionalization (LMC), which assume a sum of kernels with different coregionalization matrices:

$$\mathbf{K}(\mathbf{x}, \mathbf{x}') = \sum_{k_p \in P} \mathbf{B}_p \otimes k_p(\mathbf{x}, \mathbf{x}').$$

where P is the set of different kernels employed. Álvarez et al. (2012) argue that the LMC is much more flexible than the ICM because the latter assumes that each kernel contributes equally to the task covariances.

4 Planned Work

Our goal in this proposal is to employ GPs and the kernels introduced in Section 3 to advance the state-of-the-art in regression and classification NLP tasks. It would be unfeasible though, at least for a single thesis, to address all possible tasks so we are going to focus on three of them where kernel methods were already successfully applied.

4.1 Quality Estimation

The purpose of Machine Translation Quality Estimation is to provide a quality prediction for new, unseen machine translated texts, without relying on reference translations (Blatz et al., 2004; Bojar et al., 2013). A common use of quality predictions is the decision between post-editing a given machine translated sentence and translating its source from scratch.

GP regression models were recently successfully employed for post-editing time (Cohn and Specia, 2013) and HTER[2] prediction (Beck et al., 2013). Both used RBF kernels as the covariance function so a natural extension is to apply the structured kernels of Section 3.1. This was already been done with tree kernels by Hardmeier (2011) in the context of SVMs.

Multi-task kernels can also be applied for Quality Estimation in several ways. The model used by Cohn and Specia (2013) for modelling annotator bias can be further extended for settings with dozens or even hundreds of annotators. This is a common setting in crowdsourcing platforms like Amazon's Mechanical Turk[3].

Another plan is to use multi-task kernels to combine different datasets. Quality annotation is usually expensive, requiring post-editing or subjective scoring. Possibilities include combining datasets from different language pairs or different machine translation systems. Available datasets include those used in the WMT12 and WMT13 QE shared tasks (Callison-burch et al., 2012; Bojar et al., 2013) and others (Specia et al., 2009; Specia, 2011; Koponen et al., 2012).

4.2 Question Classification

A Question Classifier is a module that aims to restrict the answer hypotheses generated by a Question Answering system by applying a label to the input question (Li and Roth, 2002; Li and Roth, 2005). This task can be seen as an instance of text classification, where the inputs are usually composed of only one sentence.

Much of previous work in Question Classification largely used SVMs combined with structured kernels. Zhang and Lee (2003) compares String Kernels based on BOW and n-gram representations with the Subset Tree Kernel on constituent trees. Moschitti (2006) show improved results by using the Partial Tree Kernel and dependency trees instead of constituency ones. Bloehdorn and Moschitti (2007) combines a SSTK with different soft matching approaches to encode lexical similarity on tree leaves. The same soft matching idea is used by Croce et al. (2011), but applied to PTKs instead and permitting soft matches between any nodes in each tree (which is sensible when using kernels on dependency trees).

Our work proposes to address this task by employing tree kernels and GPs. Unlike Quality Estimation, this is a classification setting and our purpose is to find if this combination can also improve the state-of-the-art for tasks of this kind. We will use the TREC dataset provided by Li and Roth (2002), which assigns 6000 questions with both a coarse and a fine-grained label.

4.3 Multi-domain Sentiment Analysis

Sentiment Analysis is defined as "the computational treatment of opinion, sentiment and subjectivity in text" (Pang and Lee, 2008). In this proposal, we focus on the specific task of *polarity detection*, where the goal is to label a text as having positive or negative sentiment. State-of-the-art methods for this task use SVMs as the learning algorithm and vary between the feature sets used.

Polarity predictions can be heavily biased on the text domain. Consider the example showed by Turney (2002): the word "unpredictable" usually has a positive meaning in a movie review but a negative one when applied to an automotive review (in a phrase like "unpredictable steering", for instance). One of the first methods to tackle this issue is the Structural Correspondence Learning of Blitzer et al. (2007). Their method uses *pivot* words shared between domains to find correspondencies in words that are not shared.

A previous work that used structured kernels in Sentiment Analysis is the approach of Wu et al. (2009). Their method uses tree kernels on phrase dependency trees and outperforms bag-of-words

[2] Human Translation Error Rate (Snover et al., 2006).

[3] www.mturk.com

and word dependency approaches. They also show good results in cross-domain experiments.

We propose to apply GPs with a combination of structured and multi-task kernels for this task. The results showed by Wu et al. (2009) suggest that tree kernels on dependency trees are a good approach but we also plan to employ string kernels on this task. This is because string kernels have demonstrated promising results for text categorization in past work. Also, considering model selection is easily dealt by GPs, we can combine all those kernels in complex and heavily parameterized ways, an unfeasible setting for SVMs. We will use the Multi-Domain Sentiment Dataset (Blitzer et al., 2007), composed of Amazon product reviews in different categories.

4.4 Research Directions

In Section 2.3 we saw how the Bayesian formulation of GPs let us do model selection by maximizing the marginal likelihood. In fact, one of our main research directions in this proposal revolves around this crucial point: because we can easily fit hyperparameters to the data we have much more freedom to use richer kernel parameterizations and kernel combinations. Multi-task kernels are one example where we usually have a large number of hyperparameters because we need to fit all the elements of the coregionalization matrix. This number can get even larger if we have a LMC model, with multiple coregionalization matrices. Structured kernels can also be redefined in a richer way: tree kernels between constituency trees could have multiple decay hyperparameters, one for each POS tag. A more extreme example would be to treat all weights in a string kernel as hyperparameters. Thus, we plan to investigate these possibilities in the context of the three tasks detailed before.

As another research direction we also want to address the issue of scalability. Although GPs already showed promising results they can be slow when compared to other well established methods like SVM. Fortunately there has been a lot of advancements in the field of sparse GPs in the last years and we plan to employ them in our work. A key question is how to combine sparse GPs with the structured kernels we presented before. Although it is perfectly possible to select inducing points using greedy methods, it would be much more interesting to use the pseudo-inputs approach. However, it is not clear how to do that in conjunction with non-vectorial inputs, like the ones we plan to use in structured kernels, and this is a key direction that we also plan to investigate.

4.5 GP Toolkits

Available toolkits for GP modelling include GPML[4] (Rasmussen and Williams, 2006) and GPstuff[5] (Vanhatalo et al., 2013), which are written in Matlab. Our experiments will mainly use GPy[6], an open source toolkit written in Python. It implements models for regression and binary classification, including sparse approximations and many vectorial kernels. We plan to contribute to GPy by implementing the structured kernels of Section 3.1, effectively extending it to a GP framework for NLP.

5 Conclusions and Future Work

In this work we showed a proposal for advancing the state-of-the-art in a number of NLP tasks by combining Gaussian Process with structured and multi-task kernels. Our hypothesis is that highly parameterized kernel combinations allied with the fitting methods provided by GPs will result in better models for these tasks. We also detailed the future plans for experiments, including available datasets and toolkits.

Further research directions that can be explored by this proposal include the use of GPs in different learning settings. Models for ordinal regression (Chu and Ghahramani, 2005) and structured prediction (Altun et al., 2004; Bratières et al., 2013) were already proposed in the GP literature and a natural extension is to apply these models for their corresponding NLP tasks. Another extension is to employ other kinds of kernels. The literature on that subject is quite vast, with many approaches showing promising results.

Acknowledgements

This work was supported by funding from CNPq/Brazil (No. 237999/2012-9) and from the EU FP7-ICT QTLaunchPad project (No. 296347). The author would also like to thank Yahoo for the financial support and the anonymous reviewers for their excellent comments.

[4] www.gaussianprocess.org/gpml/code/matlab

[5] becs.aalto.fi/en/research/bayes/gpstuff

[6] github.com/SheffieldML/GPy

References

Yasemin Altun, Thomas Hofmann, and Alexander J. Smola. 2004. Gaussian Process Classification for Segmenting and Annotating Sequences. In *Proceedings of ICML*, page 8, New York, New York, USA. ACM Press.

Mauricio A. Álvarez, Lorenzo Rosasco, and Neil D. Lawrence. 2012. Kernels for Vector-Valued Functions: a Review. *Foundations and Trends in Machine Learning*, pages 1–37.

Daniel Beck, Kashif Shah, Trevor Cohn, and Lucia Specia. 2013. SHEF-Lite : When Less is More for Translation Quality Estimation. In *Proceedings of WMT13*, pages 337–342.

John Blatz, Erin Fitzgerald, and George Foster. 2004. Confidence estimation for machine translation. In *Proceedings of the 20th Conference on Computational Linguistics*, pages 315–321.

John Blitzer, Mark Dredze, and Fernando Pereira. 2007. Biographies, Bollywood, Boom-boxes and Blenders: Domain Adaptation for Sentiment Classification. In *Proceedings of ACL*.

Stephan Bloehdorn and Alessandro Moschitti. 2007. Exploiting Structure and Semantics for Expressive Text Kernels. In *Proceedings of CIKM*.

Ondřej Bojar, Christian Buck, Chris Callison-Burch, Christian Federmann, Barry Haddow, Philipp Koehn, Christof Monz, Matt Post, Radu Soricut, and Lucia Specia. 2013. Findings of the 2013 Workshop on Statistical Machine Translation. In *Proceedings of WMT13*, pages 1–44.

Sébastien Bratières, Novi Quadrianto, and Zoubin Ghahramani. 2013. Bayesian Structured Prediction using Gaussian Processes. *arXiv:1307.3846*, pages 1–17.

Chris Callison-burch, Philipp Koehn, Christof Monz, Matt Post, Radu Soricut, and Lucia Specia. 2012. Findings of the 2012 Workshop on Statistical Machine Translation. In *Proceedings of 7th Workshop on Statistical Machine Translation*.

Nicola Cancedda, Eric Gaussier, Cyril Goutte, and Jean-Michel Renders. 2003. Word-Sequence Kernels. *The Journal of Machine Learning Research*, 3:1059–1082.

Kai-Wei Chang, Vivek Srikumar, and Dan Roth. 2013. Multi-core Structural SVM Training. In *Proceedings of ECML-PHDD*.

Wei Chu and Zoubin Ghahramani. 2005. Gaussian Processes for Ordinal Regression. *Journal of Machine Learning Research*, 6:1019–1041.

Wei Chu, Zoubin Ghahramani, Francesco Falciani, and David L Wild. 2005. Biomarker discovery in microarray gene expression data with Gaussian processes. *Bioinformatics*, 21(16):3385–93, August.

Trevor Cohn and Lucia Specia. 2013. Modelling Annotator Bias with Multi-task Gaussian Processes: An Application to Machine Translation Quality Estimation. In *Proceedings of ACL*.

Trevor Cohn, Phil Blunsom, and Sharon Goldwater. 2010. Inducing tree-substitution grammars. *The Journal of Machine Learning*, 11:3053–3096.

Michael Collins and Nigel Duffy. 2001. Convolution Kernels for Natural Language. In *Advances in Neural Information Processing Systems*.

Danilo Croce, Alessandro Moschitti, and Roberto Basili. 2011. Structured Lexical Similarity via Convolution Kernels on Dependency Trees. In *Proc. of EMNLP*.

Hal Daumé III. 2007. Frustratingly easy domain adaptation. In *Proceedings of ACL*.

Scott Deerwester, Susan T. Dumais, George W. Furnas, Thomas K. Landauer, and Richard Harshman. 1990. Indexing by Latent Semantic Analysis. *Journal of the American Society For Information Science*, 41.

Thomas Gärtner, Peter Flach, and Stefan Wrobel. 2003. On Graph Kernels: Hardness Results and Efficient Alternatives. *LNAI*, 2777:129–143.

Sharon Goldwater, Thomas L. Griffiths, and Mark Johnson. 2009. A Bayesian framework for word segmentation: Exploring the effects of context. *Cognition*, 112(1):21–54, July.

Christian Hardmeier, Joakim Nivre, and Jörg Tiedemann. 2012. Tree Kernels for Machine Translation Quality Estimation. In *Proceedings of WMT12*, number 2011, pages 109–113.

Christian Hardmeier. 2011. Improving Machine Translation Quality Prediction with Syntactic Tree Kernels. In *Proceedings of EAMT*, number May.

David Haussler. 1999. Convolution Kernels on Discrete Structures. Technical report.

James Hensman, Nicolò Fusi, and Neil D. Lawrence. 2013. Gaussian Processes for Big Data. In *Proceedings of UAI*.

Matt Hoffman, David M. Blei, Chong Wang, and John Paisley. 2013. Stochastic Variational Inference. *The Journal of Machine Learning Research*.

Tommi Jaakkola, Mark Diekhans, and David Haussler. 2000. A discriminative framework for detecting remote protein homologies. *Journal of Computational Biology*, 7:95–114.

Richard Johansson and Alessandro Moschitti. 2013. Relational Features in Fine-Grained Opinion Analysis. *Computational Linguistics*, 39(3):473–509.

Jonathan Ko, Daniel J. Klein, Dieter Fox, and Dirk Haehnel. 2007. Gaussian Processes and Reinforcement Learning for Identification and Control of an Autonomous Blimp. In *Proceedings of IEEE International Conference on Robotics and Automation*, pages 742–747. Ieee, April.

Maarit Koponen, Wilker Aziz, Luciana Ramos, and Lucia Specia. 2012. Post-editing time as a measure of cognitive effort. In *Proceedings of WPTP*.

Xin Li and Dan Roth. 2002. Learning question classifiers. In *Proceedings of COLING*, volume 1, pages 1–7.

Xin Li and Dan Roth. 2005. Learning Question Classifiers: the Role of Semantic Information. *Natural Language Engineering*, 1(1).

Huma Lodhi, Craig Saunders, John Shawe-Taylor, Nello Cristianini, and Chris Watkins. 2002. Text Classification using String Kernels. *The Journal of Machine Learning Research*, 2:419–444.

Thomas P. Minka. 2001. *A family of algorithms for approximate Bayesian inference*. Ph.D. thesis.

Alessandro Moschitti. 2006. Efficient Convolution Kernels for Dependency and Constituent Syntactic Trees. In *Proceedings of ECML*.

Kevin P. Murphy. 2012. *Machine Learning: a Probabilistic Perspective*.

Radford M. Neal. 1998. Regression and Classification Using Gaussian Process Priors. *Bayesian Statistics*, 6.

Bo Pang and Lillian Lee. 2008. Opinion Mining and Sentiment Analysis. *Foundations and Trends in Information Retrieval*, 2(1–2):1–135.

Verónica Pérez-Rosas and Rada Mihalcea. 2013. Sentiment Analysis of Online Spoken Reviews. In *Proceedings of Interspeech*.

Barbara Plank and Alessandro Moschitti. 2013. Embedding Semantic Similarity in Tree Kernels for Domain Adaptation of Relation Extraction. In *Proceedings of ACL*, pages 1498–1507.

Tamara Polajnar, Simon Rogers, and Mark Girolami. 2011. Protein interaction detection in sentences via Gaussian Processes: a preliminary evaluation. *International Journal of Data Mining and Bioinformatics*, 5(1):52–72, January.

Daniel Preotiuc-Pietro and Trevor Cohn. 2013. A temporal model of text periodicities using Gaussian Processes. In *Proceedings of EMNLP*.

Carl Edward Rasmussen and Christopher K. I. Williams. 2006. *Gaussian processes for machine learning*, volume 1. MIT Press Cambridge.

Jaakko Riihimäki, Pasi Jylänki, and Aki Vehtari. 2013. Nested Expectation Propagation for Gaussian Process Classification with a Multinomial Probit Likelihood. *Journal of Machine Learning Research*, 14:75–109.

Anton Schwaighofer, Marian Grigoras, Volker Tresp, and Clemens Hoffmann. 2004. GPPS: A Gaussian Process Positioning System for Cellular Networks. In *Proceedings of NIPS*.

Matthias Seeger, Christopher K. I. Williams, and Neil D. Lawrence. 2003. Fast Forward Selection to Speed Up Sparse Gaussian Process Regression. In *Proceedings of AISTATS*.

John Shawe-Taylor and Nello Cristianini. 2004. *Kernel methods for pattern analysis*. Cambridge.

Fabian H. Sinz, Joaquin Quiñonero Candela, Gökhan H. Bakır, Carl E. Rasmussen, and Matthias O. Franz. 2004. Learning Depth from Stereo. *Pattern Recognition*, pages 1–8.

Edward Snelson and Zoubin Ghahramani. 2006. Sparse Gaussian Processes using Pseudo-inputs. In *Proceedings of NIPS*.

Matthew Snover, Bonnie Dorr, Richard Schwartz, Linnea Micciulla, and John Makhoul. 2006. A study of translation edit rate with targeted human annotation. In *Proceedings of AMTA*.

Lucia Specia and Atefeh Farzindar. 2010. Estimating machine translation post-editing effort with HTER. In *Proceedings of AMTA Workshop Bringing MT to the User: MT Research and the Translation Industry*.

Lucia Specia, Nicola Cancedda, Marc Dymetman, Marco Turchi, and Nello Cristianini. 2009. Estimating the sentence-level quality of machine translation systems. In *Proceedings of EAMT*, pages 28–35.

Lucia Specia. 2011. Exploiting objective annotations for measuring translation post-editing effort. In *Proceedings of EAMT*.

Michalis K. Titsias. 2009. Variational Learning of Inducing Variables in Sparse Gaussian Processes. In *Proceedings of AISTATS*, volume 5, pages 567–574.

Peter D. Turney. 2002. Thumbs Up or Thumbs Down?: Semantic Orientation Applied to Unsupervised Classification of Reviews. In *Proceedings of ACL*, number July, pages 417–424.

Jarno Vanhatalo, Jaakko Riihimäki, Jouni Hartikainen, Pasi Jylänki, Ville Tolvanen, and Aki Vehtari. 2013. GPstuff: Bayesian Modeling with Gaussian Processes. *The Journal of Machine Learning Research*, 14:1175–1179.

S. V. N. Vishwanathan, Nicol N. Schraudolph, Risi Kondor, and Karsten M. Borgwardt. 2010. Graph Kernels. *Journal of Machine Learning Research*, 11:1201–1242.

Christopher K. I. Williams and David Barber. 1998. Bayesian Classification with Gaussian Processes. *IEEE Transactions on Pattern Analysis and Machine Intelligence*, 20(12):1342–1351.

Yuanbin Wu, Qi Zhang, Xuanjing Huang, and Lide Wu. 2009. Phrase Dependency Parsing for Opinion Mining. In *Proceedings of EMNLP*, pages 1533–1541.

Dell Zhang and Wee Sun Lee. 2003. Question classification using support vector machines. In *Proceedings of SIGIR*, New York, New York, USA. ACM Press.

Extracting Temporal and Causal Relations between Events

Paramita Mirza
Fondazione Bruno Kessler
University of Trento
Trento, Italy
paramita@fbk.eu

Abstract

A notably challenging problem related to event processing is recognizing the relations holding between events in a text, in particular temporal and causal relations. While there has been some research on temporal relations, the aspect of causality between events from a Natural Language Processing (NLP) perspective has hardly been touched. We propose an annotation scheme to cover different types of causality between events, techniques for extracting such relations and an investigation into the connection between temporal and causal relations. In this thesis work we aim to focus especially on the latter, because causality is presumed to have a temporal constraint. We conjecture that injecting this presumption may be beneficial for the recognition of both temporal and causal relations.

1 Introduction

With the rapid growth of information available on the world wide web, especially in the form of unstructured and natural texts, *information extraction* (IE) becomes one of the most prominent fields in NLP research. IE aims to provide ways to automatically extract the available information and store them in a structured representation of knowledge. The stored knowledge can then be useful for many NLP applications, such as question answering, textual entailment, summarization, and focused information retrieval systems.

There are several subtasks within information extraction related to the type of knowledge one wishes to extract from the text, *event extraction* being one of them. Event extraction is considered to be a non-trivial task, due to the fact that mentions of an event in text could be highly varied in terms of sentence construction, and that the attributes describing an event are usually mentioned in several sentences. However, the most challenging problem in the context of event extraction is identifying the relationship between events.

Events are usually anchored to temporal expressions. The temporal attribute of an event can be used to determine the temporal relationship between events. This information can be useful for the ordering of event sequence in a timeline, e.g. for the better presentation of news or history texts. Moreover, in multi-document summarization of news articles, the relative order of events is important to merge and present information from multiple sources correctly.

A more complex type of relationship between events is causality. Identifying the causal relation between events is an important step in predicting occurrence of future events, and can be very beneficial in risk analysis as well as decision making support.

There is an overlap between causal and temporal relations, since by the definition of causality, the first event (cause) must happen *BEFORE* the second event (effect). We claim that a system for extracting both temporal and causal relations, may benefit from integrating this presumption. The main focus of this research work will be (i) investigating ways to utilize this presumption in building an integrated event relation extraction system, in addition to (ii) exploring ways to develop a robust extraction component for each type of relations (temporal and causal).

2 Background

In NLP, the definition of an event can be varied depending on the target application. In topic detection and tracking (Allan, 2002), the term *event* is used interchangeably with *topic*, which describes something that happens and is usually used to identify a cluster of documents, e.g. *Olympics*, *wars*. On the other hand, information extraction provides finer granularity of event definitions, in which events

Proceedings of the ACL 2014 Student Research Workshop, pages 10–17,
Baltimore, Maryland USA, June 22-27 2014.

are entities that happen/occur within the scope of a document.

There are several annotation frameworks for events and temporal expressions that can be viewed as *event models*,[1] TimeML (Pustejovsky et al., 2003b) and ACE (Consortium, 2005) being the prominent ones.

Both TimeML and ACE define an event as something that happens/occurs or a state that holds true, which can be expressed by a verb, a noun, an adjective, as well as a nominalization either from verbs or adjectives. Consider the following passage annotated with events and temporal expressions (TIMEX). *"A Philippine volcano, dormant* $_{\text{EVENT}}$ *for six centuries* $_{\text{TIMEX}}$, *exploded* $_{\text{EVENT}}$ *last Monday* $_{\text{TIMEX}}$. *During the eruption* $_{\text{EVENT}}$, *lava, rocks and red-hot ash are spewed* $_{\text{EVENT}}$ *onto surrounding villages. The explosion* $_{\text{EVENT}}$ *claimed* $_{\text{EVENT}}$ *at least 30 lives."*

The most important attribute of TimeML that differs from ACE is the separation of the representation of events and temporal expressions from the anchoring or ordering dependencies. Instead of treating a temporal expression as an event argument, TimeML introduces *temporal link* annotations to establish dependencies (temporal relations) between events and temporal expressions (Pustejovsky et al., 2003b). This annotation is important in (i) anchoring an event to a temporal expression (event time-stamping) and (ii) determining the temporal order between events. This distinctive feature of TimeML becomes our main consideration in choosing the event model for our research.

Moreover, TimeML is the annotation framework used in TempEval-3[2], the most recent shared task on temporal and event processing. The ultimate goal of this evaluation campaign is the automatic identification of temporal expressions, events, and temporal relations within a text (UzZaman et al., 2012).

The main tasks defined in TempEval-3 include: the automatic extraction of *TimeML entities*, i.e. temporal expressions and events, and the end-to-end automatic extraction of both TimeML entities and temporal links/relations. The result of TempEval-3 reported by UzZaman et al. (2013) shows that even though the performances of systems for extracting TimeML entities are quite good (>80% F-score), the overall performance of end-to-end event extraction systems suffers from the low performance of the temporal relation extraction system. The state-of-the-art performance on the temporal relation extraction task yields only around 36% F-score. This becomes the main reason of focusing our research on the extraction of event relations.

3 Research Problem

We consider two types of event relations to be extracted from text, which are *temporal relations* and *causal relations*. Causal relations are related to temporal relations since there is a temporal constraint in causality, i.e. the cause must precede the effect. Considering this presumption, and the assumption that there are good enough systems to extract temporal expressions and events, we define two main problems that will be addressed in this research work:

1. Given a text annotated with entities (temporal expressions and events), how to automatically extract temporal and causal relations between them.

2. Given the temporal constraint of causality, how to utilize the interaction between temporal relations and causal relations for building an integrated event relation extraction system for both types of relations.

4 Research Methodology

There are several aspects of the mentioned problems that will become our guidelines in continuing our research in this topic. The following sections will give a more detailed description of these aspects including the arising challenges, some preliminary results to address the challenges and our future research directions.

4.1 Temporal Relation Extraction

As previously mentioned, we consider the TimeML annotation framework because it explicitly encodes the temporal links between entities (events and temporal expressions) in a text. In TimeML, each temporal link has a temporal relation type assigned to it. There are 14 types of temporal relations specified in TimeML version 1.2.1 (Saurí et al., 2006),

[1]There are other event models based on web ontology (RDFS+OWL) such as LODE (Shaw et al., 2009), SEM (van Hage et al., 2011) and DOLCE (Gangemi et al., 2002), which encode knowledge about events as triples. Such models can be seen as ways to store the extracted knowledge to perform the reasoning on.

[2]http://www.cs.york.ac.uk/semeval-2013/task1/

which are defined based on Allen's interval algebra (Allen, 1983), as illustrated in Table 1.

<table>
<tr><td>a |——|
b |——|</td><td>a is BEFORE b
b is AFTER a</td></tr>
<tr><td>a |——|
b |——|</td><td>a is IBEFORE b
b is IAFTER a</td></tr>
<tr><td>a |—|
b |———|</td><td>a BEGINS b
b is BEGUN_BY a</td></tr>
<tr><td>a |—|
b |———|</td><td>a ENDS b
b is ENDED_BY a</td></tr>
<tr><td>a |—|
b |—————|</td><td>a is DURING b
b is DURING_INV a</td></tr>
<tr><td>a |—————|
b |—|</td><td>a INCLUDES b
b IS_INCLUDED in a</td></tr>
<tr><td>a |——|
b |——|</td><td>a is SIMULTANEOUS with b</td></tr>
<tr><td>a |——| b</td><td>a is IDENTITY with b</td></tr>
</table>

Table 1: Temporal relations in TimeML annotation

Recalling the low performances of currently available systems on the temporal relation extraction task, including the state-of-the-art systems according to TempEval-3, it is still insufficient to use the existing temporal relation extraction systems to support real world applications, such as creating event timelines and temporally-based question answering. Therefore, as the first step we take as an objective finding ways to improve the current state-of-the-art performance on temporal relation extraction task.

The common approach towards temporal relation extraction is dividing the task into two subtasks: *identifying the pairs* of entities having a temporal link and *determining the relation types*. The problem of identifying the entity pairs is usually simplified. In TempEval-3, the possible pairs of entities that can have a temporal link are defined as (i) main events of consecutive sentences, (ii) pairs of events in the same sentence, (iii) an event and a time expression in the same sentence, and (iv) an event and the document creation time (UzZaman et al., 2013). The problem of determining the label of a given temporal link is usually regarded as a classification problem. Given an ordered pair of entities (e_1, e_2) that could be either *event-event*, *event-timex* or *timex-timex* pair, the classifier has to assign a certain label representing the temporal relation type.

We focus on the latter subtask of classifying temporal relation types, assuming that the links between events and time expressions are already established. Several recent works have tried to address this complex multi-class classification task by using sophisticated features based on deep parsing, semantic role labelling and discourse parsing (D'Souza and Ng, 2013; Laokulrat et al., 2013). In Mirza and Tonelli (2014) we have shown that a simpler approach, based on lexico-syntactic features, can achieve comparable results.

A classification model is trained for each category of entity pair, i.e. event-event, event-timex and timex-timex, as suggested in several previous works (Mani et al., 2006; Chambers, 2013). However, because there are very few examples of timex-timex pairs in the training corpus, it is not possible to train a classifier for these particular pairs. Moreover, they only add up to 3.2% of the total number of extracted entity pairs; therefore, we decided to disregard these pairs.

We follow the guidelines and the dataset provided by the organizers of TempEval-3 so that we can compare our system with other systems participating in the challenge. The TBAQ-cleaned corpus is the training set provided for the task, consisting of the TimeBank (Pustejovsky et al., 2003a) and the AQUAINT corpora. It contains around 100K words in total, with 11K words annotated as events (UzZaman et al., 2013).

Simple Feature Set. We implement a number of features including the commonly used ones (UzZaman et al., 2013), which take into account morpho-syntactic information on events and time expressions, their textual context and their attributes. Other features rely on semantic information such as typical event durations and explicit temporal connective types. However, we avoid complex processing of data. Such semantic information is based on external lists of lexical items and on the output of the *addDiscourse* tagger (Pitler and Nenkova, 2009). We build our classification models using the Support Vector Machine (SVM) implementation provided by YamCha[3].

We perform feature engineering in order to select from our initial set of features only those that improve the accuracy of the classifiers. This allows us to select the best classification models for both event-event pairs and event-timex pairs.

Inverse Relations and Closure. Motivated by the finding of Mani et al. (2006) that bootstrapping the training data through a *temporal closure* method results in quite significant improvements, we investigate the effect of enriching the training data with *inverse relations* and *closure-based inferred*

[3] http://chasen.org/~taku/software/yamcha/

relations.

However, we adopt a simpler approach to obtain the closure graph of temporal relations, by applying the *transitive closure* only within the same relation type, e.g. e_1 BEFORE $e_2 \wedge e_2$ BEFORE $e3 \rightarrow e_1$ BEFORE $e3$. It produces only a subset of the relations produced by the *temporal closure* (Verhagen, 2005; Gerevini et al., 1995). The problem of finding the transitive closure of a directed acyclic graph can be reduced to a boolean matrix multiplication (Fischer and Meyer, 1971).

Training data	event-event	event-timex
TBAQ	**48.28%**	73.82%
TBAQ-I	47.77%	74.45%
TBAQ-IC	46.39%	**74.45%**

Table 2: Classifier accuracies with different training data: TBAQ (TimeBank+AQUAINT), TBAQ-I (TBAQ+inverse relations) and TBAQ-IC (TBAQ+inverse relations+transitive closure).

Evaluation and Analysis. Our test data is the newly annotated TempEval-3-platinum evaluation corpus provided by TempEval-3 organizers, so that we can compare our system with other systems participating in the task. First, to investigate the effect of enriching the training data with inverse relations and transitive closure, we evaluate the system performance trained with different datasets, as shown in Table 2. A randomization test between the best performing classifier and the others shows that by extending the training data with inverse relations and transitive closure, the improvement are not significant. Applying inverse relations and transitive closure extends the number of training instances but makes the already skewed dataset more imbalanced, thus it does not result in a significant improvement.

We then train our classifiers for event-event pairs and event-timex pairs by exploiting the best feature combination and using the best reported dataset for each classifier as the training data. The two classifiers are part of our temporal classification system called *TRelPro*.

Compared with the performances of other systems participating in TempEval-3 reported in UzZaman et al. (2013), *TRelPro* is the best performing system both in terms of precision and of recall. The result of our system using simpler features confirms the finding reported in UzZaman et al. (2013), that a system using basic morpho-syntactic features is hard to beat with systems using more complex semantic features, if not used properly.

System	F1	Precision	Recall
TRelPro	**58.48%**	**58.80%**	**58.17%**
UTTime-1, 4	56.45%	55.58%	57.35%
UTTime-3, 5	54.70%	53.85%	55.58%
UTTime-2	54.26%	53.20%	55.36%
NavyTime-1	46.83%	46.59%	47.07%
NavyTime-2	43.92%	43.65%	44.20%
JU-CSE	34.77%	35.07%	34.48%

Table 3: TempEval-3 evaluation on the classification of temporal relation types

4.2 Causal Relation Extraction

Unlike the *temporal order* that has a clear definition, there is no consensus in the NLP community on how to define *causality*. Causality is not a linguistic notion, meaning that although language can be used to express causality, causality exists as a psychological tool for understanding the world independently of language (van de Koot and Neeleman, 2012). There have been several attempts in the psychology field to model causality, including the *counterfactual model* (Lewis, 1973), *probabilistic contrast model* (Cheng and Novick, 1991; Cheng and Novick, 1992) and the *dynamics model* (Wolff and Song, 2003; Wolff et al., 2005; Wolff, 2007), which is based on Talmy's *force dynamic* account of causality (Talmy, 1985; Talmy, 1988).

In information extraction, modelling causality is only the first step in order to have guidelines to recognize causal relations in a text. In order to have an automatic extraction system for causal relations (particularly using a data-driven approach) and most importantly to evaluate the performance of the developed extraction system, it is important that a language resource annotated with causality is available.

Even though there are several corpora annotated with causality, e.g. Penn Discourse Treebank (PDTB) (Prasad et al., 2007) and PropBank (Palmer et al., 2005),[4] we are not aware of any standard benchmarking corpus for evaluating event causality extraction, as it is available for temporal relations in TimeML. This motivates us to create a language resource annotated with both temporal and causal relations in a unified annotation scheme, for the main purpose of investigating the interaction between both types of relations. It becomes the objective of the second stage of our research, in

[4]PDTB annotates causality between related clauses, while PropBank annotates causality between a verb and its cause clause.

addition to building an automatic extraction system for event causality using the developed corpus.

In Mirza et al. (2014) we have proposed annotation guidelines for causality between events, based on the TimeML definition of events, which considers all types of actions (punctual and durative) and states as events. Parallel to the <TLINK> tag in TimeML for temporal relations, we introduced the <CLINK> tag to signify a causal link. We also introduced the notion of causal signals through the <C-SIGNAL> tag, parallel to the <SIGNAL> tag in TimeML indicating temporal cues.

C-SIGNAL. C-SIGNAL is used to mark-up textual elements signalling the presence of causal relations, which include all causal uses of: *prepositions* (e.g. because of, as a result of, due to), *conjunctions* (e.g. because, since, so that), *adverbial connectors* (e.g. so, therefore, thus) and *clause-integrated expressions* (e.g. the reason why, the result is, that is why).

CLINK. A CLINK is a directional relation where the causing event is the *source* (indicated with $_S$ in the examples) and the caused event is the *target* (indicated with $_T$). The annotation of CLINKs also includes the *c-signalID* attribute, with the value of the ID of C-SIGNAL marking the causal relation (if available).

Wolff (2007) has shown that the dynamics model covers three main types of causal concepts, i.e. CAUSE, ENABLE and PREVENT. The model has been tested by linking it with natural language, Wolff and Song (2003) show that the three causal concepts can be lexicalized as verbs : (i) CAUSE-type verbs, e.g. *cause, prompt, force*; (ii) ENABLE-type verbs, e.g. *allow, enable, help*; and (iii) PREVENT-type verbs, e.g. *block, prevent, restrain*. Its connection with natural language becomes the main reason of basing our annotation guidelines for causality on the dynamics model.

We limit the annotation of CLINKs to the presence of an explicit causal construction linking two events, which can be one of the following cases:

1. Expressions containing **affect verbs** (*affect, influence, determine, change*), e.g. *Ogun ACN crisis* $_S$ ***influences*** *the launch* $_T$ *of the All Progressive Congress.*
2. Expressions containing **link verbs** (*link, lead, depend on*), e.g. *An earthquake* $_T$ *in North America was linked to a tsunami* $_S$ *in Japan.*
3. **Basic construction of causative verbs**, e.g. *The purchase* $_S$ ***caused*** *the creation* $_T$ *of the current building.*
4. **Periphrastic construction of causative verbs**, e.g. *The blast* $_S$ ***caused*** *the boat to heel* $_T$ *violently*, where the causative verb (*caused*) takes an embedded verb (*heel*) expressing a particular result.
5. Expressions containing **causative conjunctions and prepositions**, which are annotated as C-SIGNALs.

Note that for causative verbs we consider sets of verbs from all types of causal concepts including CAUSE-type, ENABLE-type and PREVENT-type verbs.

Manual Annotation of Event Causality. Having the annotation guidelines, we are about to complete the annotation of event causality. We have annotated a subset of training corpus from TempEval-3 used in the temporal relation extraction, i.e. TimeBank. The agreement reached by two annotators on a subset of 5 documents is 0.844 Dice's coefficient on C-SIGNALs (micro-average over markables) and 0.73 on CLINKs.

After completing causality annotation, the next step will be to build an automatic extraction system for causal relations. We will consider to use a supervised learning approach, as well as the similar features employed for temporal relation classification task, in addition to lexical information (e.g. WordNet (Fellbaum, 1998), VerbOcean (Chklovski and Pantel, 2004)) and the existing causal signals.

4.3 Integrated Event Relation Extraction

During the last stage of our research work, we will investigate the interaction between temporal and causal relations, given the temporal constraint of causality. The ultimate goal is to build an integrated event relation extraction system, that is capable of automatically extracting both temporal and causal relations from text.

Few works have investigated the interaction between these two types of relations. The corpus analysis conducted by Bethard et al. (2008) shows that although it is expected that almost every causal relation would have an underlying before relation, in reality, 32% of causal relations in the corpus are not accompanied by underlying before relations. One of the possible causes is that the considered event pairs are conjoined event pairs under the ambiguous *and* conjunctive.

Consider the sentence *"The walls were shaking* T ***because of*** *the earthquake* S." Looking at the explicit causal mark *because*, there is a causal relation between the events *shaking* and *earthquake*. However, according to Allen's interval algebra or the TimeML annotation framework we cannot say that event *earthquake* occurred `BEFORE` the event *shaking*, because both events happen almost at the same time (could be `SIMULTANOUS`), and in both frameworks there is no overlap in `BEFORE` relations. During our manual annotation process, we encountered the case where the cause event happens after the effect, as in *"Some analysts questioned* T *how much of an impact the retirement package will have,* ***because*** *few jobs will end* S *up being eliminated."* Further investigations are needed to address this issue.

Rink et al. (2010) makes use of manually annotated temporal relation types as a feature to build a classification model for causal relations between events. This results in 57.9% of F1-Score, 15% improvement of performance in comparison with the system without the additional feature of temporal relations. The significant increase of performance proves that the temporal relations between causal events have a significant role in discovering causal relations. On the other hand, a brief analysis into our preliminary result on temporal relation extraction shows that there is a possibility to employ causality to improve the temporal relation classification of event-event pairs, specifically to reduce the number of *false positives* and *false negatives* of `BEFORE` and `AFTER` relations scored by the system. Our hypothesis is that temporal and causal relations can be of mutual benefit to the extraction of each other.

Taking into account different classification frameworks and possible configurations for the integrated system, for example, cascading the temporal and causal relation extraction systems, or one system for both relation types in one pass, we will explore the possibilities and evaluate their performances. Furthermore, there is a possibility to exploit a global optimization algorithm, as explored by Chambers and Jurafsky (2008) and Do et al. (2012), to improve the performance of a pairwise classification system.

One possible classification algorithm under our considerations, which can be used for extracting both temporal and causal relations in one pass, is General Conditional Random Fields (CRFs). General CRFs allow us to train a classification model with arbitrary graphical structure, e.g. a two-dimensional CRF can be used to perform both noun phrase chunking and PoS tagging at the same time. And its skip-chain mechanism allows us to create *a chain of entity pairs*, which may improve the classification performance.

5 Conclusion

Event extraction has become one of the most investigated tasks of information extraction, since it is the key to many applications in natural language processing such as personalized news systems, question answering and document summarization. The extraction of relations that hold between events is one of the subtasks within event extraction gaining more attention in the recent years, given the beneficial and promising applications.

We have presented a research plan covering the topic of automatic extraction of two event relation types, i.e. temporal and causal relations, from natural language texts. While there has been a clearly defined framework for temporal relation extraction task, namely TempEval-3, there is none for causal relation extraction. Furthermore, since causality has a temporal constraint, we are interested in investigating the interaction between temporal and causal relations, in the context of events.

We propose a three-stage approach to cover this research topic. The first stage includes improving the state-of-the-art performance on temporal relation extraction. During the second stage we propose an annotation scheme to create a corpus for causal relations, based on the established annotation framework for events and temporal relations, namely TimeML. The created language resource will then be used to build the automatic extraction system for causal relations, and also to provide the benchmarking evaluation corpus. Finally, the last stage includes investigating the interaction between temporal and causal relations, in order to build an integrated system for event relation extraction, which is the ultimate goal of this research work.

Acknowledgments

The research leading to this paper was partially supported by the European Union's 7th Framework Programme via the NewsReader Project (ICT-316404). We also thank Google for travel and conference support for this paper.

References

James Allan, editor. 2002. *Topic Detection and Tracking: Event-based Information Organization*. Kluwer Academic Publishers, Norwell, MA, USA.

James F. Allen. 1983. Maintaining knowledge about temporal intervals. *Commun. ACM*, 26(11):832–843, November.

Steven Bethard, William Corvey, Sara Klingenstein, and James H. Martin. 2008. Building a corpus of temporal-causal structure. In *Proceedings of the Sixth International Conference on Language Resources and Evaluation (LREC'08)*, Marrakech, Morocco, May. European Language Resources Association (ELRA).

Nathanael Chambers and Dan Jurafsky. 2008. Jointly combining implicit constraints improves temporal ordering. In *Proceedings of the Conference on Empirical Methods in Natural Language Processing*, EMNLP '08, pages 698–706, Stroudsburg, PA, USA. Association for Computational Linguistics.

Nate Chambers. 2013. Navytime: Event and time ordering from raw text. In *Second Joint Conference on Lexical and Computational Semantics (*SEM), Volume 2: Proceedings of the Seventh International Workshop on Semantic Evaluation (SemEval 2013)*, pages 73–77, Atlanta, Georgia, USA, June. Association for Computational Linguistics.

Patricia W. Cheng and Laura R. Novick. 1991. Causes versus enabling conditions. *Cognition*, 40(1-2):83 – 120.

Patricia W. Cheng and Laura R. Novick. 1992. Covariation in natural causal induction. *Psychological Review*, 99(2):365–382.

Timothy Chklovski and Patrick Pantel. 2004. Verbocean: Mining the web for fine-grained semantic verb relations. In Dekang Lin and Dekai Wu, editors, *Proceedings of EMNLP 2004*, pages 33–40, Barcelona, Spain, July. Association for Computational Linguistics.

Linguistic Data Consortium, 2005. *ACE (Automatic Content Extraction) English Annotation Guidelines for Events*.

Quang Xuan Do, Wei Lu, and Dan Roth. 2012. Joint inference for event timeline construction. In *Proceedings of the 2012 Joint Conference on Empirical Methods in Natural Language Processing and Computational Natural Language Learning*, EMNLP-CoNLL '12, pages 677–687, Stroudsburg, PA, USA. Association for Computational Linguistics.

Jennifer D'Souza and Vincent Ng. 2013. Classifying temporal relations with rich linguistic knowledge. In *Proceedings of the 2013 Conference of the North American Chapter of the Association for Computational Linguistics: Human Language Technologies*, pages 918–927.

Christiane Fellbaum, editor. 1998. *WordNet: An Electronic Lexical Database*. MIT Press.

Michael J. Fischer and Albert R. Meyer. 1971. Boolean matrix multiplication and transitive closure. In *SWAT (FOCS)*, pages 129–131. IEEE Computer Society.

Aldo Gangemi, Nicola Guarino, Claudio Masolo, Alessandro Oltramari, and Luc Schneider. 2002. Sweetening ontologies with dolce. In *Proceedings of the 13th International Conference on Knowledge Engineering and Knowledge Management. Ontologies and the Semantic Web*, EKAW '02, pages 166–181, London, UK, UK. Springer-Verlag.

Alfonso Gerevini, Lenhart Schubert, and Stephanie Schaeffer. 1995. The temporal reasoning tools timegraph i-ii. *International Journal of Artificial Intelligence Tools*, 4(1-2):281–299.

Natsuda Laokulrat, Makoto Miwa, Yoshimasa Tsuruoka, and Takashi Chikayama. 2013. Uttime: Temporal relation classification using deep syntactic features. In *Second Joint Conference on Lexical and Computational Semantics (*SEM), Volume 2: Proceedings of the Seventh International Workshop on Semantic Evaluation (SemEval 2013)*, pages 88–92, Atlanta, Georgia, USA, June. Association for Computational Linguistics.

David Lewis. 1973. Causation. *The Journal of Philosophy*, 70(17):pp. 556–567.

Inderjeet Mani, Marc Verhagen, Ben Wellner, Chong Min Lee, and James Pustejovsky. 2006. Machine learning of temporal relations. In *Proceedings of the 21st International Conference on Computational Linguistics and the 44th Annual Meeting of the Association for Computational Linguistics*, ACL-44, pages 753–760, Stroudsburg, PA, USA. Association for Computational Linguistics.

Paramita Mirza and Sara Tonelli. 2014. Classifying temporal relations with simple features. In *Proceedings of the 14th Conference of the European Chapter of the Association for Computational Linguistics*.

Paramita Mirza, Rachele Sprugnoli, Sara Tonelli, and Manuela Speranza. 2014. Annotating causality in the tempeval-3 corpus. In *Proceedings of the EACL-2014 Workshop on Computational Approaches to Causality in Language (CAtoCL)*.

Martha Palmer, Daniel Gildea, and Paul Kingsbury. 2005. The proposition bank: An annotated corpus of semantic roles. *Comput. Linguist.*, 31(1):71–106, March.

Emily Pitler and Ani Nenkova. 2009. Using syntax to disambiguate explicit discourse connectives in text. In *Proceedings of the ACL-IJCNLP 2009 Conference Short Papers*, ACLShort '09, pages 13–16, Stroudsburg, PA, USA. Association for Computational Linguistics.

Rashmi Prasad, Eleni Miltsakaki, Nikhil Dinesh, Alan Lee, Aravind Joshi, Livio Robaldo, and Bonnie L Webber. 2007. The penn discourse treebank 2.0 annotation manual. Technical report.

J. Pustejovsky, P. Hanks, R. Sauri, A. See, R. Gaizauskas, A. Setzer, D. Radev, B. Sundheim, D. Day, L. Ferro, et al. 2003a. The timebank corpus. In *Corpus Linguistics*, volume 2003, page 40.

James Pustejovsky, José Castaño, Robert Ingria, Roser Saurí, Robert Gaizauskas, Andrea Setzer, and Graham Katz. 2003b. Timeml: Robust specification of event and temporal expressions in text. In *Proceedings of the Fifth International Workshop on Computational Semantics (IWCS-5)*.

Bryan Rink, Cosmin Adrian Bejan, and Sanda M. Harabagiu. 2010. Learning textual graph patterns to detect causal event relations. In *FLAIRS Conference*.

Roser Saurí, Jessica Littman, Robert Gaizauskas, Andrea Setzer, and James Pustejovsky, 2006. *TimeML Annotation Guidelines, Version 1.2.1*.

Ryan Shaw, Raphaël Troncy, and Lynda Hardman. 2009. Lode: Linking open descriptions of events. In *Proceedings of the 4th Asian Conference on The Semantic Web*, ASWC '09, pages 153–167, Berlin, Heidelberg. Springer-Verlag.

Leonard Talmy. 1985. Force dynamics in language and thought. *Chicago Linguistic Society*, 21:293337.

Leonard Talmy. 1988. Force dynamics in language and cognition. *Cognitive Science*, 12(1):49–100.

Naushad UzZaman, Hector Llorens, James F. Allen, Leon Derczynski, Marc Verhagen, and James Pustejovsky. 2012. Tempeval-3: Evaluating events, time expressions, and temporal relations. *CoRR*, abs/1206.5333.

Naushad UzZaman, Hector Llorens, Leon Derczynski, James Allen, Marc Verhagen, and James Pustejovsky. 2013. Semeval-2013 task 1: Tempeval-3: Evaluating time expressions, events, and temporal relations. In *Proceedings of the Seventh International Workshop on Semantic Evaluation*, SemEval '13, pages 1–9, Atlanta, Georgia, USA, June. Association for Computational Linguistics.

H van de Koot and A Neeleman, 2012. *The Theta System: Argument Structure at the Interface*, chapter The Linguistic Expression of Causation, pages 20 – 51. Oxford University Press: Oxford.

Willem Robert van Hage, Véronique Malaisé, Roxane Segers, Laura Hollink, and Guus Schreiber. 2011. Design and use of the simple event model (sem). *Journal of Web Semantics*, 9(2):128–136.

Marc Verhagen. 2005. Temporal closure in an annotation environment. *Language Resources and Evaluation*, 39(2-3):211–241.

Phillip Wolff and Grace Song. 2003. Models of causation and the semantics of causal verbs. *Cognitive Psychology*, 47(3):276 – 332.

Phillip Wolff, Bianca Klettke, Tatyana Ventura, and Grace Song, 2005. *Categorization inside and outside the laboratory: Essays in honor of Douglas L. Medin. APA decade of behavior series*, chapter Expressing Causation in English and Other Languages, pages 29–48. Washington, DC, US: American Psychological Association, xx, 316 pp.

Phillip Wolff. 2007. Representing causation. *Journal of Experiment Psychology: General*, 136:82–111.

Towards a Discourse Relation-aware Approach for Chinese-English Machine Translation

Frances Yung
Nara Institute of Science and Technology
8916-5 Takayama, Ikoma, Nara, 630-0192 Japan
pikyufrances-y@is.naist.jp

Abstract

Translation of discourse relations is one of the recent efforts of incorporating discourse information to statistical machine translation (SMT). While existing works focus on disambiguation of ambiguous discourse connectives, or transformation of discourse trees, only explicit discourse relations are tackled. A greater challenge exists in machine translation of Chinese, since implicit discourse relations are abundant and occur both inside and outside a sentence. This thesis proposal describes ongoing work on bilingual discourse annotation and plans towards incorporating discourse relation knowledge to a Chinese-English SMT system with consideration of implicit discourse relations. The final goal is a discourse-unit-based translation model unbounded by the traditional assumption of sentence-to-sentence translation.

1 Introduction

Human translation is created at document level, suggesting that translation of a particular sentence depends also on the 'discourse structure'. Recently, some MT researchers have started to explore the possibility to incorporate linguistic information outside the sentence boundary for MT, such as topical structure, coreference chains, and lexical coherence. Among various discourse structures, discourse relations, also known as coherence relations, are meaningful relations connecting text segments and are crucial to the human cognitive processing as well as memory of texts (Sanders and Noordman, 2000). These relations can be explicitly marked in a text by signaling phrases or implicitly implied. Even when they are explicit, some markers are ambiguous and do not always signal the same relation. In addition, strategies to represent discourse relations vary across languages. It is thus a challenging task to correctly translate discourse relations.

This thesis proposal presents my plan towards building a discourse-relation-aware machine translation system translating from Chinese to English. In particular, I would like to focus on modeling the translation of implicit discourse relations, which has not yet been exploited to date to my knowledge, but is yet a noticeable problem since implicit discourse relations are abundant in Chinese. According to the statistics of the bilingual discourse annotation in progress, about 1/4 of the Chinese implicit DCs are translated to explicit DCs in English.

A reasonable initial attempt to learn discourse-relation-aware translation rules is a knowledge-based approach based on an annotated corpus. This proposal describes my ongoing work on annotating and cross-lingually aligning discourse relations in a Chinese-English translation corpus, as well as my plans to incorporate the resulting linguistic markup into an SMT system. Motivated by the characteristics of long Chinese sentences with multiple discourse segments, a further direction of the research is to translate in units of discourse segments instead of sentences.

Section 2 gives an overview of existing literature. Section 3 explains the motivations behind my research on discourse relations for MT. Section 4 describes my ongoing work of bilingual discourse annotation, followed by statistics to date . Section 5 present my plans for next steps. Finally, a conclusion is drawn in Section 6.

2 Survey

2.1 English discourse processing

There are a number of discourse-annotated English resources, including the 'RST Treebank' (Carlson et al., 2001) and the 'Discourse GraphBank' (Wolf and Gibson, 2005), which consist

Proceedings of the ACL 2014 Student Research Workshop, pages 18–25,
Baltimore, Maryland USA, June 22-27 2014.

of 385 and 135 articles respectively. Recent discourse research often make use of the large-scaled Penn Discourse Treebank (PDTB) (Prasad et al., 2008). Departed from annotation using predefined discourse relations, such as 'Rhetorical Structure Theory' (Mann and Thompson, 1988), PDTB introduces a lexically-ground formalism to annotate discourse relations by identifying the discourse connectives (DCs). An example is shown in the following.

Example 1: <u>Since</u> **McDonald's menu prices rose this year**, *the actual decline may have been more.* (PDTB 1280)

'Since' is an explicit DC taking the *italic segment* as the first argument (Arg1), and the **bolded segment** as the second argument (Arg2), which is syntactically attached to the DC. Implicit DCs are inserted by annotators between adjacent sentences of the same paragraph to represent inferred discourse relations. Each DC is annotated with defined *senses* classified into 3 levels of granularity.

PDTB allows evaluation of English discourse parsing tasks and disambiguation tasks (Pitler and Nenkova, 2009; Lin et al., 2010), which reveal that implicit discourse relations are much harder to learn than explicit discourse relations (Pitler et al., 2009; Zhou et al., 2010). For example, classification of the 4 main relation senses (temporal, contingency, comparison, expansion) reaches 94% accuracy for explicit relations (Pitler and Nenkova, 2009), but only range from F-scores of 20% for 'temporal' to 76% for 'expansion' relations, possibly due to unbalanced number of training instances (Pitler et al., 2009; Zhou et al., 2010).

2.2 Chinese discourse processing

Schemes for Chinese discourse annotation have been proposed in the existing literature (Xue, 2005; Zhou and Xue, 2012) but the corresponding resource is not yet available. Zhou et al. (2012) proposed to project English discourse annotation and classification algorithms to Chinese data, but the transfer was based on automatic word alignment and machine translation results. Works in Chinese discourse parsing report F-scores of 64% in classification of inter-sentence discourse relations and 71% in 2-way classification of intra-sentence contingency and comparison relations (Huang and Chen, 2011; Huang and Chen, 2012), training on a moderately sized (81 articles) corpus and considering explicit and implicit relations collectively. Corelation between discourse relation and sentiment was also explored based on annotated data (Huang et al., 2013).

2.3 Discourse relations in SMT

Earlier studies of discourse relations in MT includes Marcu et al. (2000), which proposed a discourse transfer model to re-construct the target discourse tree from the source discourse tree, parsed by the (RST). However, incorporation to an SMT system was not discussed in the work. Recent works focus on the translation of ambiguous DCs, such as 'since' in the temporal sense vs. 'since' in the reason sense. This is achieved by annotating the DCs in the training data by 'translation spotting', which is to manually align the DCs of the source text to their translation in the target text, either occurring as DCs or other expressions (Meyer et al., 2011; Popescu-Belis et al., 2012; Meyer et al., 2012; Meyer and Polakova, 2013; Cartoni et al., 2013). Experiments of these works have been conducted in English-to-French, Czech and German translation and only explicit DCs were considered.

Tu et al. (2013) proposed a framework for Chinese-to-English translation, in which the source text is automatically parsed by an RST parser and translation rules are extracted from the source discourse trees aligned with the target strings. An improvement of 1.16 BLEU point is reported, considering only intra-sentential explicit relations.

Meyer et al. (2012) found that the translation of DC improves by up to 10% disregarded of BLEU, which stays around the baseline system score. To detect the improvement, they used a metric known as *ACT* (Accuracy of Connective Translation) (Hajlaoui and Popescu-Belis, 2012; Hajlaoui and Popescu-Belis, 2013), which relies on bilingual word alignment and a dictionary of DCs. In the setting, missing/additional DC (i.e. potential implicitation/explicitation of discourse relations) are to be checked manually for the validity.

3 Motivation

The motivation behind a discourse-relation-aware translation model for Chinese is two-fold. First of all, on top of ambiguous discourse connectives as in other languages, Chinese documents contain abundant implicit connectives (Xue, 2005). In particular, complex sentences often occur in the form of 'running sentences', in which loose clauses run in a sequence separated by commas yet without explicit connectives. Such sentence structures are used to represent the temporal or reasoning order or related events, or simply to achieve consistent rhythmic patterns. In contrast, syntactical constraint is prominent in English and this kind of 'paratactic' structures only occur as occasional rhetorical measures. In other cases, relations between clauses within a sentence are marked by coordinating or subordinating conjunctions in order to maintain an intact sentence structure.

Another motivation is that translation in units of sentences is not always preferable in Chinese-English translation. In fact, each comma-separated segment of a 'running sentence' can be considered as an elementary discourse units (EDU) (Yang and Xue, 2012; Zhou and Xue, 2012) and aligned across the two languages. In current SMT models, sentence splitting is the result of the language model or translation rules containing periods or sentence initial markers. A long Chinese 'running sentence' is typically translated to one English sentence with 'comma splices' (ungrammatical commas between complete sentences without connecting by conjunctions). On the other hand, discourse structure provides clues to split the source sentence. It is because some DCs only relate EDUs within the same sentences (e.g. *'but', 'because'*) while some only relate with the previous sentence (e.g. *'however', 'in addition'*)(Stepanov and Riccardi, 2013).

Example 2 shows two versions of English translation of a Chinese sentence as output by *Google Translate*. Note that in the original Chinese sentence, all the DCs are omitted to achieve a quadruplet pattern. Implicit DCs, represented by glossed words in brackets, can be inserted to each comma-separated clause to signal the discourse relations. Without explicit DCs, the MT output **(MT original)** results in a sequence of broken clauses, whereas with inserted DCs **(MT w/DC)**, the clauses are joined by the translated DCs to a complete sentence. In addition, the dropped pronoun 'you' is properly generated, potentially due to improvement in syntactical parsing of the source sentence.

Example 2
Source: (如果-if)交納税款有困難的，(便-then)可暫緩積欠，(但是-but)新税不欠，(而且-furthermore)掛税免罰，(並-and)逐年繳清。

MT original: Difficult to pay taxes, may suspend arrears, the new tex is not owed, penalties linked tax free, paid annually.

MT w/DC: **If** you have difficulty to pay taxes, you can suspend the arrears, **but** the new tax is not owed **and** taxes linked to impunity **and** paid annually.

Ref: Those having difficulty paying taxes can temporarily postponing old debt **but** not owing on new taxes, **and** suspending taxes **and** waiving fines, **and** paying off year by year.
(adapted from Chinese Tree Bank Art.89)

4 Work in progress: Cross-lingual annotation of discourse relations

Towards building a statistical machine translation system that tackles discourse relations specifically, I started manually annotating a Chinese-English translation corpus with discourse relations. The purpose of annotation is not only to create data but also to understand the problems in Chinese discourse processing and translation. The completed annotation is planned to be released.

Comparing with representation of discourse relations by analytical definitions, the PDTB-styled association of discourse relations to lexical connectives is more compatible to the procedures of statistical machine translation. Therefore, the PDTB convention is adopted for the annotation of connectives on both sides of the parallel corpus. Instead of sense annotation, the DCs are aligned in similar manner as the 'translation spotting' approach (Meyer et al., 2011; Popescu-Belis et al., 2012; Cartoni et al., 2013). In other words, the 'senses' are disambiguated by the translation of the DCs. The data used is the English Chinese Translation Treebank (Bies et al., 2007), which consists of 325 Chinese news stories translated into 146,300 words of English. Adaptations made to capture the cross-lingual difference in discourse relations are explained in the following.

4.1 EDU segmented by punctuations

In the PDTB, the span of each EDU (Arg1 or Arg2), which can range from a single noun to multiple sentences, are manually annotated. While each WSJ paragraph[1] contains three sentences on average, the typical 'running sentences' in Chinese are exceptionally long. It is hard for annotators to agree on an EDU span, and neither does it have direct effect on the DC translation. Therefore, I follow previous works (Yang and Xue, 2012; Zhou and Xue, 2012) and consider a segment separated by Chinese punctuations, especially commas, as the span of an EDU.

Nonetheless, there are exceptions since Chinese commas are used arbitrarily to signify '*pauses*' in the sentence. Three original tags are defined to annotate the exceptions: '**ATT**ribution' , 'initialized **ADV**erbial', and '**OPT**ional comma' (refer to Table 1). These are designed for training of automatic EDU segmentation.

4.2 Explicit DCs

After recognizing a valid EDU on the source text, explicit DC(s) in the EDU are tagged '**EXP**' and aligned to their translation on the target side, which are not necessarily explicit DCs. In contrast with the defined list of subordinating conjunctions, coordinating conjunctions and adverbials, DCs are not limited to any syntactical categories in this scheme so as to improve the coverage of cross-lingual annotation. For example, 'at the same time' and 'in spite of the fact that' are annotated as DC instances, since they function as the DCs 'simultaneously' and 'although' respectively, independent of context.

In addition, conjunctions between VP constructions, which are not annotated in the PDTB, are also annotated as explicit DCs. It is because subjects are often dropped in Chinese and many EDUs will be ignored if VP constructions are excluded.

4.3 Discourse markers alternative to DCs

Discourse relations can be explicitly marked by non-DC expressions that are context dependent. Following the PDTB scheme, the '**ALT**Lex' tag is used to annotate such alternative lexicalization of discourse relations. However, with a loose definition of DC, few alternative expressions are identified. Therefore, the '**ALT**' tag is defined only on the English side, which particularly serves to mark non-DC translation of Chinese DCs. Typically, English prepositions are tagged '**ALT**' and aligned to Chinese DCs that do not correspond with any English DCs. For example, '透過' is a common DC for the 'method' relation, yet there is not a DC for this relation in English and thus it is often translated to 'by' or 'through'.

[1]A paragraph is considered an independent document in the PDTB. This annotation scheme follows this assumption.

4.4 Categorization of DCs

It is observed that subtly different DCs need not be distinguished for translation, thus they are annotated as variations of a same DC. For example, explicit occurrences of *'in addition'*, *'additionally'*, *'moreover'*, *'furthermore'* and *'besides'*, all listed as distinct DCs in PDTB, are annotated as instances of *'in addition'*, and '但是', '可是', '然而', '不過' as instances of '但是' (literally *'but'*). An unambiguous DC is used to represent the DC type, such as *'since'* as an instance of *'because'* but not the reverse.

Assigning DCs variations to an unambiguous type can serve as sense annotation without an abstract taxonomy of senses. External DC lexicon can also be flexibly added by registering new DC entries to existing categories. On the other hand, DCs that are not interchangeable in the syntactical context, such as *'but'* and *'however'*, are treated as distinct DC types in order to deduce discriminative translation rules.

4.5 Implicit DCs

In order to produce translation rules for all discourse relations, including the unmarked ones, implicit DCs (**IMP**) are inserted after all explicit DCs are identified in the Chinese EDU. A corresponding implicit DC is also inserted, if possible, as translation of a Chinese DC (explicit or implicit) when explicit translation is not identified. Note that implicit DCs are always annotated by a DC type instead of a variation to avoid ambiguity.

The **IMP** tag is used to annotate parallel DC structures in Chinese. Most Chinese discourse relations are marked by 'parallel DCs', which are similar to English patterns such as *'either...or'*, *'if...then'*, *'not only...but also'*. However, one or both DCs in the parallel structure can be dropped in Chinese. The dropped DCs are inserted as **IMP** and aligned to the English side.

After the first round of the annotation, another annotator is to repeat the annotation with the set of DCs recognized by the first annotator. Since implicit discourse relations lack lexical signals, the annotator agreement is lower (72% for English (Miltsakaki et al., 2004)). I plan to include implicit DC annotations of both annotators as multiple readings or coexisting DCs of the implicit relations, thus multiplying the training instances.

4.6 Redundancy

Usually, two EDUs are related by one DC in English, thus only one of the Chinese parallel DCs is translated to explicitly. To learn this translation rule, the untranslated DC is thus aligned to a'**RED**undant' tag attached to the corresponding English EDU. To mark Chinese DCs that always occur independently rather than in parallel structure, the EDU without a DC is also annotated as '**RED**'. The various types of tags for DC annotation are summarized in Table 1.

Tags for aligned 'DC'

Chinese	English	
EXP	**EXP**	explicit DC identified
IMP	**IMP**	implicit DC insertable
-	**ALT**	expressions alternative to DC
RED	**RED**	ungrammatical to insert DC

Tags for Non-EDU Chinese segments

ATT	source of attribution
ADV	adverbial initialized
OPT	optional comma for a rhythmic pause

Table 1: Tags for Chi-Eng DC annotations

4.7 Primary analysis of the annotation

To date, 82 articles (about 33000 English words, about 1/3 of the complete dataset) have been annotated, giving rise to 2050 aligned discourse relations. In addition, 486 punctuation-separated segments on the Chinese side have been identified as non-EDU segments. 59 DC types for Chinese and 47 for English have been identified.

Chi -/- Eng	EXP.	ALT.	IMP.	RED.	Total
EXP.	291	68	23	49	**431**
IMP.	396	144	770	261	**1561**
RED.	6	0	0	52	**58**
Total	**693**	**212**	**783**	**362**	**2050**
attribute	-	-	-	-	211
optional	-	-	-	-	89
adverbial	-	-	-	-	186
Total	-	-	-	-	**486**

Table 2: Distribution of alignment between different 'DC' types

The distribution of alignments between these types is shown in Table 2. Although the statistics are not directly comparable to other existing data due to difference in definitions, it agrees with previous findings that implicit DCs are abundant in Chinese (Zhou and Xue, 2012). According to the present data, about 1/4 of the implicit DCs are translated to explicit DCs in English. However, more than half are not explicitly translated (implicit or redundant). This suggests that implicit DC recovery can be focused on the those that are likely to be translated explicitly.

It is also observable that explicit Chinese DCs are mostly translated to an explicit DC in English, while about 1/6 of them are translated to non-DC expressions. As mentioned, these are mostly prepositions corresponding to discourse relations that are not defined by any DCs in English. This suggests that bilingual discourse annotation can recover a larger variation of universal discourse relations than monolingual annotation. Further exploratory analysis will be conducted to investigate the tendency in discourse relation markedness and alignment, so as to define informative linguistic features for model training.

Currently, I am using the MAE annotation tool(Stubbs, 2011). The annotation effort can be lightened by developing an interface that assists the multilingual annotation task by, for example, automatic EDU segmentation (to be reviewed by annotators) and automatic identification and pre-alignment of DCs based on a DC dictionary.

5 Future plans

The key of this research is to integrate the annotated discourse knowledge into an SMT system. Integration of document level parse to MT, as described in Marcu et al. (2000) for Japanese-to-English translation, is complicated. In addition, comparing with Japanese, the word order in Chinese and English are not drastically different. Therefore, I plan to make use of information from DC-based shallow discourse parse. My main tasks towards this system include:

1. Cross-lingual DC annotation
2. EDU segmentation
3. Prediction of source implicit DCs
4. Integration to SMT system
5. DC-aware MT evaluation

A flowchart of these tasks is shown in Figure 1 and explained in the following.

5.1 EDU segmentation

Discourse parsing can be divided to the tasks of DC identification and argument identification,

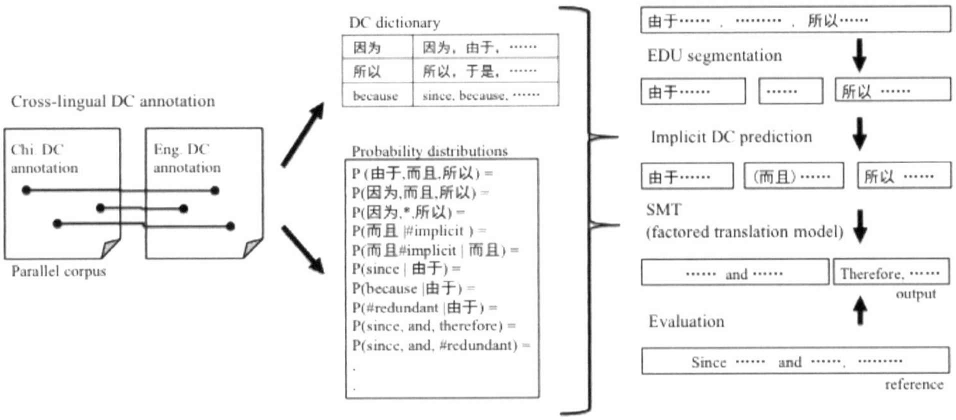

Figure 1: Main tasks for proposed DC-aware SMT system.

where the latter can be further divided into argument position and argument span identification. In Chinese, a punctuation-separated segment is basically considered an EDU, so the span is fixed. The exceptional cases of commas not segmenting an EDU are annotated in the dataset and can be predicted in a binary classification task using lexical and syntactical features, as in Yang and Xue (2012). On the other hand, a text segment can contain more than one EDU when there are multiple DCs, thus further segmentation is necessary depending on DC identification.

5.2 Prediction of source implicit DCs

One focus of this research is to explicitize implicit Chinese DCs when translating to English. I plan to construct a model to predict implicit discourse relations in the Chinese source text. Previous works on Chinese discourse relation recognitions (Yue, 2006; Huang and Chen, 2011) provide insights on the prediction task and the DC annotated corpus provides data for supervised training. Although state-of-the-art implicit discourse parsing is still of low accuracy, the preciseness can be adjusted to suit the goal of machine translation. As in other joint tasks with MT, such as Bouamor et al. (2013), features of whether the implicit DC can be translated explicitly, or correctly, can in incorporated to the prediction task, so as to predict translatable implicit DCs in particular.

5.3 Integration to SMT system

One way to exploit discourse knowledge into an SMT system is to incorporate the predicted discourse features, such as implicit DC, DC sequence or DC type, into a factored translation model (Koehn and Hoang, 2007). Another approach is to decorate identified and predicted DCs in a syntactical parsed tree, so as to enrich the tree-to-string rules with DC markedness features. Moreover, when a source DC is translated to a sentence initial DC, a source sentence is potentially split to multiple target sentences. A document level decoder (Hardmeier et al., 2012) that searches beyond the sentence boundary is thus preferred.

5.4 DC-aware MT evaluation

Comparable evaluation is essential for MT research, yet conventional MT metrics, such as BLEU, is not effective in detecting improvement in discourse relation translation (Meyer et al., 2012). One direction is to extend the *ACT* metrics (Hajlaoui and Popescu-Belis, 2013) to access also translation of implicit DCs. Another direction is to define a measure that is not reference-dependent, since implicit relations can be translated in various ways. Moreover, conventional MT metrics, which compare a candidate with the reference sentence-by-sentence, have to be modified when used to access the overall MT performance of the proposed system, since the output sentences may not align with the reference sentences one-by-one.

6 Conclusion

In this thesis proposal, ongoing work and future plans have been presented towards a discourse-relation-aware SMT system. The research can serve as basis for the goal of a document-level MT system that considers various discourse structures.

Acknowledgement

I would like to thank Baidu for travel and conference support for this paper.

References

Ann Bies, Martha Palmer, Justin Mott, and Colin Warner. 2007. English chinese translation treebank v 1.0. Linguistic Data Consortium LDC2007T02, January.

Houda Bouamor, Behrang Mohit, and Kemal Oflazer. 2013. Sumt: A framework of summarization and mt. *Proceedings of the International Conference on Natural Language Processing*.

Lynn Carlson, Daniel Marcu, and Mary Ellen Okurowski. 2001. Building a discourse-tagged corpus in the framework of rhetorical structure theory. *Proceedings of the SIGdial Workshop on Discourse and Dialogue*.

Bruno Cartoni, Sandrine Zufferey, and Thomas Meyer. 2013. Annotating the meaning of discourse connectives by looking at their translation: The translation-spotting technique. *Dialogue and Discourse*, 4(2).

Najeh Hajlaoui and Andrei Popescu-Belis. 2012. Translating english discourse connectives into arabic: a corpus-based analysis and an evaluation metric. *Proceedings of the Workshop on Computational Approaches to Arabic Script-based Languages*.

Najeh Hajlaoui and Andrei Popescu-Belis. 2013. Assessing the accuracy of discourse connective translations: Validation of an automatic metric. *Computational LInguistics and Intelligent Text Processing*, 7617.

Christian Hardmeier, Joakim Nivre, and Jörg Tiedemann. 2012. Document-wide decoding for phrase-based statistical machine translation. *Proceedings of the Joint Conference on Empirical Methods in Natural Language Processing and Computational Natural Language Learning*.

Hen-Hsen Huang and Hsin-Hsi Chen. 2011. Chinese discourse relation recognition. *Proceedings of the International Conference on Natural Language Processing*.

Hen-Hsen Huang and Hsin-Hsi Chen. 2012. Contingency and comparison relation labelling and structure prediction in chinese sentences. *Proceedings of the Annual Meeting of the Special Interest Group on Discourse and Dialogue*.

Hen-Hsen Huang, Chi-Hsin Yu, Tai-Wei Chang, Cong-Kai lin, and Hsin-Hsi Chen. 2013. Analyses of the association between discourse relation and sentiment polarity with a chinese human-annotated corpus. *Proceedings of the Linguistic Annotation Workshop and Interperability with Discourse*.

Philipp Koehn and Hieu Hoang. 2007. Factored translation models. *Proceedings of the Joint Conference on Empirical Methods in Natural Language Processing and Computational Natural Language Learning*.

Ziheng Lin, Hwee Tou Ng, and Min Yen Kan. 2010. A pdtb-styled end-to-end discourse parser. Technical report, National University of Singapore.

William C. Mann and Sandra A. Thompson. 1988. Rhetorical structure theory: Toward a functional theory of text organization. *Text*.

Daniel Marcu, Lynn Carlson, and Maki Watanabe. 2000. The automatic translation of discourse structures. *Proceedings of the North American Chapter of the Association for Computational Linguistics*.

Thomas Meyer and Lucie Polakova. 2013. Machine translation with many manually labeled discourse connectives. *Proceedings of the Discourse in Machine Translation Workshop*.

Thomas Meyer, Andrei Popescu-Belis, Sandrine Zufferey, and Bruno Cartoni. 2011. Multilingual annotation and disambiguation of discourse connectives for machine translation. *Proceedings of the Annual Meeting of the Special Interest Group on Discourse and Dialogue*.

Thomas Meyer, Andrei Popescu-Belis, and Najeh Hajlaoui. 2012. Machine translation of labeled discourse connectives. *Proceedings of the Biennial Conference of the Association for Machine Translation in the Americas*.

Eleni Miltsakaki, Rashmi Prasad, Aravind Joshi, and Bonnie Webber. 2004. Annotating discourse connectives and their arguments. *Proceedings of the Workshop on Frontiers in Corpus Annotations*.

Emily Pitler and Ani Nenkova. 2009. Using syntax to disambiguate explicit discourse connectives in text. *Proceedings of the Annual Meeting of the Association for Computational Linguistics and the International Joint Conference on Natural Language Processing*.

Emily Pitler, Annie Louis, and Ani Nenkova. 2009. Automatic sense prediction for implicit discourse relations in text. *Proceedings of the Annual Meeting of the Association for Computational Linguistics and the International Joint Conference on Natural Language Processing*.

Andrei Popescu-Belis, Thomas Meyer, Jeevanthi Liyanapathirana, Bruno Cartoni, and Sandrine Zufferey. 2012. Discourse-level annotation over europarl for machine translation: Connectives and pronouns. *Proceedings of the Language Resource and Evaluation Conference*.

Rashmi Prasad, Nikhit Dinesh, Alan Lee, Eleni Miltsakaki, Livio Robaldo, Aravind Joshi, and Bonnie Webber. 2008. The penn discourse treebank 2.0. *Proceedings of the Language Resource and Evaluation Conference*.

Ted Sanders and Leo Noordman. 2000. The role of coherence relations and their linguistic markers in text processing. *Discourse Processes*, 1.

Evgeny A. Stepanov and Giuseppe Riccardi. 2013. Comparative evaluation of argument extraction algorithms in discourse relation parsing. *Proceedings of the International Conference on Parsing Technologies.*

Amber Stubbs. 2011. Mae and mai: lightweight annotation and adjudication tools. *Proceedings of the Linguistic Annotation Workshop.*

Mei Tu, Yu Zhou, and Chengqing Zong. 2013. A novel translation framework based on rhetorical structure theory. *Proceedings of the Annual Meeting of the Association for Computational Linguistics.*

Florian Wolf and Edward Gibson. 2005. Representing discourse coherence: a corpus-based analysis. *Computational Linguistics.*

Nianwen Xue. 2005. Annotating discourse connectives in the chinese treebank. *Proceedings of the Workshop on Frontiers in Corpus Annotations.*

Yaqin Yang and Nianwen Xue. 2012. Chinese comma disambiguation for discourse analysis. *Proceedings of the Annual Meeting of the Association for Computational Linguistics.*

Ming Yue. 2006. Discursive usage of six chinese punctuation marks. *Proceedings of the Annual Meeting of the Association for Computational Linguistics and International Conference on Computational Linguistics.*

Yuping Zhou and Nianwen Xue. 2012. Pdtb-style discourse annotation of chinese text. *Proceedings of the Annual Meeting of the Association for Computational Linguistics.*

Zhi-Min Zhou, Yu Xu, Zheng-Yu Niu, Man Lan, Jian Su, and Chew Lim Tan. 2010. Predicting discourse connectives for implicit discourse relation recognition. *Proceedings of the International Conference on Computational Linguistics.*

Lan Jun Zhou, Wei Gao, Binyang Li, Zhongyu Wei, and Kam-Fat Wong. 2012. Cross-lingual identification of ambiguous discourse connectives for resource-poor language. *Proceedings of the International Conference on Computational Linguistics.*

Analyzing Positions and Topics in Political Discussions of the German Bundestag

Cäcilia Zirn
Data and Web Science Group
University of Mannheim
Germany
caecilia@informatik.uni-mannheim.de

Abstract

We present ongoing doctoral work on automatically understanding the positions of politicians with respect to those of the party they belong to. To this end, we use textual data, namely transcriptions of political speeches from meetings of the German Bundestag, and party manifestos, in order to automatically acquire the positions of political actors and parties, respectively. We discuss a variety of possible supervised and unsupervised approaches to determine the topics of interest and compare positions, and propose to explore an approach based on topic modeling techniques for these tasks.

1 Introduction

The Bundestag is the legislative institution of Germany. In its plenary sessions, the members discuss the introduction and formulation of bills. Subjects under discussion include a wide spectrum of issues, ranging from funding of public transport through fighting right-wing extremism, or the deployment of German troops in Afghanistan. For each issue, a few selected members give a speech stating their opinion towards the topic, while the audience is allowed to interact: by questions, heckles, applause or even laughter. Transcriptions of the Bundestag's sessions provide us with a gold-mine of political speech data, encoding heterogeneous political phenomena such as, for instance, the prominence or engagement of the different politicians with respect to the current political situation, or their interest for specific topics.

In our work, we propose to leverage these data to enable the analysis of the speakers' positions with respect to the party they belong to, on the basis of the content of their speech. Questions we investigate include: which party's views do different politicians support? How much are their political views aligned with those of their party? Although we know *a-priori* which party a speaker belongs to, we view their positions on different topics with respect to their party's official lines as degrees of alignment, and measure them based on the content of their speeches. There are several circumstances under which a speaker might deviate from his or her party's opinion. For instance, he might stem from an election district where membership of a particular party increases his chances of being elected. Moreover, it might just happen that a politician who generally supports his party's lines personally has a different view on one particular topic. If we are able to measure positions from text, we allow for methods of analyzing adherence to party lines, which is an important issue in political science (cf. (Clinton et al., 2004), (Ceron, 2013) and (Ansolabehere et al., 2001)).

At its heart, our work aims at modeling politicians' positions towards a specific topic, as inferred from their speech. To estimate a position, in turn, we need a statement of the party's opinion towards the topic of interest, which can be then used for comparison against the speech. Various work in political science suggests to take this from party manifestos like (Keman, 2007) and (Slapin and Proksch, 2008). Research in political science has previously focused on analyzing political positions within text, for instance (Laver and Garry, 2000), (Laver et al., 2003), (Keman, 2007) or (Sim et al., 2013). However, most of previous work focused on the general position of a party or a person, like (Slapin and Proksch, 2008), as opposed to fine-grained positions towards specific topics. In our research, we address the two following tasks:

1. *Determine the speeches' topics* – namely develop methods to determine the topic(s) covered by a political speech, such as those given in the Bundestag.

Proceedings of the ACL 2014 Student Research Workshop, pages 26–33,
Baltimore, Maryland USA, June 22-27 2014.

2. *Quantify adherence to party lines* – namely estimate the speaker's position relatively to his party's opinion towards the respective topic(s).

In the following thesis proposal we present a variety of approaches that we plan to investigate in order to address these tasks, as well as discuss their limitations and challenges.

The first task, determining the topics, could be in principle addressed using well-studied supervised approaches like state-of-the-art machine learning algorithms. However, we cannot rely on the fact that all topics are covered in the training data. Consequently, we propose to explore an unsupervised approach that integrates information from an external resource. We suggest to use a variant of topic models which allows us to influence the creation of the topics.

The second task, determining the positions, is a bigger challenge, given the current state of the art. Some previous research looked at the related field of opinion mining, also on political discussion, as in (Abu-Jbara et al., 2012), (Anand et al., 2011) or (Somasundaran and Wiebe, 2009). These methods, however, are hardly applicable to the complex data of plenary meetings. In our scenario, we have to deal with a very specific kind of text, since the discussions do not consist of spontaneous dialogues, but rather formal statements. Consequently, we are forced to deal with a type of language which lies in-between dialogue and text. More concretely, within these speeches speakers roughly assume what positions the parties have and also have expectations about their opponents' opinions. Besides, as opposed to full-fledged dialogues, our data shows a very limited amount of interaction between the speaker and the audience, solely consisting of a few questions, heckles, laughter or applause. Further, as it is the goal of the discussions to constructively develop laws and agree on formulations, the speakers do not just state reasons pro or contra some issue. They rather illustrate different aspects of the discussed items. Furthermore, they try to convince others by emphasizing what their party has achieved in the past or criticize decisions taken in the past. To address these complex problems, we propose to start by using manually annotated party manifestos in order to provide us with an upper bound. Next, we propose to investigate the applicability of topic models to provide us, again, with a flexible unsupervised approach.

2 Data

The German Bundestag meets about 60 times a year, and discusses various items in each plenary session. There are various types of items on the agenda: they can be discussions about bills, but also question times or government's statements. We are interested in the first type only. Each bill has a unique identifier which is also mentioned by the session chair. By looking it up in a database provided by the Bundestag, it is possible to filter the bill discussions from other forms of items.

For each discussed item, a few selected members are permitted to give a speech. Most of the members belong to a party and their affiliation is publicly known.

The Bundestag releases the transcripts of its sessions as plain text documents. OffenesParlament[1] is a project run by volunteers that processes these documents and publishes them in a structured form on the web as HTML documents. The data distinguishes between parts of a given speech, utterances by the chairman and heckles, each annotated with its speaker. OffenesParlament makes the attempt to divide each session's transcript into parts containing a single item of the agenda only. This is not trivial, as it is the chairman who leads over using a non-standardized formulations, and thus contains many mistakes.

We collected a number of regular expressions and hope to improve the segmentation of the items. We will evaluate the performance of this heuristic by checking a sample with human judges.

Our extracted dataset covers the time period between March 2010 and December 2012 and consists of 182 meetings.

3 Determining topics in speeches

We aim at comparing the positions stated within the speeches to the general positions of the parties represented in the Bundestag. The parties' positions can be found in their manifestos, and are commonly used as a source by scholars, as in (Keman, 2007) or (Slapin and Proksch, 2008). In order to being able to compare speakers' and parties positions, we need to address two different tasks, namely: i) identifying the topic of a speech, and ii) locating that very same topic within the party manifesto or some further resource. The latter task depends on how the comparison is done. In this

[1] `http://offenesParlament.de`

section, we will focus on the first task: determining the topic of the speech.

There are two general approaches to classify the topics of text: either the topics are known in advance and constitute a static set of categories, for example (Hillard et al., 2008), or they are unknown in advance and dynamically created depending on the data, as in (Quinn et al., 2010) (see also (Grimmer and Stewart, 2013) and (Sebastiani, 2002) for an overview). In our scenario, we assume a common set of topics over several data sources, namely the party manifestos and transcripts of speeches in our case. Therefore, we opt for a fixed set of topic categories.

3.1 Definition of topical categories

In political science, there are various schemes to categorize political topics. A well-known and important project is the Comparative Manifesto Project (Budge et al., 2001), in which party manifestos are hand-coded on sentence level with a scheme of 560 categories. A similar project is the Comparative Agendas Project[2], which uses 21 top level categories further divided into fine-grained subcategories.

An alternative approach is to use the ministries as definition of the available categories, which inspired the category scheme used in (Seher and Pappi, 2011). In our work, we develop a category scheme for our particular task on the basis of the responsibilities of committees of the Bundestag, as suggested by internal discussions with scholars of political science. Similar to the ministries in government, the responsibilities for political areas are divided among various committees (see Table 1 for a list of committees). Each item discussed in the Bundestag is assigned to all committees who investigate the issues in more detail. For instance, in our data we find that a discussion about continuing the German participation in the International Security Assistance Force in Afghanistan has been assigned to the following committees: Foreign Affairs, Internal Affairs, Legal Affairs, Defense, Human Rights and Humanitarian Aid, Economic Cooperation and Development. For each issue, one of the committees is appointed as the leading one (German: federführende Ausschuss), the Committee of Foreign Affairs in this case.

Note that, crucially for our work, this assignment process provides us with human-annotated

[2]`http://www.comparativeagendas.info`

Affairs of the European Union
Labour and social Affairs
Food, Agriculture and Consumer Protection
Family Affairs, Senior Citizens, Women and Youth
Health
Cultural and Media Affairs
Committee on Human Rights and Humanitarian Aid
Tourism
Environment, Nature Conservation and Nuclear Safety
Transport, Building and Urban Development
Scrutiny of Elections, Immunity and the Rules of Procedure
Economics and Technology
Economic Cooperation and Development
Foreign Affairs
Finance
Budget
Internal Affairs
Petitions
Legal Affairs
Sports
Defense
Education, Research and Technology Assessment

Table 1: Committees of the 17th German Bundestag.

topic labels: in fact, not only can we use the committees as category definitions, but we can also use these very same assignments as a gold standard. Consequently, we use the definitions describing the responsibilities of the committees as our category scheme for political topics. We exclude three committees from the experiments namely: a) the Committee on Scrutiny of Elections, Immunity and the Rules of Procedure, b) the Committee on Petitions, and c) the Committee of Legal Affairs. This is because these committees are not directly responsible for a particular political domain, but perform meta functions.

Descriptions of the particular committees including their responsibilities and tasks as well as concrete examples of their work, accomplished by lists of current members, can be found in flyers released by the Bundestag[3].

Given this definition of political categories on the basis of the committees, we can create a gold standard for our topic classification scenario: to label a speech, we take the item it is given about, and use the committees the item has been assigned to as labels. The committee responsible, in turn, can be seen as the most important (i.e., primary) topic label[4]. Topic assignments are automatically harvested from a freely available source of infor-

[3]`https://www.btg-bestellservice.de/index.php?navi=1&subnavi=52`

[4]Henceforth, we refer to the committees as labels for our topic classification task as "category" or "class"

mation, namely a public database offered by the German Bundestag[5]. Each item discussed in the Bundestag is associated with a printed document (*Drucksache*) tagged with a unique identifier, by which it can be tracked in the database and where the list of assigned committees can be queried.

Given these topic assignments, we aim at acquiring a model to classify the speeches with their assigned categories. To this end, we could focus on predicting the main label only (i.e. the committee responsible), or rather perform a multi-class labeling task predicting all labels (all committees the item is assigned to). We now overview a supervised and unsupervised approach to address these classification problems.

3.2 Supervised approach

Given that we have labeled data, a first solution is to opt for a supervised approach to text classification, which has been successfully used for many tasks like topic detection ((Diermeier et al., 2012), (Husby and Barbosa, 2012), or sentiment analysis (Bakliwal et al., 2013), to name a few. Consequently, in our case we could represent the speeches as a word vector and train state-of-the-art machine learning algorithms like Support Vector Machines, using the assigned committees as labels.

3.3 Unsupervised approach

In order to develop a generally applicable approach that can easily be applied to other resources such as speeches given in a context different from that of the Bundestag, we are interested to explore an unsupervised approach and compare it to the supervised one.

External definition of categories. The particular issues that fall into the responsibility of a committee are broad and might not be completely covered when using the speeches themselves as training data. As mentioned in Section 3.1, we have a clear definition of the tasks of each committee provided within the flyers. We will use them as a basis for the category definitions, and extend them with political issues discussed in party manifestos. We will explain this further in Section 3.3.

Known set of categories. Techniques such as LDA (Blei et al., 2003) create the topics dynamically during the classification process. Recently they became quite popular in political science, c.f. (Grimmer, 2010), (Quinn et al., 2010) or (Gerrish and Blei, 2011). As discussed in Section 3, we prefer to have a fixed set of categories. This allows for comparison between applications of the classification on different sources and domains separately. But while topic models do not fit this requirement, they have one property that corresponds quite well to our task: rather than assigning the text one single label, they return a distribution over topics contained by it. The items discussed in the speeches touch a range of political topics, and are assigned to various committees. There are variations of topic models that allow for influencing the creation of the topics, such as the systems of (Ramage et al., 2009) (Labeled LDA), (Andrzejewski and Zhu, 2009) or (Jagarlamudi et al., 2012). Labeled LDA is trained on a corpus of documents. In contrast to standard topic model approaches, it needs as input the information which labels (topics) are contained by the document, though not their proportions, thus uses a fixed set of categories.

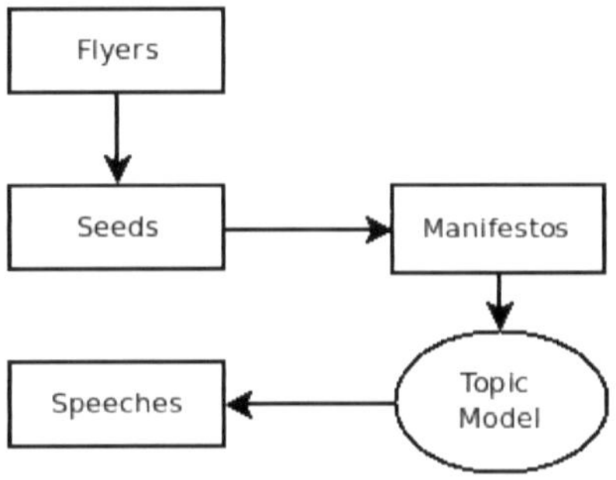

Figure 1: Approach overview

We illustrate our methodology in Figure 1. Our proposed approach starts by extracting seed words for the categories from the flyers about the committees. These seed words are then used to label training data for labeled LDA. As training data, we take an external resource: the manifestos[6] of all parties. Finally, we apply the trained model to the speeches to infer the labels. The output can be evaluated by comparing the predicted categories to the committees the issue is actually assigned to. In the following, we will explain each step in more detail.

[5] dipbt.bundestag.de/dip21.web/bt

[6] We combine the general party programs and the current election programs of each party

1) Extraction of seed words. We first download the flyers provided by the Bundestag. Then, we filter for nouns and calculate their TF-IDF values for the committee, by which we rank them. In a final step, we ask a scholar of political science to clean them, i.e. to delete nouns that are not necessarily important for the particular committee or are too ambiguous, and to cut the tail of low-ranked nouns. To give an example, we finally receive the following keywords for the committee of Labour and Social Affairs: *age-related poverty, labour-market policy, employee, social affairs, social security, labour, work, pension, basic social security, regulated rates, partial retirement, social standard, subcontracted labour.*

2) Automatically generating training data. We take the manifestos of all parties in the Bundestag to train our labeled LDA model. While topic models expect a whole collection of documents as input, we only provide a handful of them: accordingly, we generate a pseudo document collection by cutting the documents into snippets, following our previous work in (Zirn and Stuckenschmidt, 2013), and treating each of them as single documents. If a keyword for a committee is found within a snippet, we add the corresponding category to the documents labels. We finally run labeled LDA using standard configurations on the so labeled data.

3) Applying labeled LDA. Finally, we can apply the trained model on our transcribed speech data: we do this by inferring, for each speech, the distribution of topics, i.e. of categories. To evaluate the model, we check that the committee responsible corresponds to the highest probable topic inferred for the speech, and the other n assigned committees to the n most probable topics.

Currently, in our work, we are in the final stages of creating the gold standard, and evaluating our method. However, we have already implemented the proposed system as prototype, and accordingly show a part of the created topic model in Table 2 to give the reader an impression.

ENCNS	LSA	TBUD
consumer *(male)*	labour	mobility
consumer *(female)*	employee *male*	research
environment	employees *female*	infrastructure
protection	salary	railway
products	pension	traffic
farming	labour market	investments
nature	old-age provision	development
variety	unemployment	future
raw materials	employment	rails
transparency	percentage	streets

Table 2: Top 10 terms for the committees on Environment, Nature Conservation and Nuclear Safety (ENCNS), on Labour and social affairs (LSA) and on Transport, Building and Urban Development (TBUD).

4 Detecting positions

The overall goal of our work is to analyze the positions expressed by the speakers towards the debated item. As we aim at performing a fine-grained analysis, approaches merely classifying pro or contra (like those of (Walker et al., 2012) or (Somasundaran and Wiebe, 2009) are not applicable in our case. The same applies to the task of subgroup detection (as done by (Abu-Jbara et al., 2012), (Anand et al., 2011) or (Thomas et al., 2006)).

In order to produce a finer-grained model of positions, we want to develop a model that places positions stated in text along a one-dimensional scale, as done by (Slapin and Proksch, 2008) with their system called Wordfish, (Gabel and Huber, 2000),(Laver and Garry, 2000), (Laver et al., 2003) or (Sim et al., 2013). Wordfish places party manifestos on a left-right-scale, what visualizes very well which parties are close to each other and which ones are distant. This is similar in spirit to the purpose of our work, since we are interested primarily in estimating closeness and distances between the speakers' and the parties' positions. However, in contrast to their work, we are interested in positions towards specific topics, as opposed to general parties' positions.

We define our task as follows: we want to analyze the distance between the position towards a topic expressed in a speech and the position towards the same topic stated in a party manifesto. In the previous section, we described an approach to determine the topic of the speech. We now move on and present how we can retrieve the segments of the manifestos that correspond to the topic(s) addressed within the speeches, as well as how to compare these positions.

4.1 Approach A: Hand-coding of manifestos

Extract positions As part of a larger collaboration project with scholars of political science we decided to start with hand-coding a set of manifestos on sentence-level in order to have a gold standard for further work. To facilitate the manual work, we use a computer-assisted method based using the seed words created in Section 3.3. In more detail, we first use occurrences of the seed words to assign them the corresponding category label. Then, a human annotator validates these assignments, optionally adding missing labels.

If the sentence-wise labeled data proofs successful and necessary for the further analysis of political positions, we will investigate approaches to automate this process, for example with supervised learning or bootstrapping techniques starting with our seed words. For each topic, we can then accumulate the sentences assigned to its corresponding category and use this data as the party's opinion towards this topic.

Compare positions The comparison between the speech and the parties' opinions can then be performed as follows: for each party, we extract the sentences from the manifesto that are tagged with the topic covered in the speech. We then represent the extracted sentences and the speeches as word vectors, and compare them with a distance metric, e.g., a standard measure like cosine similarity, which gives us the closeness of the speech to each party's position.

4.2 Approach B: Topic Models

Extract positions Instead of selecting sentences from the manifesto that cover a topic, the position could be extracted from the manifesto using topic models, as shown in (Thomas et al., 2006) and (Gerrish and Blei, 2011). To extract the topics from the manifestos, we run labeled LDA separately on each manifesto, following the technique described in Section 3, yet with an important difference. In Section 3, we trained one common topic model on all manifestos, in order to have a broad coverage over all topics. Here, we are interested in the positions carried by the particular words chosen by the party to describe a topic. Accordingly, we train a separate topic model on each manifesto. The result is a distribution over terms for each committee, hence for each topic.

Compare positions As a result of the process to determine the topic of a speech (Section 3), the speeches also have a representation of the discussed topics as a distribution over terms. This way we can directly compare the distributions for the most probable topics in the speech with the corresponding topic in the party manifestos. This can be done using measures to estimate the distance between probability distributions like, for instance, Kullback-Leibler distance or Jensen-Shannon divergence.

5 Conclusions and Future Work

In this paper, we presented an overview of our thesis proposal on comparing positions found within political speeches against those expressed in party manifestos. To the best of our knowledge, this is the first work of this kind to aim at providing a fine-grained analysis of speakers' positions on political data. Arguably, the most exiting aspect of this work is that it grounds a variety of Natural Language Processing topics – e.g., polarity detection, topic modeling, among others – within a concrete, multi-faceted application scenario.

Being this a proposal, the first step in the future will be to complete the implementation of all above described methods and evaluate them. In our dataset, we are provided with additional information apart from the speech text: we know about heckles, laughter and applause and even know their origin. This knowledge can be used to estimate a network of support or opposition. This knowledge is also used in (Strapparava et al., 2010) to predict persuasiveness of sentences, which could constitute another source of information for our model. Another idea would be to make use of the speaker's given party affiliations and bootstrap an approach to analyze their positions: if we assume that a majority of the speakers actually does follow their parties' lines, we can train a classifier for each party for each topic, and apply it to the same data to detect outliers. Besides, a big research question would be to see how much we can complement our topic models with additional supervision in the form of symbolic knowledge sources like wide-coverage ontologies, e.g., DBpedia. Finally, while we do focus in this work on German data, we are interested in extending our model to other languages, including resource-rich ones like English as well as resource-poor ones.

Acknowledgements

We thank Google for travel and conference support for this paper.

References

Amjad Abu-Jbara, Mona Diab, Pradeep Dasigi, and Dragomir Radev. 2012. Subgroup detection in ideological discussions. In *Proceedings of the 50th Annual Meeting of the Association for Computational Linguistics: Long Papers - Volume 1*, ACL '12, pages 399–409, Stroudsburg, PA, USA. Association for Computational Linguistics.

Pranav Anand, Marilyn Walker, Rob Abbott, Jean E. Fox Tree, Robeson Bowmani, and Michael Minor. 2011. Cats rule and dogs drool!: Classifying stance in online debate. In *Proceedings of the 2Nd Workshop on Computational Approaches to Subjectivity and Sentiment Analysis*, WASSA '11, pages 1–9, Stroudsburg, PA, USA. Association for Computational Linguistics.

David Andrzejewski and Xiaojin Zhu. 2009. Latent dirichlet allocation with topic-in-set knowledge. In *Proceedings of the NAACL HLT 2009 Workshop on Semi-Supervised Learning for Natural Language Processing*, pages 43–48. Association for Computational Linguistics.

Stephen Ansolabehere, James M Snyder, and Charles Stewart III. 2001. The effects of party and preferences on congressional roll-call voting. *Legislative Studies Quarterly*, 26(4):533–572.

Akshat Bakliwal, Jennifer Foster, Jennifer van der Puil, Ron O'Brien, Lamia Tounsi, and Mark Hughes. 2013. Sentiment analysis of political tweets: Towards an accurate classifier. In *Proceedings of the Workshop on Language Analysis in Social Media*, pages 49–58, Atlanta, Georgia, June. Association for Computational Linguistics.

D.M. Blei, A.Y. Ng, and M.I. Jordan. 2003. Latent dirichlet allocation. *Journal of Machine Learning Research (JMLR)*, 3:993–1022.

Ian Budge, Hans"=Dieter Klingemann, Andrea Volkens, Judith Bara, and Eric Tanenbaum. 2001. *Mapping Policy Preferences. Estimates for Parties, Electors, and Governments 1945-1998.* Oxford University Press, Oxford u. a.

Andrea Ceron. 2013. Brave rebels stay home: Assessing the effect of intra-party ideological heterogeneity and party whip on roll-call votes. *Party Politics*, page 1354068812472581.

Joshua Clinton, Simon Jackman, and Douglas Rivers. 2004. The statistical analysis of roll call data. *American Political Science Review*, 98(02):355–370.

Daniel Diermeier, Jean-Franois Godbout, Bei Yu, and Stefan Kaufmann. 2012. Language and ideology in congress. *British Journal of Political Science*, 42:31–55, 1.

Matthew J. Gabel and John D. Huber. 2000. Putting parties in their place: Inferring party left-right ideological positions from party manifestos data. *American Journal of Political Science*, 44(1):pp. 94–103.

Sean Gerrish and David M Blei. 2011. Predicting legislative roll calls from text. In *Proceedings of the 28th International Conference on Machine Learning (ICML-11)*, pages 489–496.

Justin Grimmer and Brandon M Stewart. 2013. Text as data: The promise and pitfalls of automatic content analysis methods for political texts. *Political Analysis.*

Justin Grimmer. 2010. A bayesian hierarchical topic model for political texts: Measuring expressed agendas in senate press releases. *Political Analysis*, 18(1):1–35.

Dustin Hillard, Stephen Purpura, and John Wilkerson. 2008. Computer assisted topic classification for mixed methods social science research. *Journal of Information Technology and Politics.*

Stephanie Husby and Denilson Barbosa. 2012. Topic classification of blog posts using distant supervision. In *Proceedings of the Workshop on Semantic Analysis in Social Media*, pages 28–36, Avignon, France, April. Association for Computational Linguistics.

Jagadeesh Jagarlamudi, Hal Daumé, III, and Raghavendra Udupa. 2012. Incorporating lexical priors into topic models. In *Proceedings of the 13th Conference of the European Chapter of the Association for Computational Linguistics*, EACL '12, pages 204–213, Stroudsburg, PA, USA. Association for Computational Linguistics.

Hans Keman. 2007. Experts and manifestos: Different sources - same results for comparative research. *Electoral Studies*, 26:76–89.

Michael Laver and John Garry. 2000. Estimating policy positions from political texts. *American Journal of Political Science*, pages 619–634.

Michael Laver, Kenneth Benoit, and John Garry. 2003. Extracting policy positions from political texts using words as data. *American Political Science Review*, 97(02):311–331.

Kevin M. Quinn, Burt L. Monroe, Michael Colaresi, Michael H. Crespin, and Dragomir R. Radev. 2010. How to analyze political attention with minimal assumptions and costs. *American Journal of Political Science*, 54(1):209–228, January.

Daniel Ramage, David Hall, Ramesh Nallapati, and Christopher D Manning. 2009. Labeled lda: A supervised topic model for credit attribution in multi-labeled corpora. In *Proceedings of the 2009 Conference on Empirical Methods in Natural Language Processing: Volume 1-Volume 1*, pages 248–256. Association for Computational Linguistics.

Fabrizio Sebastiani. 2002. Machine learning in automated text categorization. *ACM computing surveys (CSUR)*, 34(1):1–47.

Nicole Michaela Seher and Franz Urban Pappi. 2011. Politikfeldspezifische positionen der landesverbände der deutschen parteien. Working Paper 139, Mannheimer Zentrum für Europäische Sozialforschung (MZES).

Yanchuan Sim, Brice D. L. Acree, Justin H. Gross, and Noah A. Smith. 2013. Measuring ideological proportions in political speeches. In *Proceedings of the 2013 Conference on Empirical Methods in Natural Language Processing*, pages 91–101, Seattle, Washington, USA, October. Association for Computational Linguistics.

Jonathan B. Slapin and Sven-Oliver Proksch. 2008. A Scaling Model for Estimating Time-Series Party Positions from Texts. *American Journal of Political Science*, 52(3):705–722, July.

Swapna Somasundaran and Janyce Wiebe. 2009. Recognizing stances in online debates. In *Proceedings of the Joint Conference of the 47th Annual Meeting of the ACL and the 4th International Joint Conference on Natural Language Processing of the AFNLP: Volume 1 - Volume 1*, ACL '09, pages 226–234, Stroudsburg, PA, USA. Association for Computational Linguistics.

Carlo Strapparava, Marco Guerini, and Oliviero Stock. 2010. Predicting persuasiveness in political discourses. In *LREC*. European Language Resources Association.

Matt Thomas, Bo Pang, and Lillian Lee. 2006. Get out the vote: Determining support or opposition from congressional floor-debate transcripts. In *Proceedings of the 2006 Conference on Empirical Methods in Natural Language Processing*, EMNLP '06, pages 327–335, Stroudsburg, PA, USA. Association for Computational Linguistics.

Marilyn A Walker, Pranav Anand, Robert Abbott, and Ricky Grant. 2012. Stance classification using dialogic properties of persuasion. In *Proceedings of the 2012 Conference of the North American Chapter of the Association for Computational Linguistics: Human Language Technologies*, pages 592–596. Association for Computational Linguistics.

Cäcilia Zirn and Heiner Stuckenschmidt. 2013. Multidimensional topic analysis in political texts. *Data & Knowledge Engineering*.

A Mapping-Based Approach for General Formal Human Computer Interaction Using Natural Language

Vincent Letard
LIMSI CNRS
letard@limsi.fr

Sophie Rosset
LIMSI CNRS
rosset@limsi.fr

Gabriel Illouz
LIMSI CNRS
illouz@limsi.fr

Abstract

We consider the problem of mapping natural language written utterances expressing operational instructions[1] to formal language expressions, applied to French and the R programming language. Developing a learning operational assistant requires the means to train and evaluate it, that is, a baseline system able to interact with the user. After presenting the guidelines of our work, we propose a model to represent the problem and discuss the fit of direct mapping methods to our task. Finally, we show that, while not resulting in excellent scores, a simple approach seems to be sufficient to provide a baseline for an interactive learning system.

1 Introduction

Technical and theoretical advances allow achieving more and more powerful and efficient operations with the help of computers. However, this does not necessarily make it easier to work with the machine. Recent supervised learning work (Allen et al., 2007; Volkova et al., 2013) exploited the richness of human-computer interaction for improving the efficiency of a human performed task with the help of the computer.

Contrary to most of what was proposed so far, our long term goal is to build an assistant system learning from interaction to construct a correct formal language (FL) command for a given natural language (NL) utterance, see Table 1. However, designing such a system requires data collection, and early attempts highlighted the importance of usability for the learning process: a system that is hard to use (*eg.* having very poor performance) would prevent from extracting useful learning examples from the interaction. We thus need to provide the system with a basis of abilities and knowledge to allow both incremental design and to keep the interest of the users, without which data turn to be way more tedious to collect. We assume that making the system usable requires the ability to provide help to the user more often than it needs help from him/her, that is an accuracy over 50%.

We hypothesize that a parametrized direct mapping between the NL utterances and the FL commands can reach that score. A knowledge set K is built from parametrized versions of the associations shown in Table 1. The NL utterance U_{best} from K that is the closest to the request-utterance according to a similarity measure is chosen and its associated command $C(U_{best})$ is adapted to the parameters of the request-utterance and returned. For example, given the request-utterance U_{req}: *"Load the file data.csv"*, the system should rank the utterances of K by similarity with U_{req}. Considering the associations represented in Table 1, the first utterance should be the best ranked, and the system should return the command:
"`var1 <- read.csv("data.csv")`".
Note that several commands can be proposed at the same time to give the user alternate choices.

We use Jaccard, tf-idf, and BLEU similarity measures, and consider different selection strategies. We highlight that the examined similarity measures show enough complementarity to permit the use of combination methods, like vote or statistical classification, to improve *a posteriori* the efficiency of the retrieval.

2 Related Work

2.1 Mapping Natural Language to Formal Language

Related problems have been previously processed using different learning methods. Branavan (2009,

[1] We call *operational instruction* the natural language expression of a command in any programming language.

Proceedings of the ACL 2014 Student Research Workshop, pages 34–40,
Baltimore, Maryland USA, June 22-27 2014.

	NL utterances	FL commands (in R)
1	Charge les données depuis **"res.csv"** Load the data from **"res.csv"**	`var1=read.csv("res.csv")`
2	Trace l'histogramme de la colonne **2** de **tab** Draw a bar chart with column **2** of **tab**	`plot(hist(tab[[2]]))`
3	Dessine la répartition de la colonne **3** de **tab** Draw the distribution of column **3** of **tab**	`plot(hist(tab[[3]]))`
4	Somme les colonnes **3** et **4** de **tab** Compute the sum of columns **3** and **4** of **tab**	`var2=c(sum(tab[3]),sum(tab[4]))`
5	Somme les colonnes **3** et **4** de **tab** Compute the sum of columns **3** and **4** of **tab**	`var3=sum(c(tab[[3]],tab[[4]]))`

Table 1: A sample of NL utterances to FL commands mapping
These examples specify the expected command to be returned for each utterance. The tokens in bold font are linked with the commands parameters, cf. section 4. Note that the relation between utterances and commands is a n to n. Several utterances can be associated to the same command and conversely.

2010) uses reinforcement learning to map English NL instructions to a sequence of FL commands. The mapping takes high-level instructions and their constitution into account. The scope of usable commands is yet limited to graphical interaction possibilities. As a result, the learning does not produce highly abstract schemes. In the problematic of interactive continuous learning, Artzi and Zettlemoyer (2011) build by learning a semantic NL parser based on combinatory categorial grammars (CCG). Kushman and Barzilay (2013) also use CCG in order to generate regular expressions corresponding to their NL descriptions. This constructive approach by translation allows to generalize over learning examples, while the expressive power of regular expressions correspond to the type-3 grammars of the Chomsky hierarchy. This is not the case for the programming languages since they are at least of type-2. Yu and Siskind (2013) use hidden Markov models to learn a mapping between object tracks from a video sequence and predicates extracted from a NL description. The goal of their approach is different from ours but the underlying problem of finding a map between objects can be compared. The matched objects constitute here a FL expression instead of a video sequence track.

2.2 Machine Translation

Machine translation usually refers to transforming a NL sentence from a source language to another sentence of the same significance in another natural language, called target language. This task is achieved by building an intermediary representation of the sentence structure at a given level of abstraction, and then encoding the obtained object into the target language. While following a different goal, one of the tasks of the XLike project (Marko Tadić et al., 2012) was to examine the possibility of translating statements from NL (English) to FL (Cycl). Adapting such an approach to operational formal target language can be interesting to investigate, but we will not focus on that track for our early goal.

2.3 Information Retrieval

The issue of information retrieval systems can be compared with the operational assistant's (OA), when browsing its knowledge. Question answering systems in particular (Hirschman and Gaizauskas, 2001), turn out to be similar to OA since both types of systems have to respond to a NL utterance of the user by generating an accurate reaction (which is respectively a NL utterance containing the wanted information, or the execution of a piece of FL code). However, as in (Toney et al., 2008), questions answering systems usually rely on text mining to retrieve the right information. Such a method demands large sets of annotated textual data (either by hand or using an automatic annotator). Yet, tutorials, courses or manuals which could be used in order to look for responses for operational assistant systems are heterogeneous and include complex or implicit references to operational knowledge. This makes the annotation of such data difficult. Text mining methods are thus not yet applicable to operational assistant systems but could be considered once some annotated data is collected.

3 Problem Formulation

As we introduced in the first section, we represent the knowledge K as a set of examples of a binary relation $R : NL \rightarrow FL$ associating a NL utterance to a FL command. If we consider the simple case of a functional and injective relation, each utterance is associated to exactly one command. This is not realistic since it is possible to reformulate nearly any NL sentence. The case of a non injective relation covers better the usual cases: each command can be associated with one or more utterances, this situation is illustrated by the second and third examples of Table 1. Yet, the real-life case should be a non injective nor functional relation. Not only multiple utterances can refer to a same command, but one single utterance can also stand for several distinct commands (see the fourth and fifth examples[2] in Table 1). We must consider all these associations when matching a request-utterance U_{req} for command retrieval in K.

At this point, several strategies can be used to determine what to return, with the help of the similarity measure $\sigma : NL \times NL \rightarrow \mathbb{R}$ between two NL utterances. Basically, we must determine if a response should be given, and if so how many commands to return. To do this, two potential strategies can be considered for selecting the associated utterances in K.

The first choice focuses on the number of responses that are given for each request-utterance. The n first commands according to the rankings of their associated utterances in K are returned. The rank r of a given utterance U is computed with:

$$r(U|U_{req}) = \left|\{U' \in K : \sigma(U_{req}, U') > \sigma(U_{req}, U)\}\right| \quad (1)$$

The second strategy choice can be done by determining an absolute similarity threshold below which the candidate utterances from K and their associated sets of commands are considered too different to match. The resulting set of commands is given by:

$$Res = \{C \in FL : (U, C) \in K, \sigma(U_{req}, U) < t\} \quad (2)$$

with t the selected threshold. Once selected the set of commands to be given as response, if there are more than one, the choice of the one to execute can be done interactively with the help of the user.

[2]The command 4 returns a vector of the sums of each column, while the command 5 returns the sum of the columns as a single integer.

4 Approach

We are given a simple parsing result of both the utterance and the command. The first step to address is the acquisition of examples and the way to update the knowledge. Then we examine the methods for retrieving a command from the knowledge and a given request-utterance.

Correctly mapping utterances to commands requires at least to take their respective parameters into account (variable names, numeric values, and quoted strings). We build generic representations of utterances and commands by identifying the parameters in the knowledge example pair (see Table 1), and use them to reconstruct the command with the parameters of the request-utterance.

4.1 Retrieving the Commands

We applied three textual similarity measures to our model in order to compare their strengths and weaknesses on our task: the Jaccard similarity coefficient (Jaccard index), a tf-idf (Term frequency-inverse document frequency) aggregation, and the BLEU (Bilingual Evaluation Understudy) measure.

4.1.1 Jaccard index

The Jaccard index measures a similarity between two sets valued in the same superset. For the present case, we compare the set of words of the input NL instruction and the one of the compared candidate instruction, valued in the set of possible tokens. The adapted formula for two sentences S_1 and S_2 results in:

$$J(s_1, s_2) = \frac{|W(s_1) \cap W(s_2)|}{|W(s_1) \cup W(s_2)|} \quad (3)$$

where $W(S)$ stands for the set of words of the sentence S. The Jaccard index is a baseline to compare co-occurences of unigrams, and should be efficient mainly with corpora containing few ambiguous examples.

4.1.2 tf-idf

The tf-idf measure permits, given a word, to classify documents on its importance in each one, regarding its importance in the whole set. This measure should be helpful to avoid noise bias when it comes from frequent terms in the corpus. Here, the documents are the NL utterances from K, and they are classified regarding the whole request-utterance, or input sentence s_i. We then use the following aggregation of the tf-idf values for each word of $\overline{s_i}$.

$$tfidf_S(s_i, s_c) = \frac{1}{|W(s_i)|} \sum_{w \in W(s_i)} tfidf(w, s_c, S) \quad (4)$$

with $S = \{s | (s, com) \in K\}$, where s_i is the input sentence, $s_c \in S$ is the compared sentence, and where the tf-idf is given by:

$$tfidf(w, s_c, S) = f(w, s_c) idf(w, S) \quad (5)$$

$$idf(w, S) = log\left(\frac{|S|}{|\{s \in S | w \in s\}|}\right) \quad (6)$$

where at last $f(w, s)$ is the frequency of the word w in the sentence s. As we did for the Jaccard index, we performed the measures on both raw and lemmatized words. On the other hand, getting rid of the function words and closed class words is not here mandatory since the tf-idf measure already takes the global word frequency into account.

4.1.3 The BLEU measure

The bilingual evaluation understudy algorithm (Papineni et al., 2002) focuses on n-grams co-occurrences. This algorithm can be used to discard examples where the words ordering is too far from the candidate. It computes a modified precision based on the ratio of the co-occurring n-grams within candidate and reference sentences, on the total size of the candidate normalized by n.

$$P_{BLEU}(s_i, S) = \sum_{gr_n \in s_i} \frac{\max_{s_c \in S} occ(gr_n, s_c)}{grams(s_i, n)} \quad (7)$$

where $grams(s, n) = |s| - (n - 1)$ is the number of n-grams in the sentence s and $occ(gr_n, s) = \sum_{gr_n' \in s} [gr_n = gr_n']$ is the number of occurrences of the n-gram gr_n in s. BLEU also uses a brevity penalty to prevent long sentences from being too disadvantaged by the n-gram based precision formula. Yet, the scale of the length of the instructions in our corpus is sufficiently reduced not to require its use.

4.2 Optimizing the similarity measure

We applied several combinations of filters to the utterances compared before evaluating their similarity. We can change the set of words taken into account, discarding or not the non open-class words[3]. Identified non-lexical references such as variable names, quoted character strings and numeric values can also be discarded or transformed to standard substitutes. Finally, we can apply or not a lemmatization[4] on lexical tokens.By discarding non open-class words, keeping non-lexical references and applying the lemmatization, the second utterance of Table 1 would then become:

draw bar chart column xxVALxx xxVARxx

5 Experimental Setup

5.1 Parsing

The NL utterances first pass through an arithmetic expression finder to completely tag them before the NL analyzer. They are then parsed using WMATCH, a generic rule-based engine for language analysis developed by Olivier Galibert (2009). This system is modular and dispose of rules sets for both French and English. As an example, the simplified parsing result of the first utterance of Table 1 looks like:

```
<_operation>
  <_action> charge|_~V </_action>
  <_det> les </_det>
  <_subs> données|_~N </_subs>
  <_prep> depuis </_prep>
  <_unk> "res.csv" </_unk>
</_operation>
```

Words tagged as unknown are considered as potential variable or function names. We also added a preliminary rule to identify character strings and count them among the possibly linked features of the utterance. The commands are normalized by inserting spaces between every non semantically linked character pair and we identify numeric values, variable/function names and character strings as features.

Only generative forms of the commands are associated to utterances in the knowledge. This form consists in a normalized command with unresolved references for every parameter linked with the learning utterance. These references are resolved at the retrieving phase by matching with the tokens of the request-utterance.

5.2 Corpus Constitution

Our initial corpus consists in 605 associations between 553 unique NL utterances in French and 240 unique R commands.

[3]Open-class words include nouns, verbs, adjectives, adverbs and interjections.

[4]Lemmatization is the process of transforming a word to its canonical form, or lemma, ignoring the inflections. It can be performed with a set of rules or with a dictionary. The developed system uses a dictionary.

The low number of documents describing a majority of R commands and their heterogeneity make automatic example gathering not yet achievable. These documentations are written for human readers having global references on the task. Thus, we added each example pair manually, making sure that the element render all the example information and that the format correspond to the corpus specifications. Those specifications are meant to be the least restrictive, that is: a NL utterance must be written as to ask for the execution of the associated R task. It therefore should be mostly in the imperative form and reflect, for experienced people, a usual way they would express the concerned operation for non specialists.

5.3 Evaluation Metrics

The measures that can contribute to a relevant evaluation of the system depend on its purpose. Precision and recall values of information retrieval systems are computed as follows:

$$P = \frac{\text{\# correct responses}}{\text{\# responses given}} \qquad (8)$$

$$R = \frac{\text{\# correct responses}}{\text{\# responses in K}} \qquad (9)$$

Note that the recall value is not as important as for information retrieval: assuming that the situation showed by the fourth and fifth associations of Table 1 are not usual[5], there should be few different valid commands for a given request-utterance, and most of them should be equivalent. Moreover, the number of responses given is fixed (so is the number of responses in K), the recall thus gives the same information as the precision, with a linear coefficient variation.

These formulae can be applied to the "command level", that is measuring the accuracy of the system in terms of its good command ratio. However, the user satisfaction can be better measured at the "utterance level" since it represents the finest granularity for the user experience. We define the utterance precision uP as:

$$uP = \frac{\text{\# correct utterances}}{\text{\# responses given}} \qquad (10)$$

where "# correct utterances" stands for the number of request-utterances for which the system provided at least one good command.

[5]Increasing the tasks covering of the corpus will make these collisions more frequent, but this hypothesis seems reasonable for a first approach.

6 Results and Discussion

The system was tested on 10% of the corpus (61 associations). The set of known associations K contains 85% of the corpus (514 associations), instead of 90% in order to allow several distinct drawings (40 were tested), and thus avoid too much noise.

6.1 Comparing similarity measures

As shown in Table 2 the tf-idf measure outperforms the Jaccard and BLEU measures, whichever filter combination is applied. The form of the utterances in the corpus causes indeed the repetition of a small set of words across the associations. This can explain why the inverse document frequency is that better.

non-lexical	included		not included	
lemmatize	yes	no	yes	no
Jaccard	36.5	36.5	21.2	23.0
tf-idf	**48.0**	**51.9**	**36.5**	**40.4**
BLEU	30.8	32.7	26.9	30.8
chance	1.9			

Table 2: Scores of precision by utterance (uP), providing 3 responses for each request-utterance.

The lemmatization and the inclusion of non open-class words (not shown here) does not seem to have a clear influence on uP, whereas including the non-lexical tokens allows a real improvement. This behaviour must result from the low length average (7.5 words) of the utterances in the corpus.

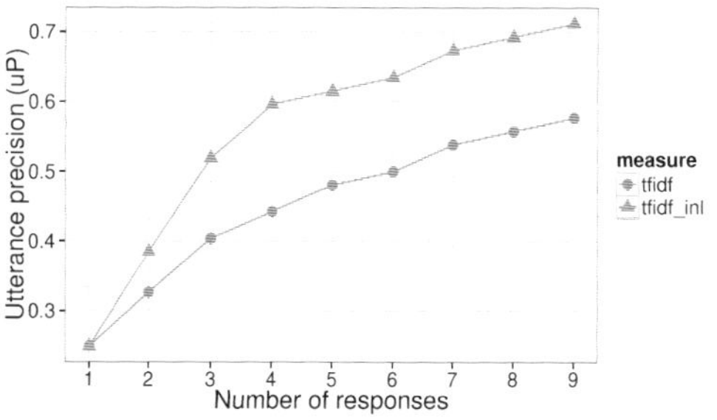

Figure 1: Utterance precision (uP) for a fixed number of responses by utterance. The tfidf_inl curve includes the non-lexical tokens.
Note that uP is obtained with Equation 10, which explains the increase of the precision along the number of responses.

Figure 1 shows the precision obtained with tfidf while increasing the number of commands given for each request-utterance. It comes out that it is useful to propose at least 3 commands to the user. It would not be interesting, though, to offer a choice of more than 5 items, because the gain on uP would be offset by the time penalty for retrieving the good command among the proposals.

6.2 Allowing silence

We also tested the strategy of fixing an absolute threshold to decide between response and silence. Given a request-utterance and an associated ordering of K according to σ, the system will remain silent if the similarity of the best example in K is below the defined threshold.

Surprisingly, it turned out that for every measure, the 6 best similar responses at least were all wrong. This result seems to be caused by the existence, in the test set of commands uncovered by K, of some very short utterances that contain only one or two lexical tokens.

6.3 Combinations

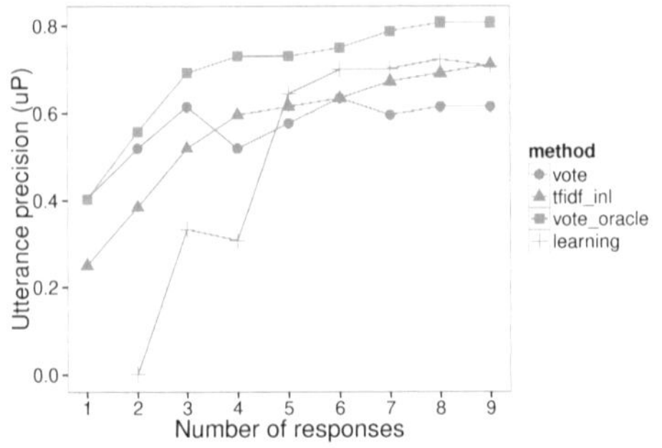

Figure 2: Comparison of the combinations with the tf-idf_inl method. Oracle and actual vote are done using tf-idf, Jaccard, and BLEU, with and without non-lexical tokens. The training set for learning is the result of a run on K.

Having tested several methods giving different results, combining these methods can be very interesting depending on their complementarity. The oracle vote using the best response among the 6 best methods shows an encouraging progression margin (*cf.* Figure 2). The actual vote itself outperforms the best method for giving up to 3 responses (reaching 50% for only 2 responses). However, the curve position is less clear for more responses, and tests must be performed on other drawings of K to measure the noise influence.

The complementarity of the methods can also be exploited by training a classification model to identify when a method is better than the others. We used the similarity values as features and the measure that gave a good response as the reference class label (best similarity if multiple, and "none" class if no good response). This setup was tested with the support vector machines using libsvm (Chang and Lin, 2011) and results are shown in Figure 2. As expected, machine learning performs poorly on our tiny corpus. The accuracy is under 20% and the system only learned when to use the best method, and when to give no response. Still, it manages to be competitive with the best method and should be tested again with more data and multiple drawings of K.

7 Conclusion and Future Work

The simple mapping methods based on similarity ranking showed up to 60% of utterance precision[6] remaining below a reasonable level of user sollicitation, which validate our prior hypothesis. A lot of approaches can enhance that score, such as adding or developing more suitable similarity measures (Achananuparp et al., 2008), combining learning and vote or learning to rerank utterances.

However, while usable as a baseline, these methods only allow poor generalization and really need more corpus to perform well. As we pointed out, the non-functionality of the mapping relation also introduces ambiguities that cannot be solved using the only knowledge of the system.

Thanks to this baseline method, we are now able to collect more data by developing an interactive agent that can be both an intelligent assistant and a crowdsourcing platform. We are currently developing a web interface for this purpose. Finally, situated human computer interaction will allow the real-time resolving of ambiguities met in the retrieval with the help of the user or with the use of contextual information from the dialogue.

Aknowledgements

The authors are grateful to every internal and external reviewer for their valuable advices. We also would like to thank Google for the financial support for the authors participation to the conference.

[6]The corpus will soon be made available.

References

Palakorn Achananuparp, Xiaohua Hu, and Xiajiong Shen. 2008. *The Evaluation of Sentence Similarity Measures*. In Data Warehousing and Knowledge Discovery, Springer.

James Allen, Nathanael Chambers, George Ferguson, Lucian Galescu, Hyuckchul Jung, Mary Swift, and William Tayson. 2007. *PLOW: A Collaborative Task Learning Agent*. In Proceedings of the 22nd National Conference on Artificial Intelligence.

Yoav Artzi, and Luke S. Zettlemoyer. 2011. *Bootstrapping semantic parsers from conversations*. Proceedings of the conference on empirical methods in natural language processing.

S.R.K. Branavan, Luke S. Zettlemoyer, and Regina Barzilay. 2010. *Reading Between the Lines: Learning to Map High-level Instructions to Commands*. In Proceedings of the 48th Annual Meeting of the Association for Computational Linguistics.

S.R.K. Branavan, Harr Chen, Luke S. Zettlemoyer, and Regina Barzilay. 2009. *Reinforcement Learning for Mapping Instructions to Actions*. In Proceedings of the Joint Conference of the 47th Annual Meeting of the ACL and the 4th International Joint Conference on Natural Language Processing of the AFNLP.

Chih-Chung Chang, and Chih-Jen Lin. 2011. *LIBSVM: A Library for Support Vector Machines*. ACM Transactions on Intelligent Systems and Technology

Olivier Galibert. 2009. *Approches et méthodologies pour la réponse automatique à des questions adaptées à un cadre interactif en domaine ouvert*. Doctoral dissertation, Université Paris Sud XI.

Lynette Hirschman, and Robert Gaizauskas. 2001. *Natural language question answering: The view from here*. Natural Language Engineering 7. Cambridge University Press.

Nate Kushman, and Regina Barzilay. 2013. *Using Semantic Unification to Generate Regular Expressions from Natural Language*. In Proceedings of the Conference of the North American Chapter of the Association for Computational Linguistics.

Kishore Papineni, Salim Roukos, Todd Ward, and Wei-Jing Zhu. 2002. *Bleu: a Method for Automatic Evaluation of Machine Translation*. In Proceedings of the 40th Annual Meeting of the Association for Computational Linguistics.

Marko Tadić, Božo Bekavac, Željko Agić, Matea Srebačić, Daša Berović, and Danijela Merkler. 2012. *Early machine translation based semantic annotation prototype* XLike project www.xlike.org .

Dave Toney, Sophie Rosset, Aurélien Max, Olivier Galibert, and éric Billinski. 2008. *An Evaluation of Spoken and Textual Interaction on the RITEL Interactive Question Answering System* In Proceedings of the Sixth International Conference on Language Resources and Evaluation.

Svitlana Volkova, Pallavi Choudhury, Chris Quirk, Bill Dolan, and Luke Zettlemoyer. 2013. *Lightly Supervised Learning of Procedural Dialog System* In Proceedings of the 51st Annual Meeting of the Association for Computational Linguistics.

Haonan Yu, and Jeffrey Mark Siskind. 2013. *Grounded Language Learning from Video Described with Sentences*. In Proceedings of the 51st Annual Meeting of the Association for Computational Linguistics.

An Exploration of Embeddings for Generalized Phrases

Wenpeng Yin and Hinrich Schütze
Center for Information and Language Processing
University of Munich, Germany
wenpeng@cis.lmu.de

Abstract

Deep learning embeddings have been successfully used for many natural language processing problems. Embeddings are mostly computed for word forms although lots of recent papers have extended this to other linguistic units like morphemes and word sequences. In this paper, we define the concept of *generalized phrase* that includes conventional linguistic phrases as well as skip-bigrams. We compute embeddings for generalized phrases and show in experimental evaluations on coreference resolution and paraphrase identification that such embeddings perform better than word form embeddings.

1 Motivation

One advantage of recent work in deep learning on natural language processing (NLP) is that linguistic units are represented by rich and informative embeddings. These embeddings support better performance on a variety of NLP tasks (Collobert et al., 2011) than symbolic linguistic representations that do not directly represent information about similarity and other linguistic properties. Embeddings are mostly derived for word forms although a number of recent papers have extended this to other linguistic units like morphemes (Luong et al., 2013), phrases and word sequences (Socher et al., 2010; Mikolov et al., 2013).[1] Thus, an important question is: what are the basic linguistic units that should be represented by embeddings in a deep learning NLP system? Building on the prior work in (Socher et al., 2010; Mikolov et al., 2013), we generalize the notion of phrase to include *skip-bigrams* (SkipBs) and lexicon entries, where lexicon entries can be both "continuous" and "noncontinuous" *linguistic phrases*. Examples of skip-bigrams at distance 2 in the sentence "this tea helped me to relax" are: "this*helped", "tea*me", "helped*to" ... Examples of linguistic phrases listed in a typical lexicon are continuous phrases like "cold_cuts" and "White_House" that only occur without intervening words and discontinous phrases like "take_over" and "turn_off" that can occur with intervening words. We consider it promising to compute embeddings for these phrases because many phrases, including the four examples we just gave, are noncompositional or weakly compositional, i.e., it is difficult to compute the meaning of the phrase from the meaning of its parts. We write gaps as "*" for SkipBs and "_" for phrases.

We can approach the question of what basic linguistic units should have representations from a practical as well as from a cognitive point of view. In practical terms, we want representations to be optimized for good generalization. There are many situations where a particular task involving a word cannot be solved based on *the word itself*, but it can be solved by analyzing *the context of the word*. For example, if a coreference resolution system needs to determine whether the unknown word "Xiulan" (a Chinese first name) in "he helped Xiulan to find a flat" refers to an animate or an inanimate entity, then the SkipB "helped*to" is a good indicator for the animacy of the unknown word – whereas the unknown word itself provides no clue.

From a cognitive point of view, it can be argued that many basic units that the human cognitive system uses have multiple words. Particularly convincing examples for such units are phrasal verbs in English, which often have a non-compositional meaning. It is implausible to suppose that we retrieve atomic representations for, say, "keep", "up", "on" and "from" and then combine them to

[1] Socher et al. use the term "word sequence". Mikolov et al. use the term "phrase" for word sequences that are mostly frequent continuous collocations.

Proceedings of the ACL 2014 Student Research Workshop, pages 41–47,
Baltimore, Maryland USA, June 22-27 2014.

form the meanings of the expressions "keep your head up," "keep the pressure on," "keep him from laughing". Rather, it is more plausible that we recognize "keep up", "keep on" and "keep from" as relevant basic linguistic units in these contexts and that the human cognitive systems represents them as units.

We can view SkipBs and discontinuous phrases as extreme cases of treating two words that do not occur next to each other as a unit. SkipBs are defined purely statistically and we will consider any pair of words as a potential SkipB in our experiments below. In contrast, discontinuous phrases are well motivated. It is clear that the words "picked" and "up" in the sentences "I picked it up" belong together and form a unit very similar to the word "collected" in "I collected it". The most useful definition of discontinuous units probably lies in between SkipBs and phrases: we definitely want to include all phrases, but also some (but not all) statistical SkipBs. The initial work presented in this paper may help in finding a good "compromise" definition.

This paper contributes to a preliminary investigation of generalized phrase embeddings and shows that they are better suited than word embedding for a coreference resolution classification task and for paraphrase identification. Another contribution lies in that the phrase embeddings we release[2] could be a valuable resource for others.

The remainder of this paper is organized as follows. Section 2 and Section 3 introduce how to learn embeddings for SkipBs and phrases, respectively. Experiments are provided in Section 4. Subsequently, we analyze related work in Section 5, and conclude our work in Section 6.

2 Embedding learning for SkipBs

With English Gigaword Corpus (Parker et al., 2009), we use the *skip-gram model* as implemented in word2vec[3] (Mikolov et al., 2013) to induce embeddings. Word2vec skip-gram scheme is a neural network language model, using a given word to predict its context words within a window size. To be able to use word2vec directly without code changes, we represent the corpus as a sequence of sentences, each consisting of two tokens: a SkipB and a word that occurs between the two enclosing words of the SkipB. The distance k between the two enclosing words can be varied. In our experiments, we use either distance $k = 2$ or distance $2 \leq k \leq 3$. For example, for $k = 2$, the trigram $w_{i-1}\ w_i\ w_{i+1}$ generates the single sentence "$w_{i-1}*w_{i+1}\ w_i$"; and for $2 \leq k \leq 3$, the fourgram $w_{i-2}\ w_{i-1}\ w_i\ w_{i+1}$ generates the four sentences "$w_{i-2}*w_i\ w_{i-1}$", "$w_{i-1}*w_{i+1}\ w_i$", "$w_{i-2}*w_{i+1}\ w_{i-1}$" and "$w_{i-2}*w_{i+1}\ w_i$".

In this setup, the middle context of SkipBs are kept (i.e., the second token in the new sentences), and the surrounding context of words of original sentences are also kept (i.e., the SkipB in the new sentences). We can run word2vec without any changes on the reformatted corpus to learn embeddings for SkipBs. As a baseline, we run word2vec on the original corpus to compute embeddings for words. Embedding size is set to 200.

3 Embedding learning for phrases

3.1 Phrase collection

Phrases defined by a lexicon have not been deeply investigated before in deep learning. To collect canonical phrase set, we extract two-word phrases defined in Wiktionary[4], and two-word phrases defined in Wordnet (Miller and Fellbaum, 1998) to form a collection of size 95218. This collection contains phrases whose parts always occur next to each other (e.g., "cold cuts") and phrases whose parts more often occur separated from each other (e.g., "take (something) apart").

3.2 Identification of phrase continuity

Wiktionary and WordNet do not categorize phrases as continuous or discontinous. So we need a heuristic for determining this automatically.

For each phrase "A_B", we compute $[c_1, c_2, c_3, c_4, c_5]$ where $c_i, 1 \leq i \leq 5$, indicates there are c_i occurrences of A and B in that order with a distance of i. We compute these statistics for a corpus consisting of Gigaword and Wikipedia. We set the maximal distance to 5 because discontinuous phrases are rarely separated by more than 5 tokens.

If c_1 is 10 times higher than $(c_2+c_3+c_4+c_5)/4$, we classify "A_B" as *continuous*, otherwise as *discontinuous*. Taking phrase "pick_off" as an example, it gets vector [1121, 632, 337, 348, 4052], c_1 (1121) is smaller than the average 1342.25, so

[2] http://www.cis.lmu.de/pub/phraseEmbedding.txt.bz2

[3] https://code.google.com/p/word2vec/

[4] http://en.wiktionary.org/wiki/Wiktionary:Main_Page

"pick_off" is set as "discontinuous". Further consider "Cornell University" which gets [14831, 16, 177, 331, 3471], satisfying above condition, hence it is treated as a continuous phrase.

3.3 Sentence reformatting

Given the continuity information of phrases, sentence "$\cdots A \cdots B \cdots$" is reformated into "$\cdots A\_B \cdots A\_B \cdots$" if "A_B" is a discontinuous phrase and is separated by maximal 4 words, and sentence "$\cdots AB \cdots$" into "$\cdots A\_B \cdots$" if "A_B" is a continuous phrase.

In the first case, we use phrase "A_B" to replace each of its component words for the purpose of making the context of both constituents available to the phrase in learning. For the second situation, it is natural to combine the two words directly to form an independent semantic unit.

Word2vec is run on the reformatted corpus to learn embeddings for both words and phrases. Embedding size is also set to 200.

3.4 Examples of phrase neighbors

Usually, compositional methods for learning representations of multi-word text suffer from the difficulty in integrating word form representations, like word embeddings. To our knowledge, there is no released embeddings which can directly facilitate measuring the semantic affinity between linguistic units of arbitrary lengths. Table 1 attempts to provide some nearest neighbors for given typical phrases to show the promising perspective of our work. Note that discontinuous phrases like "turn_off" have plausible single word nearest neighbors like "unplug".

4 Experiments

Our motivation for generalized phrases in Section 1 was that they can be used to infer the attributes of the context they enclose and that they can capture non-compositional semantics. Our hypothesis was that they are more suitable for this than word embeddings. In this section we carry out two experiments to test this hypothesis.

4.1 Animacy classification for markables

A *markable* in coreference resolution is a linguistic expression that refers to an entity in the real world or another linguistic expression. Examples of markables include noun phrases ("the man"), named entities ("Peter") and nested nominal expressions ("their"). We address the task of *animacy classification* of markables: classifying them as animate/inanimate. This feature is useful for coreference resolution systems because only animate markables can be referred to using masculine and feminine pronouns in English like "him" and "she". Thus, this is an important clue for automatically clustering the markables of a document into correct coreference chains.

To create training and test sets, we extract all 39,689 coreference chains from the CoNLL2012 OntoNotes corpus.[5] We label chains that contain an animate pronoun markable ("she", "her", "he", "him" or "his") and no inanimate pronoun markable ("it" or "its") as animate; and chains that contain an inanimate pronoun markable and no animate pronoun markable as inanimate. Other chains are discarded.

We extract 39,942 markables and their contexts from the 10,361 animate and inanimate chains. The context of a markable is represented as a SkipB: it is simply the pair of the two words occurring to the left and right of the markable. The gold label of a markable and its SkipB is the animacy status of its chain: either animate or inanimate. We divide all SkipBs having received an embedding in the embedding learning phase into a training set of 11,301 (8097 animate, 3204 inanimate) and a balanced test set of 4036.

We use LIBLINEAR (Fan et al., 2008) for classification, with penalty factors 3 and 1 for inanimate and animate classes, respectively, because the training data are unbalanced.

4.1.1 Experimental results

We compare the following representations for animacy classification of markables. (i) Phrase embedding: Skip-bigram embeddings with skip distance $k = 2$ and $2 \leq k \leq 3$; (ii) Word embedding: concatenation of the embeddings of the two enclosing words where the embeddings are either standard word2vec embeddings (see Section 2) or the embeddings published by (Collobert et al., 2011);[6] (iii) the one-hot vector representation of a SkipB: the concatentation of two one-hot vectors of dimensionality V where V is the size of the vocabulary. The first (resp. second) vector

[5] http://conll.cemantix.org/2012/data.html

[6] http://metaoptimize.com/projects/wordreprs/

turn_off	caught_up	take_over	macular_degeneration	telephone_interview
switch_off	mixed_up	take_charge	eye_disease	statement
unplug	entangled	replace	diabetic_retinopathy	interview
turning_off	involved	take_control	cataracts	conference_call
shut_off	enmeshed	stay_on	periodontal_disease	teleconference
block_out	tangled	retire	epilepsy	telephone_call
turned_off	mired	succeed	glaucoma	told
fiddle_with	engaged	step_down	skin_cancer	said

Table 1: Phrases and their nearest neighbors

is the one-hot vector for the left (resp. right) word of the SkipB. Experimental results are shown in Table 2.

representation		accuracy
phrase embedding	$k = 2$	0.703
	$2 \leq k \leq 3$	0.700
word embedding	word2vec	$0.668^{*\dagger}$
	Collobert et al.	$0.662^{*\dagger}$
one-hot vectors		$0.638^{*\dagger}$

Table 2: Classification accuracy. Mark "*" means significantly lower than "phrase embedding", $k = 2$; "†" means significantly lower than "phrase embedding", $2 \leq k \leq 3$. As significance test, we use the test of equal proportion, $p < .05$, throughout.

The results show that phrase embeddings have an obvious advantage in this classification task, both for $k = 2$ and $2 \leq k \leq 3$. This validates our hypothesis that learning embeddings for discontinuous linguistic units is promising.

In our error analysis, we found two types of frequent errors. (i) **Unspecific SkipBs.** Many SkipBs are equally appropriate for animate and inanimate markables. Examples of such SkipBs include "take*in" and "then*goes". (ii) **Untypical use of specific SkipBs.** Even SkipBs that are specific with respect to what type of markable they enclose sometimes occur with the "wrong" type of markable. For example, most markables occurring in the SkipB "of*whose" are animate because "whose" usually refers to an animate markable. However, in the context "...the southeastern area of Fujian whose economy is the most active" the enclosed markable is Fujian, a province of China. This example shows that "whose" occasionally refers to an inanimate entity even though these cases are infrequent.

4.1.2 Nearest neighbors of SkipBs

Table 3 shows some SkipBs and their nearest neighbors in descending order, where similarity is computed with cosine measure.

A general phenomenon is that phrase embeddings capture high degree of consistency in inferring the attributes of enclosed words. Considering the neighbor list in the first column, we can estimate that a *verb* probably appears as the middle token. Furthermore, *noun*, *pronoun*, *adjective* and *adverb* can roughly be inferred for the remaining columns, respectively.[7]

4.2 Paraphrase identification task

Paraphrase identification depends on semantic analysis. Standard approaches are unlikely to assign a high similarity score to the two sentences "he started the machine" and "he turned the machine on". In our approach, embedding of the phrase "turned on" can greatly help us to infer correctly that the sentences are paraphrases. Hence, phrase embeddings and in particular embeddings of discontinuous phrases seem promising in paraphrase detection task.

We use the Microsoft Paraphrase Corpus (Dolan et al., 2004) for evaluation. It consists of a training set with 2753 true paraphrase pairs and 1323 false paraphrase pairs, along with a test set with 1147 true and 578 false pairs. After discarding pairs in which neither sentence contains phrases, 3027 training pairs (2123 true vs. 904 false) and 1273 test pairs (871 true vs. 402 false) remain.

[7] A reviewer points out that this is only a suggestive analysis and that corpus statistics about these contexts would be required to establish that phrase embeddings can predict part-of-speech with high accuracy.

who*afghanistan,	some*told	women*have	with*responsibility	he*worried
had*afghanistan	other*told	men*have	of*responsibility	she*worried
he*afghanistan	two*told	children*have	and*responsibility	was*worried
who*iraq	–*told	girls*have	“*responsibility	is*worried
have*afghanistan	but*told	parents*have	that*responsibility	said*worried
fighters*afghanistan	one*told	students*have	’s*responsibility	that*worried
who*kosovo	because*told	young*have	the* responsibility	they*worried
was*afghanistan	and*told	people*have	for*responsibility	’s*worried

Table 3: SkipBs and their nearest neighbors

We tackle the paraphrase identification task via supervised binary classification. Sentence representation equals to the addition over all the token embeddings (words as well as phrases). A slight difference is that when dealing with a sentence like “$\cdots A\_B \cdots A\_B \cdots$” we only consider “A_B” embedding once. The system “word embedding” is based on the embeddings of single words only. Subsequently, pair representation is derived by concatenating the two sentence vectors. This concatentation is then classified by LIBLINEAR as “paraphrase” or “no paraphrase”.

4.2.1 Experimental results and analysis

Table 4 shows the performance of two methods. Phrase embeddings are apparently better. Most work on paraphrase detection has devised intricate features and achieves performance numbers higher than what we report here (Ji and Eisenstein, 2013; Madnani et al., 2012; Blacoe and Lapata, 2012). Our objective is only to demonstrate the superiority of considering phrase embedding over merely word embedding in this standard task.

We are interested in how phrase embeddings make an impact on this task. To that end, we perform an analysis on test examples where word embeddings are better than phrase embeddings and vice versa.

Table 5 shows four pairs, of which “phrase embedding” outperforms “word embedding” in the first two examples, “word embedding” defeats “phrase embedding” in the last two examples. In the first pair, successful phrase detection enables to split sentences into better units, thus the generated representation can convey the sentence meaning more exactly.

Methods	Accuracy	F1
baseline	0.684	0.803
word embedding	0.695	0.805
phrase embedding	**0.713**	**0.812**

Table 4: Paraphrase task results.

The meaning difference in the second pair originates from the synonym substitution between “take over as chief financial officer” and “fill the position”. The embedding of the phrase “take_over” matches the embedding of the single word “fill” in this context.

“Phrase embedding” in the third pair suffers from wrong phrase detection. Actually, “in” and “on” can not be treated as a sound phrase in that situation even though “in_on” is defined by Wiktionary. Indeed, this failure, to some extent, results from the shortcomings of our method in discovering true phrases. Furthermore, figuring out whether two words are a phrase might need to analyse syntactic structure in depth. This work is directly based on naive intuitive knowledge, acting as an initial exploration. Profound investigation is left as future work.

Our implementation discovers the contained phrases in the fourth pair perfectly. Yet, “word embedding” defeats “phrase embedding” still. The pair is not a paraphrase partly because the numbers are different; e.g., there is a big difference between “5.8 basis points” and “50 basis points”. Only a method that can correctly treat numerical information can succeed here. However, the appearance of phrases “central_bank”, “interest_rates” and “basis_points” makes the non-numerical parts more expressive and informative, leading to less dominant for digital quantifications. On the contrary, though “word embedding” fails to split the sen-

GWP	sentence 1	sentence 2
1 0 1	Common **side_effects** include **nasal_congestion**, **runny_nose**, **sore_throat** and cough, the FDA said .	The most common **side_effects** after getting the nasal spray were **nasal_congestion**, **runny_nose**, **sore_throat** and cough .
1 0 1	Douglas Robinson, a senior **vice_president** of finance, will **take_over** as chief financial officer on an interim basis .	Douglas Robinson, CA senior **vice_president**, finance, will fill the position in the interim .
1 1 0	They were being held Sunday in the Camden County Jail on $ 100,000 bail each .	The Jacksons remained **in_on** Camden County jail $ 100,000 bail .
0 0 1	The **interest_rate** sensitive two year Schatz yield was down 5.8 **basis_points** at 1.99 percent .	The Swedish **central_bank** cut **interest_rates** by 50 **basis_points** to 3.0 percent .

Table 5: Four typical sentence pairs in which the predictions of word embedding system and phrase embedding system differ. G = gold annotation, W = prediction of word embedding system, P = prediction of phrase embedding system. The formatting used by the system is shown. The original word order of sentence 2 of the third pair is "··· in Camden County jail on $ 100,000 bail".

tences into better units, it weakens unexpectedly the expressiveness of subordinate context. This example demonstrates the difficulty of paraphrase identification. Differing from simple similarity tasks, two sentences are often not paraphrases even though they may contain very similar words.

5 Related work

To date, approaches to extend embedding (or more generally "representation") beyond individual words are either *compositional* or *holistic* (Turney, 2012).

The best known work along the first line is by (Socher et al., 2010; Socher et al., 2011; Socher et al., 2012; Blacoe and Lapata, 2012), in which distributed representations of phrases or even sentences are calculated from the distributed representations of their parts. This approach is only plausible for units that are compositional, i.e., whose properties are systematically predictable from their parts. As well, how to develop a robust composition function still faces big hurdles; cf. Table 5.1 in (Mitchell and Lapata, 2010). Our approach (as well as similar work on continuous phrases) makes more sense for noncompositional units.

Phrase representations can also be derived by methods other than deep learning of embeddings, e.g., as vector space representations (Turney, 2012; Turney, 2013; Dinu et al., 2013). The main point of this paper – generalizing phrases to discontinuous phrases and computing representations for them – is orthogonal to this issue. It would be interesting to evaluate other types of representations for generalized phrases.

6 Conclusion and Future Work

We have argued that generalized phrases are part of the inventory of linguistic units that we should compute embeddings for and we have shown that such embeddings are superior to word form embeddings in a coreference resolution task and standard paraphrase identification task.

In this paper we have presented initial work on several problems that we plan to continue in the future: (i) How should the inventory of continuous and discontinous phrases be determined? We used a purely statistical definition on the one hand and dictionaries on the other. A combination of the two methods would be desirable. (ii) How can we distinguish between phrases that only occur in continuous form and phrases that must or can occur discontinuously? (iii) Given a sentence that contains the parts of a discontinuous phrase in correct order, how do we determine that the cooccurrence of the two parts constitutes an instance of the discontinuous phrase? (iv) Which tasks benefit most significantly from the introduction of generalized phrases?

Acknowledgments

This work was funded by DFG (grant SCHU 2246/4). We thank Google for a travel grant to support the presentation of this paper.

References

William Blacoe and Mirella Lapata. 2012. A comparison of vector-based representations for semantic composition. In *Proceedings of the 2012 Joint Conference on Empirical Methods in Natural Language Processing and Computational Natural Language Learning*, pages 546–556. Association for Computational Linguistics.

Ronan Collobert, Jason Weston, Léon Bottou, Michael Karlen, Koray Kavukcuoglu, and Pavel Kuksa. 2011. Natural language processing (almost) from scratch. *The Journal of Machine Learning Research*, 12:2493–2537.

Georgiana Dinu, Nghia The Pham, and Marco Baroni. 2013. General estimation and evaluation of compositional distributional semantic models. In *Proceedings of the Workshop on Continuous Vector Space Models and their Compositionality*, pages 50–58.

Bill Dolan, Chris Quirk, and Chris Brockett. 2004. Unsupervised construction of large paraphrase corpora: Exploiting massively parallel news sources. In *Proceedings of the 20th international conference on Computational Linguistics*, page 350. Association for Computational Linguistics.

Rong-En Fan, Kai-Wei Chang, Cho-Jui Hsieh, Xiang-Rui Wang, and Chih-Jen Lin. 2008. Liblinear: A library for large linear classification. *The Journal of Machine Learning Research*, 9:1871–1874.

Yangfeng Ji and Jacob Eisenstein. 2013. Discriminative improvements to distributional sentence similarity. In *Proceedings of the 2013 Conference on Empirical Methods in Natural Language Processing*, pages 891–896.

Minh-Thang Luong, Richard Socher, and Christopher D Manning. 2013. Better word representations with recursive neural networks for morphology. In *Proceedings of the Conference on Computational Natural Language Learning*, pages 104–113.

Nitin Madnani, Joel Tetreault, and Martin Chodorow. 2012. Re-examining machine translation metrics for paraphrase identification. In *Proceedings of the 2012 Conference of the North American Chapter of the Association for Computational Linguistics: Human Language Technologies*, pages 182–190. Association for Computational Linguistics.

Tomas Mikolov, Ilya Sutskever, Kai Chen, Greg Corrado, and Jeffrey Dean. 2013. Distributed representations of words and phrases and their compositionality. *arXiv preprint arXiv:1310.4546*.

George Miller and Christiane Fellbaum. 1998. Wordnet: An electronic lexical database.

Jeff Mitchell and Mirella Lapata. 2010. Composition in distributional models of semantics. *Cognitive science*, 34(8):1388–1429.

Robert Parker, Linguistic Data Consortium, et al. 2009. *English gigaword fourth edition*. Linguistic Data Consortium.

Richard Socher, Christopher D Manning, and Andrew Y Ng. 2010. Learning continuous phrase representations and syntactic parsing with recursive neural networks. In *Proceedings of the NIPS-2010 Deep Learning and Unsupervised Feature Learning Workshop*, pages 1–9.

Richard Socher, Jeffrey Pennington, Eric H Huang, Andrew Y Ng, and Christopher D Manning. 2011. Semi-supervised recursive autoencoders for predicting sentiment distributions. In *Proceedings of the Conference on Empirical Methods in Natural Language Processing*, pages 151–161.

Richard Socher, Brody Huval, Christopher D Manning, and Andrew Y Ng. 2012. Semantic compositionality through recursive matrix-vector spaces. In *Proceedings of the 2012 Joint Conference on Empirical Methods in Natural Language Processing and Computational Natural Language Learning*, pages 1201–1211.

Peter D Turney. 2012. Domain and function: A dual-space model of semantic relations and compositions. *Journal of Artificial Intelligence Research*, 44:533–585.

Peter D Turney. 2013. Distributional semantics beyond words: Supervised learning of analogy and paraphrase. *Transactions of the Association for Computational Linguistics*, 1:353–366.

Learning Grammar with Explicit Annotations for Subordinating Conjunctions

Dongchen Li, Xiantao Zhang and Xihong Wu
Key Laboratory of Machine Perception and Intelligence
Speech and Hearing Research Center
Peking University, Beijing, China
{lidc,zhangxt,wxh}@cis.pku.edu.cn

Abstract

Data-driven approach for parsing may suffer from data sparsity when entirely unsupervised. External knowledge has been shown to be an effective way to alleviate this problem. Subordinating conjunctions impose important constraints on Chinese syntactic structures. This paper proposes a method to develop a grammar with hierarchical category knowledge of subordinating conjunctions as explicit annotations. Firstly, each part-of-speech tag of the subordinating conjunctions is annotated with the most general category in the hierarchical knowledge. Those categories are human-defined to represent distinct syntactic constraints, and provide an appropriate starting point for splitting. Secondly, based on the data-driven state-split approach, we establish a mapping from each automatic refined subcategory to the one in the hierarchical knowledge. Then the data-driven splitting of these categories is restricted by the knowledge to avoid over refinement. Experiments demonstrate that constraining the grammar learning by the hierarchical knowledge improves parsing performance significantly over the baseline.

1 Introduction

Probabilistic context-free grammars (PCFGs) underlie most of the high-performance parsers (Collins, 1999; Charniak, 2000; Charniak and Johnson, 2005; Zhang and Clark, 2009; Chen and Kit, 2012; Zhang et al., 2013). However, a naive PCFG which simply takes the empirical rules and probabilities off of a Treebank does not perform well (Klein and Manning, 2003; Levy and Manning, 2003; Bansal and Klein, 2012), because its context-freedom assumptions are too strong in some cases (e.g. it assumes that subject and object NPs share the same distribution). Therefore, a variety of techniques have been developed to enrich PCFG (Klein and Manning, 2005; Matsuzaki et al., 2005; Zhang and Clark, 2011; Shindo et al., 2012).

Hierarchical state-split approach (Petrov et al., 2006; Petrov and Klein, 2007; Petrov and Klein, 2008a; Petrov and Klein, 2008b; Petrov, 2009) refines and generalizes the original grammars in a data-driven manner, and achieves state-of-the-art performance. Starting from a completely markovized X-Bar grammar, each category is split into two subcategories. EM is initialized with this starting point and used to climb the highly non-convex objective function of computing the joint likelihood of the observed parse trees. Then a merging step applies a likelihood ratio test to reverse the least useful half part of the splits. Learning proceeds by iterating between those two steps for six rounds. Spectral learning of latent-variable PCFGs (Cohen et al., 2012; Bailly et al., ; Cohen et al., 2013b; Cohen et al., 2013a) is another effective manner of state-split approach that provides accurate and consistent parameter estimates. However, this two complete data-driven approaches are likely to be hindered by the overfitting issue.

Incorporating knowledge (Zhang et al., 2013; Wu et al., 2011) to refine the categories in training a parser has been proved to remedy the weaknesses of probabilistic context-free grammar (PCFG). The knowledge contains content words semantic resources base (Fujita et al., 2010; Agirre et al., 2008; Lin et al., 2009), named entity cues (Li et al., 2013) and so on. However, they are limited in that they do not take into account the knowledge about subordinating conjunctions.

Subordinating conjunctions are important indications for different syntactic structure, espe-

Proceedings of the ACL 2014 Student Research Workshop, pages 48–55,
Baltimore, Maryland USA, June 22-27 2014.

cially for Chinese. For example, the subordinating conjunction "无论" (no matter what) is typically ahead of a sentence with pros and cons of the situation; on the contrary, a sufficient condition often occurs after the subordinating conjunction "如果" (if). Those two cases are of distinct syntactic structure. Figure 1 demonstrates that although the sequences of the part-of-speech of the input words are similar, these two subordinating conjunctions exert quite different syntactic constraints to the following clauses.

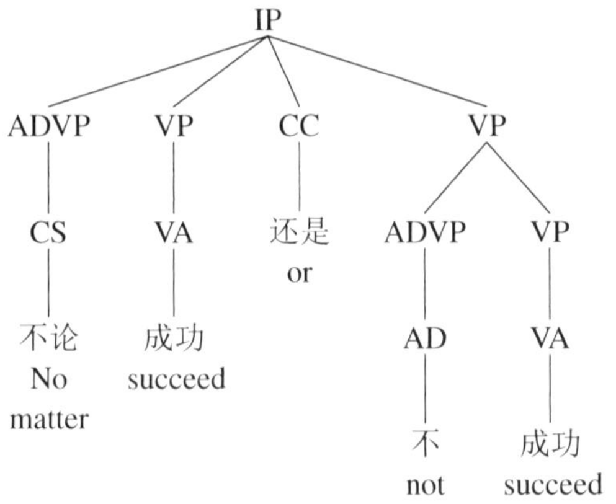

(a) "无论" (no matter what) is typically ahead of a sentence with pros and cons of the situation.

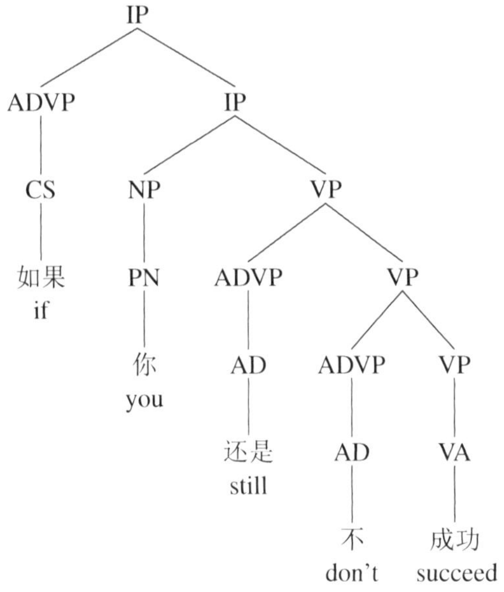

(b) "如果" (if) often precedes a sufficient condition.

Figure 1: Different types of subordinating conjunctions indicate distinct syntactic structure.

Based on the hierarchical state-split approach, this paper proposes a data-oriented model supervised by our hierarchical subcategories of subordinating conjunctions. In order to constrain the automatic subcategory refinement, we firstly establish the mapping between the automatic clustered subcategories and the predefined subcategories. Then we employ a knowledge criterion to supervise the hierarchical splitting of these subordinating conjunction subcategories by the automatic state-split approach, which can alleviate over-fitting. The experiments are carried out on Penn Chinese Treebank and Tsinghua Treebank, which verify that the refined grammars with refined subordinating conjunction categories can improve parsing performance significantly.

The rest of this paper is organized as follows. We first describe our hierarchical subcategories of subordinating conjunction. Section 3 illustrates the constrained grammar learning process in details. Section 4 presents the experimental evaluation and the comparison with other approaches.

2 Hierarchical Subcategories of Subordinating Conjunction

The only tag "CS" for all the various subordinating conjunctions is too coarse to indicate the intricate subordinating relationship. The words indicating different grammatical features share the same tag "CS", such as transition relationship, progression relationship, preference relationship, purpose relationship and condition relationship. In each case, the context is different, and the subordinating conjunction is an obvious indication for the parse disambiguation for the context. The existing resources for computational linguistic, like HowNet (Dong and Dong, 2003) and Cilin (Mei et al., 1983), have classified all subordinating conjunctions as one category, which is too coarse to capture the syntactic implication.

To make use of the indication, we subdivide the subordinating conjunctions according to its grammatical features in our scheme. Subordinating conjunctions indicating each relationship is further subdivided into two subcategories: one is used before the principal clause, the other is before the subordinate clause. For example, the conjunctions representing cause and effect contains "because" and "so", where "because" should modify the cause, and "so" should modify the effect. In addition, we found that there are several cases in the conditional clause. Accordingly, we subdivide the conditional subordinating conjunctions into seven types: assumption, universalization,

- *SubordinatingConjunction*
  - *Transition*
    - *LatterOf"Transition"* 却
    - *Formerof"Transition"* 虽然
    - *Progression*
      - *FormerOf"Progression"* 不但
      - *LatterOf"Progression"* 甚至
    - *Preference*
      - *LatterOf"Preference"* 不如
      - *FormerOf"Preference"* 与其
  - *LogicCoordination*
    - *LatterOfTheCoordination* 又
    - *Logic"And"* 并且
  - *Condition*
    - *Assumption* 如果
    - *Universalization* 不论
    - *UnnecessaryCondition* 既然
    - *InsufficientCondition* 即使
    - *SufficientCondition* 只要
    - *NecessaryCondition* 只有
    - *Equality* 除非
  - *Purpose*
    - *LatterOf"Purpose"* 以便
    - *FormerOf"Purpose"* 以免
  - *CauseAndEffect*
    - *Cause* 由于
    - *Effect* 果

Figure 2: Hierarchical subcategories of subordinating conjunctions with examples.

equality, sufficient condition, necessary condition, sufficient but unnecessary condition and necessary but insufficient condition (concession). The detailed hierarchical subcategories of subordinating conjunctions are displayed in Figure 2.

3 Parsing with Hierarchical Categories

The automatic state-split approach is designed to refine all symbols together through a data-driven manner, which takes the over-fitting risk. Instead of splitting and merging all symbols together automatically, we employ a knowledge-based criterion with hierarchical refinement knowledge to constraint the splitting of these new refined tags for subordinating conjunctions.

At the beginning, we produce a good starting annotation with the top subcategories in the hierarchical subcategories, which is of great use to constraining the automatic splitting process. As demonstrated in Figure 4, our parser is trained on the good initialization with the automatic hierarchical state-split process, and gets improvements compared with the original training data. For example, as shown in Figure 2, the category for 却(but) and "Cause" for 由于(because) is annotated as the top category "Transition" and "Cause And Effect" respectively.

However, during this process, only the most general hypernyms are used as the semantic representation of words, and the lower subcategory knowledge in the hierarchy is not explored. Thus, we further constraint the split of the subordinating conjunctions subcategories to be consistent with the hierarchical subcategories to alleviate the overfitting issue. The top class is only used as the starting annotations of POS tags to reduce the search space for EM in our method. It is followed by the hierarchical state-split process to further refine the starting annotations based on the hierarchical subcategories.

3.1 Mapping from Automatic Subcategories to Predefined Subcategories

With the initialization proposed above, the automatically split-merge approach produces a series of refined categories for each tag. We restrict each automatically refined subcategory of subordinating conjunctions to correspond to a special node

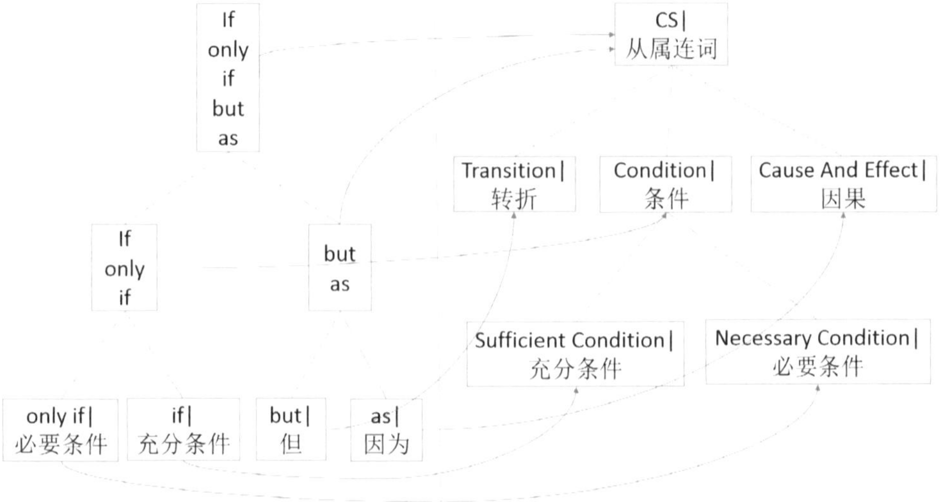

Figure 3: A schematic figure for the hierarchical state-split process of the tag "CS". Each subcategory of this tag has its own word set, and corresponds to one layer at the appropriate level in the hierarchical subcategories.

in the hierarchical subcategories, as a hyponym of "CS". The hierarchical subcategories are employed in the hierarchical state-split process to impose restrictions on the subcategory refinement.

First of all, it is necessary to establish the mapping from each subcategory in the data-driven hierarchical subcategories to the subcategory in the predefined hierarchical subcategories. We transfer the method for semantic-related labels (Lin et al., 2009) to our case here. The mapping is implemented with the word set related to each automatically refined granularity of clustered subordinating conjunctions and the node at the special level in the subcategory knowledge. The schematic in Figure 3 demonstrates this supervised splitting process for CS. The left part of this figure is the word sets of automatic clustered subcategories of the CS, which is split hierarchically. As expressed by the lines, each subcategory corresponds to one node in the right part of this figure, which is our hierarchical subcategory knowledge of subordinating conjunctions.

As it is shown in Figure 3, the original tag "CS" treats all the words it produces as its word set. Upon splitting each coarse category into two more specific subcategories, its word set is also cut into two subsets accordingly, through forcedly dividing each word in the word set into one subcategory which is most probable for this word in the lexical grammar. And each automatic refinement is mapped to the most specific subcategory (that is to say, the lowest node) that contains the entirely corresponding word set in the human-defined knowledge. On this basis, the new knowledge-based criterion is introduced to enrich and generalize these subcategories, with the purpose of fitting the refinement to the subcategory knowledge rather than the training data.

3.2 Knowledge-based Criterion for Subordinating Conjunctions Refinement

With the mapping between the automatic refined subcategories and the human-defined hierarchical subcategory knowledge, we could supervise the automatic state refinement by the knowledge.

Instead of being merged by likelihood, a knowledge-based criterion is employed, to decide whether or not to go back to the upper layer in the hierarchical subcategories and thus remove the new subcategories of these tags. The criterion is that, we assume that the bottom layer in the hierarchical subcategories is special enough to express the distinction of the subordinating conjunctions. If the subcategories of the subordinating conjunctions has gone beyond the bottom layer, then the new split subcategories are deemed to be unnecessary and should be merged back. That is to say, once the parent layer of this new subcategory is mapped onto the most special subcategory, it should be removed immediately. As illustrated

Treebank	Train Dataset	Develop Dataset	Test Dataset
CTB5	Articles 1-270	Articles 400-1151, 301-325	Articles 271-300
TCT	16000 sentences	800 sentences	758 sentences

Table 1: Data allocation of our experiment.

in Figure 3, if the node has no hyponym, this subcategory has been specialized enough according to the knowledge, and thus the corresponding subcategory will stop splitting.

By introducing a knowledge-based criterion, the issue is settled whether or not to further split subcategories from the perspective of predefined knowledge. To investigate the effectiveness of the presented approach, several experiments are conducted on both Penn Chinese Treebank and Tsinghua Treebank. They reveal that the subcategory knowledge of subordinating conjunctions is effective for parsing.

4 Experiments

4.1 Experimental Setup

We present experimental results on both Chinese Treebank (CTB) 5.0 (Xue et al., 2002) (All traces and functional tags were stripped.) and Tsinghua Treebank (TCT) (Zhou, 2004). All the experiments were carried out after six cycles of split-merge.

The data set allocation is described in Table 1. We use the EVALB parseval reference implementation (Sekine, 1997) for scoring. Statistical significance was checked by Bikel's randomized parsing evaluation comparator (Bikel, 2000).

4.2 Parsing Performance with Hierarchical Subcategories

We presented a flexible approach which refines the subordinating conjunctions in a hierarchy fashion where the hierarchical layers provide different granularity of specificity. To facilitate the comparisons, we set up 6 experiments on CTB5.0 with different strategies of choosing the subcategory layers in the hierarchical subcategory knowledge:

- baseline: Training without hierarchical subcategory knowledge
- top: Choosing the top layer in hierarchical subcategories (using "Transition", "Condition" , "Purpose" and so on)
- bottom: Choosing the bottom layer in hierarchical subcategories (the most specified subcategories)
- word: Substituting POS tag with the word itself
- knowledge criterion: Automatically choosing the appropriate layer through the knowledge criterion

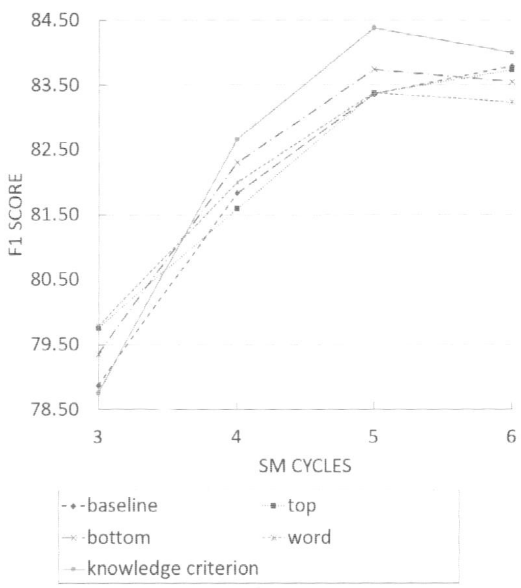

Figure 4: Comparison of parsing performance for each model in the split-merge cycles.

Figure 4 shows the F_1 scores of the last 4 cycles in the 6 split-merge cycles. The results are just as expectation, through which we can tell that the "top" model performs slightly better than the baseline owing to a better start point of the state-splitting. This result confirms the value of our initial explicit annotations. While the "bottom" model doesn't improve the performance due to excessive refinement and causes over-fitting, the "word" model behaves even worse for the same reason. In the 5th split-merge cycle, the "knowledge criterion" model picks the appropriate layer in hierarchical subcategories and achieves the best result.

We also test our method on TCT. Table 2 compares the accuracies of the baseline, initialization with top subcategories and the "knowledge criterion" model, and confirms that the subcategory knowledge helps parse disambiguation.

Parser	P	R	F_1
baseline	74.40	74.28	74.34
top	75.12	75.17	75.14
knowledge criterion	76.18	76.27	76.22

Table 2: Our parsing performance with different criterions on TCT.

4.3 Final Results

Our final results are achieved using the "knowledge criterion" model. As we can see from the table 3, our final parsing performance is higher than the unlexicalized parser (Levy and Manning, 2003; Petrov, 2009) and the parsing system in Qian and Liu (2012), but falls short of the systems using semantic knowledge of Lin et al. (2009) and exhaustive word formation knowledge of Zhang et al. (2013).

Parser	P	R	F_1
Levy(2003)	78.40	79.20	78.80
Petrov(2009)	84.82	81.93	83.33
Qian(2012)	84.57	83.68	84.13
Zhang(2013)	84.42	84.43	84.43
Lin(2009)	86.00	83.10	84.50
This paper	85.93	82.87	84.32

Table 3: Our final parsing performance compared with the best previous works on CTB5.0.

The improvement on the hierarchical state-split approach verifies the effectiveness of the subcategory knowledge of subordinating conjunctions for alleviating over-fitting. And the subcategory knowledge could be integrated with the knowledge base employed in Lin et al. (2009) and Zhang et al. (2013) to contribute more on parsing accuracy improvement.

5 Conclusion

In this paper, we present an approach to constrain the data-driven state-split method by hierarchical subcategories of subordinating conjunctions, which appear as explicit annotations in the grammar. The parsing accuracy is improved by this method owing to two reasons. Firstly, the most general hypernym of subordinating conjunctions exerts an initial restrict to the following splitting step. Secondly, the splitting process is confined by a knowledge-based criterion with the human-defined hierarchical subcategories to avoid over refinement.

Acknowledgments

We thank Baidu for travel and conference support for this paper. We thank Meng Zhang and Dingsheng Luo for their valuable advice. This work was supported in part by the National Basic Research Program of China (973 Program) under grant 2013CB329304, the Research Special Fund for Public Welfare Industry of Health under grant 201202001, the Key National Social Science Foundation of China under grant 12&ZD119, the National Natural Science Foundation of China under grant 91120001.

References

Eneko Agirre, Timothy Baldwin, and David Martinez. 2008. Improving parsing and pp attachment performance with sense information. *Proceedings of ACL-08: HLT*, pages 317–325.

Raphaël Bailly, Xavier Carreras Pérez, Franco M Luque, and Ariadna Julieta Quattoni. Unsupervised spectral learning of wcfg as low-rank matrix completion. Association for Computational Linguistics.

Mohit Bansal and Daniel Klein. 2012. An all-fragments grammar for simple and accurate parsing. Technical report, DTIC Document.

Bikel. 2000. Dan bikel's randomized parsing evaluation comparator. In *http://www.cis.upenn.edu/dbikel/software.html*.

Eugene Charniak and Mark Johnson. 2005. Coarse-to-fine n-best parsing and maxent discriminative reranking. In *Proceedings of the 43rd annual meeting on Association for Computational Linguistics*, pages 173–180. Association for Computational Linguistics.

Eugene Charniak. 2000. A maximum-entropy-inspired parser. In *Proceedings of the 1st North*

American chapter of the association for computational Linguistics conference, pages 132–139. Association for Computational Linguistics.

Xiao Chen and Chunyu Kit. 2012. Higher-order constituent parsing and parser combination. In *Proceedings of the 50th annual meeting of the Association for Computational Linguistics: Short papers-Volume 2*, pages 1–5. Association for Computational Linguistics.

Shay B Cohen, Karl Stratos, Michael Collins, Dean P Foster, and Lyle Ungar. 2012. Spectral learning of latent-variable pcfgs. In *Proceedings of the 50th annual meeting of the Association for Computational Linguistics: Long Papers-Volume 1*, pages 223–231. Association for Computational Linguistics.

Shay B Cohen, Giorgio Satta, and Michael Collins. 2013a. Approximate pcfg parsing using tensor decomposition. In *Proceedings of NAACL-HLT*, pages 487–496.

Shay B Cohen, Karl Stratos, Michael Collins, Dean P Foster, and Lyle Ungar. 2013b. Experiments with spectral learning of latent-variable pcfgs. In *Proceedings of NAACL-HLT*, pages 148–157.

Michael Collins. 1999. *Head-driven statistical models for natural language parsing*. Ph.D. thesis, University of Pennsylvania.

Zhendong Dong and Qiang Dong. 2003. Hownet-a hybrid language and knowledge resource. In *Proceedings of the international conference on natural language processing and knowledge engineering*, pages 820–824. IEEE.

Sanae Fujita, Francis Bond, Stephan Oepen, and Takaaki Tanaka. 2010. Exploiting semantic information for hpsg parse selection. *Research on language and computation*, 8(1):1–22.

Dan Klein and Christopher D Manning. 2003. Accurate unlexicalized parsing. In *Proceedings of the 41st annual meeting on Association for Computational Linguistics-Volume 1*, pages 423–430. Association for Computational Linguistics.

Dan Klein and Christopher D Manning. 2005. Parsing and hypergraphs. In *New developments in parsing technology*, pages 351–372. Springer.

Roger Levy and Christopher D Manning. 2003. Is it harder to parse chinese, or the chinese treebank? In *Proceedings of the 41st annual meeting on Association for Computational Linguistics-Volume 1*, pages 439–446. Association for Computational Linguistics.

Dongchen Li, Xiantao Zhang, and Xihong Wu. 2013. Improved chinese parsing using named entity cue. In *Proceeding of the 13th international conference on parsing technology*, pages 45–53.

Xiaojun Lin, Yang Fan, Meng Zhang, Xihong Wu, and Huisheng Chi. 2009. Refining grammars for parsing with hierarchical semantic knowledge. In *Proceedings of the 2009 conference on empirical methods in natural language processing: Volume 3-Volume 3*, pages 1298–1307. Association for Computational Linguistics.

Takuya Matsuzaki, Yusuke Miyao, and Jun'ichi Tsujii. 2005. Probabilistic cfg with latent annotations. In *Proceedings of the 43rd annual meeting on Association for Computational Linguistics*, pages 75–82. Association for Computational Linguistics.

Jia-Ju Mei, YM Li, YQ Gao, et al. 1983. Chinese thesaurus (tong-yi-ci-ci-lin).

Slav Petrov and Dan Klein. 2007. Improved inference for unlexicalized parsing. In *Human language technologies 2007: the conference of the North American chapter of the Association for Computational Linguistics*, pages 404–411.

Slav Petrov and Dan Klein. 2008a. Discriminative log-linear grammars with latent variables. *Advances in neural information processing systems*, 20:1153–1160.

Slav Petrov and Dan Klein. 2008b. Sparse multi-scale grammars for discriminative latent variable parsing. In *Proceedings of the conference on empirical methods in natural language processing*, pages 867–876. Association for Computational Linguistics.

Slav Petrov, Leon Barrett, Romain Thibaux, and Dan Klein. 2006. Learning accurate, compact, and interpretable tree annotation. In *Proceedings of the 21st international conference on computational linguistics and the 44th annual meeting of the Association for Computational Linguistics*, pages 433–440. Association for Computational Linguistics.

Slav Orlinov Petrov. 2009. *Coarse-to-Fine natural language processing*. Ph.D. thesis, University of California.

Xian Qian and Yang Liu. 2012. Joint chinese word segmentation, pos tagging and parsing. In *Proceedings of the 2012 Joint Conference on Empirical Methods in Natural Language Processing and Computational Natural Language Learning*, pages 501–511. Association for Computational Linguistics.

Collins Sekine. 1997. Evalb bracket scoring program. In *http://nlp.cs.nyu.edu/evalb/*.

Hiroyuki Shindo, Yusuke Miyao, Akinori Fujino, and Masaaki Nagata. 2012. Bayesian symbol-refined tree substitution grammars for syntactic parsing. In *Proceedings of the 50th annual meeting of the Association for Computational Linguistics: Long Papers-Volume 1*, pages 440–448. Association for Computational Linguistics.

Xihong Wu, Meng Zhang, and Xiaojun Lin. 2011. Parsing-based chinese word segmentation integrating morphological and syntactic information. In *Proceedings of 7th international conference on natural language processing and knowledge engineering (NLP-KE)*, pages 114–121. IEEE.

Nianwen Xue, Fu-Dong Chiou, and Martha Palmer. 2002. Building a large-scale annotated chinese corpus. In *Proceedings of the 19th international conference on computational linguistics-Volume 1*, pages 1–8. Association for Computational Linguistics.

Yue Zhang and Stephen Clark. 2009. Transition-based parsing of the chinese treebank using a global discriminative model. In *Proceedings of the 11th International Conference on Parsing Technologies*, pages 162–171. Association for Computational Linguistics.

Yue Zhang and Stephen Clark. 2011. Syntactic processing using the generalized perceptron and beam search. *Computational linguistics*, 37(1):105–151.

Meishan Zhang, Yue Zhang, Wanxiang Che, and Ting Liu. 2013. Chinese parsing exploiting characters. *51st annual meeting of the Association for Computational Linguistics*.

Qiang Zhou. 2004. Annotation scheme for chinese treebank. *Journal of Chinese information processing*, 18(4):1–8.

Going beyond sentences when applying tree kernels

Dmitry Ilvovsky
School of Applied Mathematics and Information Science
National Research University Higher School of Economics
Moscow, Russia
dilvovsky@hse.ru

Abstract

We go beyond the level of individual sentences applying parse tree kernels to paragraphs. We build a set of extended trees for a paragraph of text from the individual parse trees for sentences and learn short texts such as search results and social profile postings to take advantage of additional discourse-related information. Extension is based on coreferences and rhetoric structure relations between the phrases in different sentences. We evaluate our approach, tracking relevance classification improvement for multi-sentence search task. The search problem is formulated as classification of search results into the classes of relevant and irrelevant, learning from the Bing search results. We compare performances of individual sentence kernels with the ones for extended parse trees and show that adding discourse information to learning data helps to improve classification results.

1 Introduction

In spite of substantial efforts to formulate a complete linking theory between syntax and semantics, it is not available yet. Hence the design of syntactic features for automated learning of syntactic structures is still an art. One of the solutions to systematically treat these syntactic features – tree kernels built over syntactic parse trees. Convolution tree kernel (Collins and Duffy, 2002) defines a feature space consisting of all subtree types of parse trees and counts the number of common subtrees as the syntactic similarity between two parse trees. They have found a number of applications in several natural language tasks, e.g. syntactic parsing re-ranking, relation extraction (Zelenko et al., 2003; Zhang et al 2006), named entity recognition (Cumby and Roth, 2003) and Semantic Role Labeling (Moschitti, 2004), pronoun resolution (Yang et al., 2006), question classification (Zhang and Lee, 2003) and machine translation (Zhang and Li, 2009).

The kernel ability to generate large feature sets is useful to quickly model new and not well understood linguistic phenomena in learning machines. However, it is often possible to manually design features for linear kernels that produce high accuracy and fast computation time whereas the complexity of tree kernels may prevent their application in real scenarios.

Many learning algorithms, such as SVM (Vapnik, 1998) can work directly with kernels by replacing the dot product with a particular kernel function. This useful property of kernel methods, that implicitly calculates the dot product in a high-dimensional space over the original representations of objects such as sentences, has made kernel methods an effective solution to modeling structured objects in NLP. A number of NL tasks require computing of semantic features over paragraphs of text containing multiple sentences. Doing it in a sentence pair-wise manner is not always accurate, since it is strongly dependent on how information (phrases) is distributed through sentences.

An approach to build a kernel based on more than a single parse tree has been proposed (Severyn et.al., 2012), however without any relations between parse trees or for a different purpose than treating multi-sentence portions of text. To compensate for parsing errors (Zhang et al., 2008), a convolution kernel over packed parse forest (Severyn and Moschitti, 2012; Aioli et.al, 2007) is used to mine syntactic features from it directly. A packed forest compactly encodes exponential number of n-best parse trees, and thus containing much more rich structured features than a single parse tree. This advantage enables the forest kernel not only to be more robust against parsing errors, but also to be able to learn more reliable feature values and help to

Proceedings of the ACL 2014 Student Research Workshop, pages 56–63,
Baltimore, Maryland USA, June 22-27 2014.

solve the data sparseness issue that exists in the traditional tree kernel.

On the contrary, in this study we form a tree forest of sequence of sentences in a paragraph of text. Currently, kernel methods tackle individual sentences. However, in learning settings where texts include multiple sentences, structures which include paragraph-level information need to be employed. We demonstrate that in certain domains and certain cases discourse structure is essential for proper classification of texts.

2 Necessity to extend parse trees

We introduce a domain where a pair-wise comparison of sentences is insufficient to properly learn certain semantic features of texts. This is due to the variability of ways information can be communicated in multiple sentences, and variations in possible discourse structures of text which needs to be taken into account.

We consider an example of text classification problem, where short portions of text belong to two classes:

- Tax liability of a landlord renting office to a business.
- Tax liability of a business owner renting an office from landlord.

> I rent an office space. This office is for my business. I can deduct office rental expense from my business profit to calculate net income.
>
> To run my business, I have to rent an office. The net business profit is calculated as follows. Rental expense needs to be subtracted from revenue.
>
> To store goods for my retail business I rent some space. When I calculate the net income, I take revenue and subtract business expenses such as office rent.
>
> ---
>
> I rent out a first floor unit of my house to a travel business. I need to add the rental income to my profit. However, when I repair my house, I can deduct the repair expense from my rental income.
>
> I receive rental income from my office. I have to claim it as a profit in my tax forms. I need to add my rental income to my profits, but subtract rental expenses such as repair from it.
>
> I advertised my property as a business rental. Advertisement and repair expenses can be subtracted from the rental income. Remaining rental income needs to be added to my profit and be reported as taxable profit.

Firstly, note that keyword-based analysis does not help to separate the first three paragraphs and the second three paragraphs. They all share the same keywords *rental/office/income/profit/add/subtract*. Phrase-based analysis does not help, since both sets of paragraphs share similar phrases. Secondly, pair-wise sentence comparison does not solve the problem either. Anaphora resolution is helpful but insufficient. All these sentences include 'I' and its mention, but other links between words or phrases in different sentences need to be used.

Rhetoric structures need to come into play to provide additional links between sentences. The structure to distinguish between

renting for yourself and deducting from total income

and

renting to someone and adding to income

embraces multiple sentences. The second clause about adding/subtracting incomes is linked by means of the rhetoric relation of elaboration with the first clause for *landlord/tenant*. This rhetoric relation may link discourse units within a sentence, between consecutive sentences and even between first and third sentence in a paragraph. Other rhetoric relations can play similar role for forming essential links for text classification.

Which representations for these paragraphs of text would produce such common sub-structure between the structures of these paragraphs? We believe that extended trees, which include the first, second, and third sentence for each paragraph together can serve as a structure to differentiate the two above classes.

The dependency parse trees for the first text in our set and its coreferences are shown in Fig. 1. There are multiple ways the nodes from parse trees of different sentences can be connected: we choose the rhetoric relation of elaboration which links the same entity office and helps us to form the structure rent-office-space – for-my-business – deduct-rental-expense which is the base for our classification. We used Stanford Core NLP, coreferences resolution (Lee et al., 2012) and its visualization to form Figs. 1 and 2.

Fig. 2 shows the resultant extended tree with the root 'I' from the first sentence. It includes the whole first sentence, a verb phrase from the second sentence and a verb phrase from the third sentence according to rhetoric relation of elaboration. Notice that this extended tree can be intuitively viewed as representing the 'main idea' of this text compared to other texts in our set. All extended trees need to be formed for a text and then compared with that of the other texts, since we don't know in advance which extended tree is essential. From the standpoint of tree kernel learning, extended trees are learned the same way as regular parse trees.

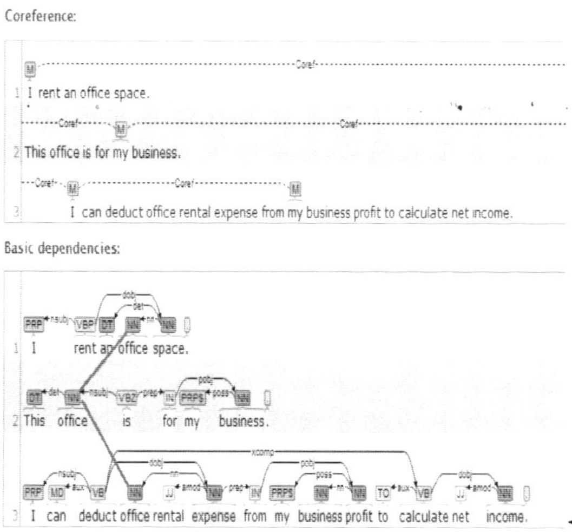

Fig.**1**: Coreferences and the set of dependency trees for the first text.

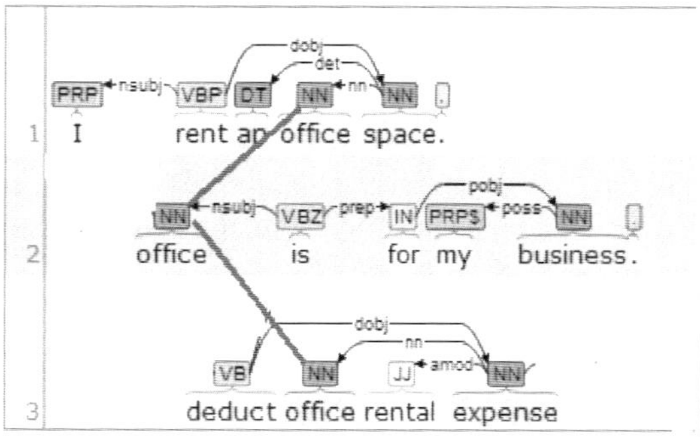

Fig. **2**: Extended tree which includes 3 sentences

3 Building extended trees

For every arc which connects two parse trees, we derive the extension of these trees, extending branches according to the arc (Fig. 3).

In this approach, for a given parse tree, we will obtain a set of its extension, so the elements of kernel will be computed for many extensions, instead of just a single tree. The problem here is that we need to find common sub-trees for a much higher number of trees than the number of sentences in text, however by subsumption (sub-tree relation) the number of common sub-trees will be substantially reduced.

If we have two parse trees P_1 and P_2 for two sentences in a paragraph, and a relation R_{12}: $P_{1i} \rightarrow P_{2j}$ between the nodes P_{1i} and P_{2j}, we form the pair of extended trees $P_1 * P_2$:

$\ldots, P_{1i-2}, P_{1i-1}, P_{1i}, P_{2j}, P_{2j+1}, P_{2j+2}, \ldots$

$\ldots, P_{2j-2}, P_{2j-1}, P_{2j}, P_{1i}, P_{1i+1}, P_{2i+2}, \ldots,$

which would form the feature set for tree kernel learning in addition to the original trees P_1 and P_2. Notice that the original order of nodes of parse trees is retained under operation '*' (Fig. 3).

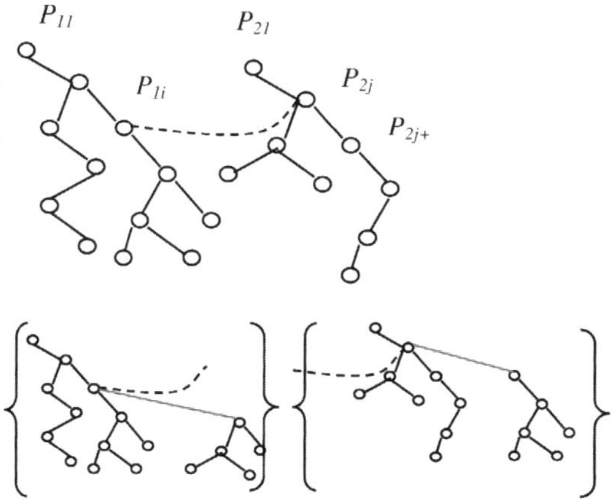

Fig. **3**: An arc which connects two parse trees for two sentences in a text (on the top) and the derived set of extended trees (on the bottom).

The algorithm for building an extended tree for a set of parse trees *T* is presented below:

Input:
1) Set of parse trees *T*.
2) Set of relations *R*, which includes relations R_{ijk} between the nodes of T_i and T_j: $T_i \in T$, $T_j \in T$, $R_{ijk} \in R$. We use index *k* to range over multiple relations between the nodes of parse tree for a pair of sentences.

Output: the exhaustive set of extended trees *E*.

Set $E = \varnothing$;
For each tree i=1:|T|
  For each relation R_{ijk}, k= 1: |R|
    Obtain T_j
    Form the pair of extended trees $T_i * T_j$;
    Verify that each of the extended trees do not have a super-tree in *E*
      If verified, add to *E*;
Return *E*.

Notice that the resultant trees are not the proper parse trees for a sentence, but nevertheless form an adequate feature space for tree kernel learning.

To obtain the inter-sentence links, we employed the following sources:

- Coreferences from Stanford NLP (Recasens et al., 2013, Lee et al., 2013).
- Rhetoric relation extractor based on the rule-based approach to finding relations between elementary discourse units (Galitsky et al., 2013). We combined manual rules with automatically learned derived from the available discourse corpus by means of syntactic generalization.

4 Assessment of classification improvement

To confirm that using a set of extended parse trees for paragraphs leverages additional semantic information compared to a set of parse trees for all sentences in a paragraph, we perform an evaluation of relevance in search domain:

- As a baseline, we take all trees for sentences in paragraphs
- As an expected improvement, we take all extended trees in a paragraph.

Since a benchmarking database for answering complex multi-sentence questions is not available, we form our own dataset for product-related opinions. The question answering problem is formulated as finding information on the web, relevant to a user posting / opinion expression in a blog, forum or social network.

For the purpose of this evaluation it is not essential to provide the best possible set of answers. Instead, we are concerned with the comparison of relevance improvement by using extended parse tree, as long as the evaluation settings of question answering are identical. The details of the evaluation are given in Section 7.

5 Implementation of kernel learning for extended trees

The evaluation framework described here is implemented as an OpenNLP contribution. It relies on the following systems:

- OpenNLP/Stanford NLP parser;
- Stanford NLP Coreference;
- Bing search;
- Wrapper of TK-Light kernel learner (Moschitti, 2006).

Framework includes the following components of Apache OpenNLP.similarity project:

- Rhetoric parser
- Parse thicket builder and generalizer (Galitsky et al., 2012). Not used in this evaluation.
- A number of applications based on the above component, including search (request handler for SOLR), speech recognition, content generation and others.

One of the use cases of this OpenNLP.similarity component is a Java wrapper for tree kernel algorithms implemented in C++. It allows seamless integration of tree kernel algorithms into other open source systems available in Java for search, information retrieval and machine learning. Moreover, tree kernel algorithms can be embedded into Hadoop framework in the domains where offline performance is essential. Libraries and evaluation results described in this paper are also available at http://code.google.com/p/relevance-based-on-parse-trees and http://svn.apache.org/repos/asf/opennlp/sandbox/opennlp-similarity/.

6 Complexity estimation

To estimate the complexity of building extended trees, let us consider an average case with 5 sentences in each paragraph and 15 words in each sentence. We have on average 10 inter-sentence arcs, which give us up to 20 extended trees formed from two sentences, and 60 extended trees formed from 3 sentences. Hence we have to apply tree learning to up to 100 trees (of a bigger size) instead of just 5 original trees. We observe that kernel learning of extended trees has to handle at least 20 times bigger input set.

However, most of the smaller subtrees are repetitive and will be reduced in the course of dimensionality reduction.

7 Evaluation

To estimate whether additional high-level semantic and discourse information contributes to classical kernel based approach, we compare two sources for trees:

- Regular parse trees
- Extended parse trees

To perform this estimation, we need a corpus including a high number of short texts similar to our example in Introduction. These texts should have high similarity (otherwise keyword approach would do well), certain discourse structure, and describe some objects (products) in a meaningful application domain. Unfortunately, to the best of our knowledge such corpus is not available. Therefore, for comparison of tree kernel performances we decided to use search results, given the query which is a short text. We rely on search engine APIs following the evaluation settings in the studies on answering complex questions (Galitsky et al., 2013).

Search results typically include texts of fairly high similarity, which is leveraged in our evaluation. To formulate classification problem on the set of texts obtained as search results, we need to form positive and negative sets. To do that, we select the first ***n*** search results as relevant (positive) and also ***n*** results towards to tail of search results lists as irrelevant (negative). In this case each search session yields an individual training (and evaluation) dataset. The same nature of such data allows averaging of precision and recall, having individual training dataset of a limited size. Hence reliability of our results is achieved not via the size of individual dataset, but instead by the increased number of search sessions. To assure an abrupt change in relevance proceeding from the head to the tail of search results lists, we use complicated queries including multiple sentences, which are not handled by modern search engines well.

The preparation of search queries (which include multiple sentences) is based on the following steps:

1. Forming the names of products and their short descriptions
2. Given (1), find a text including an extended review or opinion about this product.
3. Texts (2) cannot be used as queries as they are. To form the queries from (2), we need to extract most significant phrases from them; otherwise, search engines are confused which keywords to choose and give either duplicate, or irrelevant results. These were the longest noun and selected verb phrases from (2).

The analogous steps were conducted for Yahoo Answers data. We manually select a 100 most interesting search queries for each domain.

The training/evaluation datasets is formed from search results in the following way. We obtain a first hundred search results (or less if hundred is not available). We select 1..20 (or first 20%) of search results as a positive set, and 81..100 as a negative set. Search results 21..80 form the basis of evaluation dataset, from which we randomly select 10 texts to be classified into the classes of positive or negative. Hence we have the ratio 4:1 between the training and evaluation datasets.

To motivate our evaluation setting, we rely on the following observations. In case of searching for complex multi-sentence queries, relevance indeed drops abruptly with proceeding from the first 10-20 search results, as search evaluation results demonstrated (Galitsky et al., 2013). The order of search results in first 20% and last 20% does not affect our evaluation. Although the last 20% of search results is not really a "gold standard", it is nevertheless a set that can be reasonably separated from the positive set. If such separation is too easy or too difficult, it would be hard to adequately evaluate the difference between regular parse trees and extended trees for text classification. Search-based approach to collect texts for evaluation of classification allows reaching maximum degree of experiment automation.

It turned out that the use of tail search results as negative set helps to leverage the high level semantic and discourse information. Negative examples, as well as positive ones, include most keywords from the queries. However, the main difference between the positive and negative search results is that the former include much more coreferences and rhetoric structures similar to the query, than the latter set. The use of the extended trees was beneficial in the cases where phrases from queries are distributed through multiple sentences in search results.

We conducted two independent experiments for each search session, classifying search result snippets and also original texts, extracted from webpages. For the snippets, we split them into sentence fragments and built extended trees for these fragments of sentences. For original texts, we extracted all sentences related to the snippet fragments and built extended trees for these sentences.

Training and classification occurs in the automated mode, and the classification assessment is conducted by the members of research group guided by the authors. The assessors only consulted the query and answer snippets.

We used the standard parameters of tree sequence kernels from http://disi.unitn.it/moschitti/Tree-Kernel.htm (Moschitti, 2006). Tree kernel is applied to all tree pairs from two forests. The latest version of tree kernel learner was obtained from the author.

Products		*Basic kernels*	*Extended kernels (corefs+RST)*
Texts from the pages	*Precision*	0,5679	0,5868
	Recall	0,7516	0,8458
	F-measure	0,6485	0,6752
Snippets	*Precision*	0,5625	0,6319
	Recall	0,7840	0,8313
	F-measure	0,6169	0,6695

Table **1**: Evaluation results for products domain

Answers		*Basic kernels*	*Extended kernels (corefs)*	*Extended kernels (corefs+ RST)*
Texts from the pages	*P*	0,5167	0,5083	0,5437
	R	0,7361	0,7917	0,8333
	F	0,6008	0,5458	0,6278
Snippets	*P*	0,5950	0,6264	0,6794
	R	0,7329	0,7492	0,7900
	F	0,6249	0,6429	0,7067

Table **2**: Evaluation results for popular answers domain

Evaluation results show visible improvement of classification accuracy achieved by extended trees. For Yahoo Answers one can observe that coreferences only provide a slight improvement of accuracy, whereas RST added to coreferences gives a stronger improvement. Stronger increase of recall in comparison to precision can be explained by the following. It is due to the acquired capability of extended trees to match phrases from the search results distributed through multiple sentences, with questions.

8 Conclusions and future work

In this study we focused on how discourse information can help with text relevance tasks irrespectively of learning mechanisms. We compared two sets of linguistic features:

- The baseline, parse trees for individual sentences,
- Parse trees and discourse information,

and demonstrated that the enriched set of features indeed improves the classification accuracy, having the learning framework fixed. This improvement varies from 2 to 8 % in different domains with different structure of texts. To tackle such enriched set of linguistic features, an adjustment of tree kernel algorithm itself was not necessary.

The approach developed in this paper can also be applied to parse tree querying and manipulation problem (Levy and Galen, 2006). A system such as Tregex is an expressive and flexible way for single sentence parse tree querying and manipulation. Extending parse trees of individual sentences towards paragraph of text, the recall of a tree querying system would dramatically increase, and dependence on how phrases are distributed through sentences would decrease.

There are a few possible directions of future development. One interesting continuation of this study is to applying standard ranking mechanisms such as NDCG. We can draw the comparison between the standard and extended kernels in terms of standard Bing ranking, as well as special ranking based on syntactic similarity between the query and search results (Galitsky et al., 2013).

We also plan to generalize extended tree kernels towards graphs (DAGs) (Suzuki et al., 2003). In this case we can perform learning on Parse thickets (Galitsky et al., 2013) – the structures which are the sets of parse trees for a paragraph. It will be fruitful to compare performances of various ways of kernel computation and estimate the contribution of a particular way of paragraph representation to the quality of classification.

It is possible to apply the outlined approach to perform question answering in the case where the latter are extensive portions of paragraph-sized text and the former include multiple sentences.

Another obvious direction is applying tree kernels to classify short texts based on standard corpus data. However, a corpus of short texts, where advantages of kernel methods over alternatives would become visible, does not exist. One of our next tasks is to form such a corpus.

Acknowledgments

We would like to thank Baidu for travel and conference support for this paper.

References

Cumby, C., Roth, D. 2003. *Kernel methods for relational learning.* In: ICML.

Kim, Jung-Jae, Pezik, P. and Rebholz-Schuhmann, D. 2008. *MedEvi: Retrieving textual evidence of relations between biomedical concepts from Medline.* Bioinformatics. Volume 24, Issue 11 pp. 1410-1412.

Zelenko, D., Aone, C., Richardella, A. 2003. *Kernel methods for relation extraction.* JMLR (2003).

Suzuki, J., Hirao, H., Sasaki, Y and Maeda, E., *Hierarchical Directed Acyclic Graph Kernel: Methods for Structured Natural Language Data.* In Proceedings of the 41th Annual Meeting of Association for Computational Linguistics (ACL). 2003.

Galitsky, B. *Natural Language Question Answering System: Technique of Semantic Headers.* Advanced Knowledge International, Australia (2003).

Galitsky, B., de la Rosa, J., Dobrocsi, G. 2012. *Inferring the semantic properties of sentences by mining syntactic parse trees.* Data & Knowledge Engineering. Volume 81-82, November (2012) 21-45.

Galitsky, B., Usikov, D. Kuznetsov, S. 2013. *Parse Thicket Representations for Answering Multi-sentence questions.* 20th International Conference on Conceptual Structures, ICCS 2013.

Galitsky, B., Kuznetsov, S. 2008. *Learning communicative actions of conflicting human agents.* J. Exp. Theor. Artif. Intell. 20(4): 277-317.

Galitsky, B. 2012. *Machine Learning of Syntactic Parse Trees for Search and Classification of Text.* Engineering Application of AI, http://dx.doi.org/10.1016/j.engappai.2012.09.017.

Galitsky, B., Ilvovsky, D., Kuznetsov, S., Strok, F. 2013. *Improving Text Retrieval Efficiency with Pattern Structures on Parse Thickets,* Workshop "Formal Concept Analysis meets Information Retrieval" at ECIR 2013, Moscow, Russia.

Ehrlich H.-C., Rarey M. 2011. *Maximum common subgraph isomorphism algorithms and their applications in molecular science: review.* Wiley Interdisciplinary Reviews: Computational Molecular Science, 2011, vol. 1 (1), pp. 68-79.

Yan, X., Han, J. 2002. *gSpan: Graph-Based Substructure Pattern Mining.* In: Proc. IEEE Int. Conf. on Data Mining, ICDM'02, IEEE Computer Society (2002), pp 721–724.

Jiangning Wu, Zhaoguo Xuan and Donghua Pan, *Enhancing text representation for classification tasks with semantic graph structures,* International Journal of Innovative Computing, Information and Control (ICIC), Volume 7, Number 5(B).

Haussler, D. 1999. *Convolution kernels on discrete structures.*

Moschitti, A. 2006. *Efficient Convolution Kernels for Dependency and Constituent Syntactic Trees.* In Proceedings of the 17th European Conference on Machine Learning, Berlin, Germany.

Severyn, A., Moschitti, A. 2012. *Structural relationships for large-scale learning of answer reranking.* SIGIR 2012: 741-750.

Severyn, A., Moschitti, A. 2012. *Fast Support Vector Machines for Convolution Tree Kernels.* Data Mining Knowledge Discovery 25: 325-357.

Aiolli, F., Da San Martino, G., Sperduti, A. and Moschitti, A. 2007. *Efficient Kernel-based Learning for Trees,* Proceeding of the IEEE Symposium on Computational Intelligence and Data Mining (CIDM), Honolulu, Hawaii.

Punyakanok, V., Roth, D., & Yih, W. 2004. *Mapping dependencies trees: an application to question answering.* In: Proceedings of AI & Math, Florida, USA.

Mann, William C., Christian M. I. M. Matthiessen and Sandra A. Thompson. 1992. *Rhetorical Structure Theory and Text Analysis. Discourse Description: Diverse linguistic analyses of a fund-raising text.* ed. by W. C. Mann and S. A. Thompson. Amsterdam, John Benjamins: 39-78.

Sun, J., Min Zhang, Chew Lim Tan. 2011. *Tree Sequence Kernel for Natural Language.* AAAI-25, 2011.

Zhang, M.; Che, W.; Zhou, G.; Aw, A.; Tan, C.; Liu, T.; and Li, S. 2008. *Semantic role labeling using a grammar-driven convolution tree kernel.* IEEE transactions on audio, speech, and language processing 16(7):1315–1329.

Montaner, M.; Lopez, B.; de la Rosa, J. L. (June 2003). *A Taxonomy of Recommender Agents on the Internet.* Artificial Intelligence Review 19 (4): 285–330.

Collins, M., and Duffy, N. 2002. *Convolution kernels for natural language. In Proceedings of NIPS,* 625–632, 2002.

Heeyoung Lee, Angel Chang, Yves Peirsman, Nathanael Chambers, Mihai Surdeanu and Dan Jurafsky. 2013. *Deterministic coreference resolution based on entity-centric, precision-ranked rules.* Computational Linguistics 39(4).

Daniel Jurafsky, James H. Martin. 2008. *Speech and Language Processing. An Introduction to Natural Language Processing,* Computational Linguistics, and Speech Recognition.

Robinson J.A. 1965. *A machine-oriented logic based on the resolution principle.* Journal of the Association for Computing Machinery, 12:23-41.

Mill, J.S. 1843. *A system of logic, ratiocinative and inductive*. London.

Fukunaga, K. *Introduction to statistical pattern recognition (2nd ed.)*, Academic Press Professional, Inc., San Diego, CA, 1990.

Mitchell, T. 1997. *Machine Learning*. McGraw Hill.

Furukawa, K. 1998. *From Deduction to Induction: Logical Perspective. The Logic Programming Paradigm*. In Apt, K.R., Marek V.W., Truszczynski, M., Warren, D.S., Eds. Springer.

Bharat Bhasker; K. Srikumar. 2010. *Recommender Systems in E-Commerce*. CUP. ISBN 978-0-07-068067-8.

Trias i Mansilla, A., JL de la Rosa i Esteva. 2012. *Asknext: An Agent Protocol for Social Search*. Information Sciences 190, 144–161.

Punyakanok, V.,Roth, D. and Yih, W. 2005. *The Necessity of Syntactic Parsing for Semantic Role Labeling*. IJCAI-05.

Domingos P. and Poon, H. 2009. *Unsupervised Semantic Parsing*, In: Proceedings of the 2009 Conference on Empirical Methods in Natural Language Processing, Singapore: ACL.

Marcu, D. 1997. *From Discourse Structures to Text Summaries*, in I. Mani and M.Maybury (eds) Proceedings of ACL Workshop on Intelligent Scalable Text Summarization, pp. 82–8, Madrid, Spain.

Abney, S. 1991. *Parsing by Chunks, Principle-Based Parsing*, Kluwer Academic Publishers, 1991, pp. 257-278.

Hyeran Byun, Seong-Whan Lee. 2002. *Applications of Support Vector Machines for Pattern Recognition: A Survey*. In Proceedings of the First International Workshop on Pattern Recognition with Support Vector Machines (SVM '02), Seong-Whan Lee and Alessandro Verri (Eds.). Springer-Verlag, London, UK, UK, 213-236.

Chris Manning and Hinrich Schütze, *Foundations of Statistical Natural Language Processing, MIT Press*. Cambridge, MA: May 1999.

Sun, J.; Zhang, M.; and Tan, C. 2010. *Exploring syntactic structural features for sub-tree alignment using bilingual tree kernels*. In *Proceedings of ACL*, 306–315.

Kohavi, Ron. 1995. *A Study of Cross-Validation and Bootstrap for Accuracy Estimation and Model Selection*. International Joint Conference on Artificial Intelligence IJCAI 1995.

Kalervo Jarvelin, Jaana Kekalainen. 2002. *Cumulated gain-based evaluation of IR techniques*. ACM Transactions on Information Systems 20(4), 422–446.

Roger Levy and Galen Andrew, Tregex and Tsurgeon: tools for querying and manipulating tree data structures. 5th International Conference on Language Resources and Evaluation (LREC 2006), 2006.

Heeyoung Lee, Marta Recasens, Angel Chang, Mihai Surdeanu, and Dan Jurafsky. 2012. *Joint Entity and Event Coreference Resolution across Documents*. In EMNLP-CoNLL 2012.

Marta Recasens, Marie-Catherine de Marneffe, and Christopher Potts. 2013. The Life and Death of Discourse Entities: Identifying Singleton Mentions. In Proceedings of NAACL 2013.

Multi-Document Summarization Using Distortion-Rate Ratio

Ulukbek Attokurov
Department of Computer Engineering
Istanbul Technical University
attokurov@itu.edu.tr

Ulug Bayazit
Department of Computer Engineering
Istanbul Technical University
ulugbayazit@itu.edu.tr

Abstract

The current work adapts the optimal tree pruning algorithm(BFOS) introduced by Breiman et al.(1984) and extended by Chou et al.(1989) to the multi-document summarization task. BFOS algorithm is used to eliminate redundancy which is one of the main issues in multi-document summarization. Hierarchical Agglomerative Clustering algorithm(HAC) is employed to detect the redundancy. The tree designed by HAC algorithm is successively pruned with the optimal tree pruning algorithm to optimize the distortion vs. rate cost of the resultant tree. Rate parameter is defined to be the number of the sentences in the leaves of the tree. Distortion is the sum of the distances between the representative sentence of the cluster at each node and the other sentences in the same cluster. The sentences assigned to the leaves of the resultant tree are included in the summary. The performance of the proposed system assessed with the Rouge-1 metric is seen to be better than the performance of the DUC-2002 winners on DUC-2002 data set.

1 Introduction

Nowadays, the massive amount of information available in the form of digital media over the internet makes us seek effective ways of accessing this information. Textual documents, audio and video materials are uploaded every second. For instance, the number of Google's indexed web pages has exceeded 30 billion web pages in the last two years. Extraction of the needed information from a massive information pool is a challenging task. The task of skimming all the documents in their entirety before deciding which information is relevant is very time consuming.

One of the well known and extensively studied methods for solving this problem is summarization. Text summarization produces a short version of a document that covers the main topics in it (Mani and Hahn, 2000). It enables the reader to determine in a timely manner whether a given document satisfies his/her needs or not.

A single document summarization system produces a summary of only one document whereas a multi-document summarization system produces a summary based on multiple documents on the same topic. Summarization systems can also be categorized as generic or query-based . A generic summary contains general information about particular documents. It includes any information supposed to be important and somehow linked to the topics of the document set. In contrast, a query based summary comprises information relevant to the given query. In this case, query is a rule according to which a summary is to be generated.

Summarization systems can be also classified as extractive or abstractive. In extractive systems, a summary is created by selecting important sentences from a document. Here, only sentences containing information related to the main topics of the document are considered to be important. These sentences are added to the summary without any modification. On the other hand, abstractive systems can modify the existing sentences or even generate new sentences to be included in the summary. Therefore, abstractive summarization is typically more complex than extractive summarization.

The main goal in multi-document summarization is redundancy elimination. Since the documents are related to the same topics, similar text units(passages, sentences etc.) are encountered frequently in different documents. Such text units that indicate the importance of the topics discussed within them should be detected in order to reduce the redundancy. Some of the well-known ap-

Proceedings of the ACL 2014 Student Research Workshop, pages 64–70,
Baltimore, Maryland USA, June 22-27 2014. ©2014 Association for Computational Linguistics

proaches that address this problem are briefly explained in the following section.

Although much work has been done to eliminate the redundancy in multi-document summarization, the problem is still actual and addressed in the current work as well. The current work proposes to integrate the generalized BFOS algorithm (Breiman et al., 1984) adopted by Chou et.al (1989) for pruned tree structured quantizer design with the HAC (Hierarchical Agglomerative Clustering) algorithm. The two main parameters (distortion and rate) in the latter work are adopted to the multi-document summarization task. Distortion can be succinctly defined as the information loss in the meaning of the sentences due to their representation with other sentences. More specifically, in the current context, distortion contribution of a cluster is taken to be the sum of the distances between the vector representations of the sentences in the cluster and representative sentence of that cluster. Rate of a summary is defined to be the number of sentences in the summary, but more precise definitions involving word or character counts are also possible. BFOS based tree pruning algorithm is applied to the tree built with the HAC algorithm. HAC algorithm is used for clustering purposes since BFOS algorithm gets tree structured data as an input. It is found that the suggested approach yields better results in terms of the ROUGE-1 Recall measure (Lin et al., 2003) when compared to 400 word extractive summaries(400E) included in DUC-2002 data set. Also, the results with the proposed method are higher than the ones obtained with the best systems of DUC-2002 in terms of sentence recall and precision(Harabagiu, 2002; Halteren, 2002).

2 Related Works

Term frequency (Luhn, 1958), lexical chains (Barzilay and Elhadad, 1997), location of the sentences (Edmundson, 1969) and the cue phrases (Teufel et al., 1997) are used to determine the important lexical units. Goldstein et al. (2000) proposed a measure named Maximal Marginal Relevance which assigns a high priority to the passages relevant to the query and has minimal similarity to the sentences in the summary. Radev et al. (2001) developed a system called MEAD based on the centroid of the cluster. The words that are most relevant to the main topics are included in the centroid. Lin et al. designed a statistic-based summarization system (Summarist) which incorporated NLP(Natural Language Processing) and IR(Information Retrieval) methods. LSA(Latent Semantic Analysis) (Landauer et al., 1998) has also been used extensively in recent years for multi-document summarization. By applying SVD(Singular Value Decomposition) to the term-document matrix, it determines the most important topics and represents the term and documents in the reduced space (Murray et al., 2005; Steinberger and Jezek , 2004; Geiss, 2011). Rachit Arora et al. (2008) combined LDA(Latent Dirichlet Allocation) and SVD. In this approach, LDA is used to detect topics and SVD is applied to select the sentences representing these topics.

Clustering of the sentences has also been used to determine the redundant information. In this approach, the sentences are first clustered. The sentences in each cluster share common information about the main topics of the documents to be summarized. Then a sentence is selected (Radev et al., 2004) or generated (McKeown et al., 1999) from each cluster that represents the sentences in the cluster. Finally, selected sentences are added to the summary until a predetermined length is exceeded (Aliguliyev, 2006; Hatzivassiloglou et al., 1999; Hatzivassiloglou et al., 2001).

3 Background

3.1 Generalized BFOS Algorithm

Let us assume that we have a tree T with the set of leaves $\tilde{T}$. Also let us denote a sub-tree of T rooted at any node of T as S. The leaves of the sub-trees may happen to be the inner nodes of T. If the root node of the sub-tree S is not identical to the root node of T and the set of leaves $\tilde{S}$ is a sub-set of $\tilde{T}$ then S is called a branch. But if the sub-tree S is rooted at the root node of T then S is named a pruned sub-tree of T. Function defined on the tree T and on any sub-tree S is called a tree functional. Monotonic tree functional is a class of functional where it increases or decreases depending on the tree size. In our case, tree size is the number of the nodes of T.

Two main tree functionals($u1$ and $u2$) need to be defined in the generalized $BFOS$ algorithm. They are adapted to the problem under consideration. In regression trees, $u1$ is the number of the leaves and $u2$ is the mean squared distortion error. In TSVQ(Tree Structured Vector Quantization), $u1$ and $u2$ are the length of the code and the expected distortion, respectively. In the current context, distortion(D) and rate(R) defined in the next section are used as the tree functionals $u1$ and $u2$.

As shown in Chou et al., the set of distortion and rate points of the pruned sub-trees of T generate a convex hull if distortion is an increasing and rate is a decreasing function. Also it is stated that if the tree T is pruned off until the root node remains, then it is possible to generate the sub-trees which correspond to the vertices on the lower boundary of the convex hull. Thus it is sufficient to consider the sub-trees corresponding to the vertices of the boundary to trade off between rate and distortion.

A parameter $\lambda = -\frac{\Delta D}{\Delta R}$ may be used to locate the vertices on the lower boundary of the convex hull. ΔD and ΔR indicate the amount of distortion increase and rate decrease when branch subtree S is pruned off. It can be shown that a step on the lower boundary can be taken by pruning off at least one branch sub-tree rooted at a particular inner node. The λ value of this sub-tree is minimal among all the other branch sub-trees rooted at various inner nodes of T, because it is a slope of the lower boundary. At each pruning iteration, the algorithm seeks the branch sub-tree rooted at an inner node with the minimal lambda and prunes it off the tree. After each pruning step, the inner node at which the pruned branch sub-tree is rooted becomes a leaf node. The pruning iterations continue until the root node remains or the pruned sub-tree meets a certain stopping criterion.

4 The Proposed Summarization System

In the current work, BFOS and HAC algorithm were incorporated to the multi-document summarization system. Generalized version of the BFOS algorithm discussed in the work of Chou et al. (1989) with previous applications to TSVQ, speech recognition etc. was adapted for the purpose of pruning the large tree designed by the HAC algorithm. Generalized BFOS algorithm was preferred in the current context because it is believed that the generated optimal trees yield the best trade-off between the semantic distortion and rate (the summary length in terms of number of sentences).

The proposed system consists of the following stages: preprocessing, redundancy detection, redundancy elimination and the summary generation.

In preprocessing stage, the source documents are represented in the vector space. Towards this end, the sentences are parsed, stemmed and a feature set is created (terms (stems or words, n-grams etc.) that occur in more than one document are extracted). The sentences of the document set are then represented by a sentence X term matrix with n columns and m rows, where n is the number of the sentences and m is the number of the terms in the feature set. TF-IDF is used to determine the values of the matrix elements. TF-IDF assigns a value according to the importance of the terms in the collection of the sentences. If the term t occurs frequently in the current document but the opposite is true for other documents then tf-idf value of t is high.

$$TF - IDF = TF * \log \frac{N}{DF} \qquad (1)$$

where TF is the term frequency, DF is the document frequency and N is the number of sentences. Term frequency is the number of the occurrences of the term in the sentence. Document frequency is the number of the sentences in which the term is found.

Redundancy detection is facilitated by applying the Hierarchical Agglomerative Clustering(HAC) algorithm. Initially, individual sentences are considered to be singletons in the HAC algorithm. The most similar clusters are then successively merged to form a new cluster that contains the union of the sentences in the merged clusters. At each step, a new (inner) node is created in the tree as the new cluster appears and contains all the sentences in the union of the merged clusters. HAC merge operations continue until a single cluster remains. The tree built after HAC operation is referred to as the HAC tree.

The third stage is the redundancy elimination. To this end, generalized BFOS algorithm discussed previously is applied to the HAC tree. In order to adapt the generalized BFOS algorithm to the current context, distortion contribution of each cluster (node) is defined as follows:

$$D = \sum_{s \in cluster} d(rs, s) \qquad (2)$$

where d is the distance between the representative sentence(rs) and a sentence(s) in the cluster.

By definition, the distortion contribution of each leaf node of the HAC tree is zero.

Rate is defined to be the number of sentences in the leaves of the tree. A branch sub-tree is removed at each pruning step of the generalized BFOS algorithm. Correspondingly, the sentences at the leaf nodes of the pruned branch subtree are eliminated. As a result, the rate decreases to the number of leaf nodes remaining after pruning.

The centroid of the cluster can be used as the representative sentence of the cluster. Centroid can be constituted of the important (with TF-IDF values exceeding a threshold) words of the cluster (Radev et al., 2004) or can be generated using Natural language processing techniques (McKeown et al., 1999). In the current work, the simpler approach of selecting the sentence from the cluster yielding the minimal distortion as the representative sentence is employed.

λ parameter is used to determine the branch sub-trees that are successively pruned. In each pruning step, the branch sub-tree with minimum λ is identified to minimize the increase in total distortion(ΔD) per discarded sentence(ΔR).

In accordance with the definition of rate given above, ΔR is the change in the number of sentences in the summary before and after the pruning of the branch sub-tree. It also equals to the number of pruned leaf nodes, because rate equals to the number of the sentences stored in the leaf nodes of the current tree. For instance, let us assume that the number of sentences before pruning is 10 and a sub-tree A is cut off. If A has 4 leaf nodes, than 3 of them is eliminated and one is left to represent the cluster of sentences corresponding to the sub-tree A. Since 3 leaf nodes are removed and each leaf node is matched to the certain sentence, the current rate equals to 7. The increase in total distortion is written as

$$\Delta D = D_{post} - D_{prev} \tag{3}$$

where D_{prev} is set equal to the sum of distortions in the leaves of the tree before pruning and D_{post} is set equal to the sum of distortions in the leaves of the tree after pruning.

The application of the generalized BFOS algorithm to the HAC tree can be recapped as follows. At the initial step, a representative sentence is selected for each inner node and λ is determined for each inner node. At each generic pruning step, the node with the minimum lambda value is identified, the sub-tree rooted at that node is pruned, the root node of the sub-tree is converted to a leaf node. After each pruning step, the λ values of the ancestor nodes of this new leaf node are updated. We summarize the generalized BFOS algorithm with a pseudocode in Algorithm 1.

Algorithm 1: PRUNING THE TREE. Prunes a tree T created by using Hierarchical Agglomerative Clustering Algorithm

Input: A tree T produced by using Hierarchical Clustering Algorithm
Output: Optimal sub-tree O obtained by pruning T

For each leaf node,
  $\lambda \leftarrow \infty, distortion(D) \leftarrow 0$
For each inner node calculate $\lambda = \frac{\Delta D}{\Delta R}$, where ΔD and ΔR are change in distortion(D) and rate(R) respectively
$rate(R) \leftarrow$ the number of the leaves of T
while *the number of the nodes > 1* **do**
  find a node A with minimum λ value among the inner nodes
  prune the sub-tree S rooted at the node A
  convert the pruned inner node A to the leaf node containing the representative sentence of the sub-tree S
  update the ancestor nodes of the node A: update ΔD, ΔR and λ
  update rate(R)
return O

A summary of desired length can be created by selecting a threshold based on rate (the number of remaining sentences after pruning, the number of leaf nodes of the pruned tree). Another possibility for the choice of the stopping criterion may be based on the λ parameter which monotonically increases with pruning iterations. When a large enough λ value is reached, it may be assumed that shortening the summary further eliminates informative sentences.

The proposed method of summarization has a few drawbacks. The main problem is that the pruning algorithm is highly dependent on the distortion measure. If the distortion measure is not defined appropriately, the representative sentence can be selected incorrectly. Another issue is the inclusion of the irrelevant sentences into the summary. This problem may occur if the sentences remaining after pruning operation are included in the summary without filtering.

5 Evaluation

The testing of the system performed on DUC-2002 data set (Document Understanding Conference, 2002) since the proposed system is designed to produce a generic summary without specified information need of users or predefined user profile. This data set contains 59 document sets. For each document set extraction based summaries with the length 200 and 400 words are provided. Document sets related to the single event are used for testing purposes.

Evaluation of the system is carried out using ROUGE package (Lin C, 2004). Rouge is a summary evaluation approach based on n-gram co-occurrence , longest common subsequence and skip bigram statistics (Lin et al., 2003). The performance of the summarizing system is measured with Rouge-1 Recall, Rouge-1 Precision and F1 measure(Table 1). 400E stood for the extractive 400 word summary provided by DUC-2002 data set. It was created manually as an extractive summary for evaluation purposes. Candidate summary(CS) was produced by the proposed system. Both summaries were compared against a 200 word abstractive summary included in DUC-2002 data set. 200 word abstractive summary was considered as the model summary in ROUGE package. As shown, the summary of the proposed system gives better results in Rouge-1 recall measure. However, the highest precision is achieved in the 400E summary. Generally, the proposed system outperforms the 400E summary, since F1-score which takes into account precision and recall is higher.

In addition, the performance of the system was compared with the best systems(BEST) of DUC-2002(Halteren, 2002; Harabagiu, 2002)(Table 2). The results of the best systems(BEST) in terms of sentence recall and sentence precision are provided by DUC-2002. Sentence recall and sentence precision of the candidate summary(produced by the proposed system) were calculated by using 400 word extract based summary(provided by DUC-2002) and a candidate summary. Sentence recall and sentence precision are defined as follows:

$$sentence\ recall = \frac{M}{B} \quad (4)$$

$$sentence\ precision = \frac{M}{C} \quad (5)$$

where M is the number of the sentences included in both of the summaries(a candidate and 400 word summary provided by DUC-2002(400E)), C,B are the number of the sentences in the candidate summary and in a 400E summary, respectively.

summary	P	R	F1
400E	0.313	0.553	0.382
candidate	0.3	0.573	0.394

Table 1: ROUGE-1 Results. Candidate summary(produced by the proposed system) and 400E summary provided by DUC 2002 are compared with 200 word abstract created manually.

summary	Sentence Precision	Sentence Recall
BEST	0.271	0.272
candidate	0.273	0.305

Table 2: Results. The best systems of DUC-2002 results and the results of the proposed system. Proposed system is compared with 400 word extracts provided by DUC-2002.

As shown, the proposed system performs better than the best systems of DUC-2002 in terms of sentence recall. We are more interested in sentence recall because it states the ratio of the important sentences contained in the candidate summary if the sentences included in the 400E summary are supposed to be important ones. Furthermore, sentence precision is affected from the length of the candidate summary.

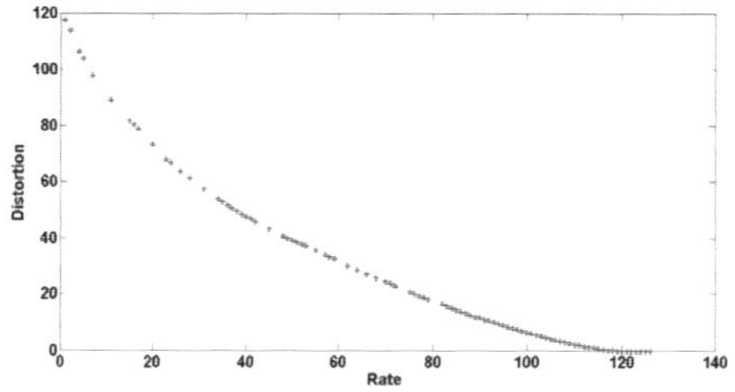

Figure 1: The relationship between distortion and rate. While rate is decreasing distortion is increasing.

Summarizing the text can be considered as the compression of the text. Thus it is possible to depict the graph of dependence of distortion on rate (Figure 1). The graph shows that as rate decreases distortion increases monotonically. Therefore, if distortion is assumed to be the information loss occurred when the original text is summarized then the summaries of different quality can be produced by restricting rate (the number of sentences).

Another graph shows the change of the *lambda* value(Figure 2). The iteration number of the pruning is on X axis and lambda value is on Y one. If λ value of the pruned points are sorted in ascending order and then the graph of ordered λ values is depicted according to their order then the graph identical to the one shown below is obtained(Figure 2). This indicates that the node with minimal lambda value is selected in each iteration. Consequently, the sentences are eliminated so that increase in distortion is minimal for decrease in rate.

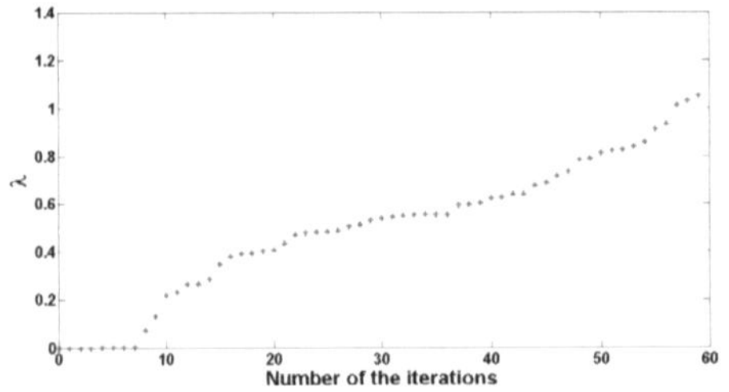

Figure 2: λ value of the pruned node. The change of λ value has upward tendency.

All in all, the quantitative analyses show that the proposed system can be used as one of the redundancy reduction methods. However, in order to achieve the good results, the parameters of BFOS algorithm have to be set appropriately.

6 Conclusion

In this paper , the combination of tree pruning and clustering is explored for the purpose of multi-document summarization. Redundancy in the text detected by the HAC algorithm is eliminated by the generalized BFOS algorithm. It is shown that if the parameters(distortion and rate) are set properly, generalized BFOS algorithm can be used to reduce the redundancy in the text. The depicted graph (Figure 1) shows that the proposed definitions of distortion and rate are eligible for the multi-document summarization purpose.

The performance evaluation results in terms of ROUGE-1 metric suggest that the proposed system can perform better with additional improvements (combining with LSI). Also it is stated that distance measure selection and noisy sentence inclusion have significance impact on the summarization procedure.

Future research will deal with the abstraction. A new sentence will be created(not extracted) when two clusters are merged. It will represent the cluster of sentences as well as summarize the other sentences in the same cluster.

Acknowledgments

We thank Google for travel and conference support for this paper.

References

Aliguliyev R. 2006. A Novel Partitioning-Based Clustering Method and Generic Document Summarization. In *WI-IATW 06: Proceedings of the 2006 IEEE/WIC/ACM international conference on Web Intelligence and Intelligent Agent Technology*,pages 626–629,Washington,DC, USA.

Arora R. and Ravindran B. 2008. Latent Dirichlet Allocation Based Multi-Document Summarization. In *Proceedings of the Second Workshop on Analytics for Noisy Unstructured Text Data (AND 2008)*,91-97.

Barzilay R. and Elhadad M. 1997. Using Lexical Chains for Text Summarization. In *Proceedings of the ACL/EACL'97 Workshop on Intelligent Scalable Text Summarization*,pages 10-17.

Barzilay R. 2003. Information fusion for multi-document summarization: Paraphrasing and generation, PhD thesis, DigitalCommons@Columbia.

Breiman L., Friedman J.H., Olshen R.A., and Stone C.J. 1984. Classification and Regression Trees. *The Wadsworth Statistics/Probability Series*,Belmont, CA: Wadsworth.

Chou A. Philip, Tom Lookabaugh, and Gray M. Robert. 1989. Optimal Pruning with Applications to Tree-Structured Source Coding and Modeling. *IEEE transactions on information theory*, volume 35, no 2.

DUC–2002. 2002. *Document Understanding Conference*.

Edmundson H. P. 1969. New methods in automatic extracting. *Journal of the ACM*,16:264-285.

Goldstein J., Mittal V., Carbonell J., and Kantrowitz M. 2000. Multi-document summarization by sentence extraction. In *Proceedings of the ANLP/NAACL Workshop on Automatic Summarization*,pages 40-48.

H. van Halteren. 2002. Writing style recognition and sentence extraction. In *Proceedings of the workshop on automatic summarization*,pages 66–70.

Harabagiu S.M. and Lacatusu F. 2002. Generating single and multi-document summaries with gistexter. In *Proceedings of the workshop on automatic summarization*,pages 30–38.

Hatzivassiloglou V., Klavans J. L., Holcombe M. L., Barzilay R., Kan M.-Y., and McKeown K. R. 1999. Detecting text similarity over short passages: Exploring Linguistic Feature Combinations via Machine Learning. In *Proceedings of the 1999 Joint SIGDAT Conference on empirical Methods in Natural Language Processing and very large corpora*,pages 203-212. College Park, MD, USA.

Hatzivassiloglou V., Klavans J. L., Holcombe M. L., Barzilay, R., Kan M.-Y., and McKeown K. R. 2001. SIMFINDER: A Flexible Clustering Tool for Summarization. In *NAACL Workshop on Automatic Summarization*,pages 41-49. Pittsburgh, PA, USA.

Hahn U. and Mani I. 2000. Computer. The challenges of automatic summarization. *IEEE Computer*,33(11),29–36.

Hovy E. and Lin C.Y. 1999. Automated Text Summarization in SUMMARIST. *Mani I and Maybury M (eds.), Advances in Automatic Text Summarization*,pages 81–94. The MIT Press.

Johanna Geiss. 2011. Latent semantic sentence clustering for multi-document summarization, PhD thesis. Cambridge University.

"Towards Multidocument Summarization by Reformulation: Progress and Prospects",

Kathleen McKeown, Judith Klavans, Vasilis Hatzivassiloglou, Regina Barzilay, Eleazar Eskin. 1999. Towards Multidocument Summarization by Reformulation: Progress and Prospects. In *Proceedings of AAAI*,Orlando, Florida.

Landauer T.K., Foltz P.W., and Laham D. 1998. Introduction to Latent Semantic Analysis. *Discourse Processes*,25,pages 259–284.

Lin C.Y. and Hovy E. 2003. Automatic Evaluation of Summaries Using N-gram Co-occurrence Statistics. In *North American Chapter of the Association for Computational Linguistics on Human Language Technology (HLTNAACL- 2003)*,pages 71-78.

Lin C–Y. 2004. Rouge: A package for automatic evaluation of summaries. In *Proceedings of Workshop on Text Summarization Branches Out, Post-Conference Workshop of ACL 2004*.

Luhn H.P. 1958. The Automatic Creation of Literature Abstracts. *IBM Journal of Research Development*,2(2):159-165.

Murray G., Renals S., and Carletta J. 2005. Extractive summarization of meeting recordings. In *Proceedings of the 9th European Conference on Speech Communication and Technology*.

Radev D. R., Jing H., and Budzikowska M. 2000. Centroid-based summarization of multiple documents: sentence extraction, utility-based evaluation, and user studies, pages 21-29. In *ANLP/NAACL Workshop on Summarization*, Morristown, NJ, USA.

Radev R., Blair–goldensohn S,Zhang Z. 2001. Experiments in Single and Multi-Docuemtn Summarization using MEAD. In*First Document Under- standing Conference*,New Orleans,LA.

Radev D. R., Jing H., Stys M., and Tam D. 2004. Centroid-based summarization of multiple documents. *Information Processing and Management*,40:919-938.

Scott Deerwester, Dumais T. Susan, Furnas W George , Landauer Thomas K., and Richard Harshman. 1990. Indexing by latent semantic analysis. *Journal of the American Society of Information Science*,41(6):391-407.

Steinberger J. and Jezek K. 2004. Using Latent Semantic Analysis in Text Summarization and Summary Evaluation. *Proceedings of ISIM '04*, pages 93-100.

Teufel, Simone, and Marc Moens. 1997. Sentence extraction as a classification task. *ACL/EACL workshop on Intelligent and scalable Text summarization*,58-65.

Disambiguating prepositional phrase attachment sites with sense information captured in contextualized distributional data

Clayton Greenberg
Department of Computational Linguistics and Phonetics
Universität des Saarlandes
cgreenbe@alumni.princeton.edu

Abstract

This work presents a supervised prepositional phrase (PP) attachment disambiguation system that uses contextualized distributional information as the distance metric for a nearest-neighbor classifier. Contextualized word vectors constructed from the GigaWord Corpus provide a method for implicit Word Sense Disambiguation (WSD), whose reliability helps this system outperform baselines and achieve comparable results to those of systems with full WSD modules. This suggests that targeted WSD methods are preferable to ignoring sense information and also to implementing WSD as an independent module in a pipeline.

1 Introduction

Arriving at meaning from a linguistic expression is hardly a trivial process, but a "simple" four-word expression shows some of the kinds of knowledge and interactions involved:

(1) a. *eat* [*seeds* [*in plants*]]
b. [*eat seeds*] [*in plants*]

(a) and (b) illustrate two possible interpretations for the expression. In (a), the seeds are part of larger organic units, and in (b), the eating takes place in refineries. Choosing (a) or (b) helps the system construct accurate relationships between the events and participants mentioned, which is essential for many natural language processing tasks including machine translation, information extraction, and textual inference.

These two groupings represent an example of the widely-studied phenomenon of prepositional phrase (PP) attachment ambiguity. We define the governor of a PP as the word or phrase that the PP modifies. Ambiguity arises from multiple candidates for the governor. Strings such as in (1) can be represented by quadruples of the form (V, N_1, P, N_2), where V is a transitive verb, N_1 is the head noun of an object of V, P is a preposition, and N_2 is the head noun of the object of P. Then, (a) and (b) reflect the two possible choices of governor for the PP: V (adverbial PP) and N_1 (adjectival PP). Therefore, disambiguation for such quadruples is a binary classification of the PP as adjectival or adverbial, or equivalently, noun-attach or verb-attach.

In our example, classifying the sense of the word *plant* as either `organic_unit` or `refinery` is key to choosing the correct structure. These senses have significantly different respective relationships to *eat* and *seeds*. In particular, we often eat most except, or only, the seeds from an organic unit, but we have no such intuitions about refineries. The training data must be analyzed carefully in order to prevent unwanted mixing of senses, since that causes noise in predictions about word relationships.

Given that $V-N_2$ and N_1-N_2 relationships are very important for PP-attachment disambiguation, it is not surprising that leading PP-attachment disambiguation systems include a Word Sense Disambiguation (WSD) module. The challenging aspect of this is that it introduces a subtask that in the general case has lower accuracy levels than the entire system. Hence, its place and form within the system deserves to be examined closely. Since a representation of the predicted sense is not part of the attachment decision, it does not need to be explicitly present within the procedure. In this paper, we investigate the importance of proper word sense decisions for PP-attachment disambiguation, and describe a highly-accurate system that encodes sense information in contextualized distributional data. Its high performance shows the benefit of representing and handling sense information in a targeted fashion for the task.

Proceedings of the ACL 2014 Student Research Workshop, pages 71–77,
Baltimore, Maryland USA, June 22-27 2014.

2 Background and related work

Sense information provides an illuminating through line for many previous PP-attachment disambiguation systems. We begin by describing a very popular dataset for the problem and its subsequent development, and then trace through the two main approaches to sense information representation and the results obtained using this dataset.

2.1 The corpus

A standard corpus for the binary classification problem described above was developed by Ratnaparkhi, Reynar and Roukos (1994). They systematically extracted (V, N_1, P, N_2) quadruples from the Penn Treebank Wall Street Journal (WSJ) corpus and used the manually-generated constituency parses to obtain attachment decisions for each of the extracted PPs. The final dataset contained 27,937 quadruples. These were divided into 20,801 training quadruples, 4,039 development quadruples, and 3,097 test quadruples. Their maximum entropy model achieved 81.6% accuracy on this dataset and their decision tree achieved 77.7%. Accuracy on this corpus is defined to be the number of quadruples for which the classifier assigned the same attachment site as the site indicated in that sentence's parse tree, divided by the total number of quadruples. Although some parse trees in the corpus are known to have errors, the accuracy figures do not take this into account.

Also, Ratnaparkhi et al. (1994) conducted human experiments with a subset of their corpus. They found that humans, when given just the quadruple, were accurate 88.2% of the time. When given the entire sentence for context, accuracy improved to 93.2%. The perhaps underwhelming human performance is partially due to misclassifications by the Treebank assemblers who made these determinations by hand, and also unclear cases, which we discuss in the next section.

Collins and Brooks (1995) introduced modifications to the Ratnaparkhi et al. (1994) dataset meant to combat data sparsity and used the modified version to train their backed-off model. They replaced four digit numbers with `YEAR`, other numbers with `NUM`. Verbs and prepositions were converted to all lowercase. In nouns, all words that started with an uppercase letter followed by a lowercase letter were replaced with `NAME`. Then, all strings `NAME-NAME` were replaced with `NAME`. Finally all verbs were automatically lemmatized. They did not release statistics on how these modifications affected performance, so it is unclear how to allocate the performance increase between the backed-off model and the modifications to the dataset. The paper also provided some baselines: they achieve 59.0% accuracy on the Ratnaparkhi et al. (1994) corpus by assigning noun-attach to every quadruple, and 72.2% accuracy by assigning a default classification determined for each preposition. They show, and many subsequent papers confirm, that the preposition is the most predictive dimension in the quadruple.

Abney, Schapire, and Singer (1999) used the dataset from Collins and Brooks (1995) with a boosting algorithm and achieved 85.4% accuracy. Their algorithm also was able to order the specific data points by how much weight they were assigned by the learning algorithm. The highest data points tended to be those that contained errors. Thus, they were able to improve the quality of the dataset in a systematic way.

2.2 The WordNet approach

WordNet (Fellbaum, 1998) can be quite a powerful aid to PP-attachment disambiguation because it provides a way to systematically quantify semantic relatedness. The drawback is, though, that since WordNet semantic relations are between explicit word senses (SynSets), the words in the quadruples must be associated with these explicit word senses. The systems described below outline the different ways to make those associations.

Brill and Resnik (1994) trained a transformation-based learning algorithm on 12,766 quadruples from WSJ, with modifications similar to those by Collins and Brooks (1995). As a particularly human-interpretable feature, the rules used word sense hierarchies. Namely, a WordNet rule applied to the named node and all of its hyponyms. For example, a rule involving *boat* would apply to instances of *kayak*. Importantly, each noun in the corpus inherited hypernyms from all of its senses. Therefore, they did not perform explicit WSD. Their accuracy was 81.8%.

The neural network by Nadh and Huyck (2012) also used WordNet word sense hierarchies. Only the first (intended to be the most frequent) sense of the word was used in computations. Hence, they explicitly perform WSD using a baseline method.

On a training corpus of 4,810 quadruples and a test corpus of 3,000 quadruples from WSJ, they achieve 84.6% accuracy. This shows the success of performing baseline WSD as part of a PP-attachment disambiguation system, although the different dataset makes comparison less direct.

At the other extreme, Stetina and Nagao (1997) developed a customized, explicit WSD algorithm as part of their decision tree system. For each ambiguous word in each quadruple, this algorithm selected a most semantically similar quadruple in the training data using unambiguous or previously disambiguated terms. Then, the word was assigned the WordNet sense that was semantically closest to the sense of the corresponding word in the other quadruple. Their distance metric was $L_1/D_1 + L_2/D_2$, where L_i is the distance from word sense i to the common ancestor, and D_i is the depth of the tree (distance to root) at word sense i. Such a metric captures the notion that more fine grained distinctions exist deeper in the WordNet graph, so the same absolute distance between nodes matters less at greater depths. Stetina and Nagao (1997) trained on a version of the Ratnaparkhi et al. (1994) dataset that contained modifications similar to those by Collins and Brooks (1995) and excluded forms not present in WordNet. The system achieved 88.1% accuracy on the entire test set and 90.8% accuracy on the subset of the test set in which all four of the words in the quadruple were present in WordNet.

Finally, Greenberg (2013) implemented a decision tree that reimplemented the WSD module from Stetina and Nagao (1997), and also used WordNet morphosemantic (teleological) links, WordNet evocations, and a list of phrasal verbs as features. The morphosemantic links and evocations brought more semantic relatedness information after the cost of explicit WSD had already been incurred. The system achieved 89.0% on a similarly modified Ratnaparkhi et al. (1994) dataset.

2.3 The distributional approach

As an alternative to the WordNet approach, the distributional tradition allows for implicit sense handling given that contexts from all senses of the word are represented together in the vector. Without modification, the senses are represented according to their relative frequencies in the data. Pantel and Lin (2000) created a collocation database that, for a given word, tracked the words that appeared in specific syntactic relations to it, such as subject (for verbs), adjective-modifier (for nouns), etc. Then, they used the collocation database to construct a corpus-based thesaurus that evaluated semantic relatedness between quadruples. With a mix of unsupervised learning algorithms, they achieved 84.3% accuracy. They also argued that rules involving both V and N_1 should be excluded because they cause over-fitting.

Zhao and Lin (2004) implemented a nearest neighbor system that used various vector similarity metrics to calculate distances between quadruples. The vectors were generated from the ACQUAINT corpus with both syntactic relation and proximity-based (bag of words) models. They found that the cosine of pointwise mutual information metric on a syntactic model performed with the greatest accuracy (86.5%, $k = 33$). They used a version of the Ratnaparkhi et al. (1994) dataset that had all words lemmatized and all digits replaced by `@`.

Using the Web as a large unsupervised corpus, Nakov and Hearst (2005) created a PP-attachment disambiguation system that exploits n-grams, derived surface features, and paraphrases to predict classifications. The system searched for six specific disambiguating paraphrases such as *opened the door (with a key)*, which suggests verb-attach, and *eat: spaghetti with sauce*, which suggests noun-attach. Paraphrases and n-gram models represent the aim to gather context beyond the quadruple as a disambiguation method. Their final system had 85.0% precision and 91.8% recall on the Ratnaparkhi et al. (1994) dataset. When assigning unassigned quadruples to verb-attach, it had 83.6% accuracy and 100% recall. Their system continued the trend that the most common error is classifying a noun-attach quadruple as verb-attach. This is because the majority of difficult cases are verb-attach, so all of the difficult cases get assigned verb-attach as a default.

3 Linguistic analysis

In this section, we will discuss some difficulties with and observations about the task of PP-attachment disambiguation. The analyses and conclusions drawn here set the linguistic foundation for the structure of the system described in the next section.

3.1 Lexically-specified prepositions

Hindle and Rooth (1993) provided many linguistic insights for the PP-attachment disambiguation problem, including the tendency to be verb-attach if N_1 is a pronoun, and that idiomatic expressions (e.g. *give way to mending*) and light verb constructions (e.g. *make cuts to Social Security*) are particularly troublesome for humans to classify. The defining feature of such constructions is a semantically-vacuous preposition. For example, in (2), we have semantically similar verbs appearing with different prepositions and yet the meanings of these sentences are still similar.

(2) a. *She was blamed for the crime.*
b. *She was accused of the crime.*
c. *She was charged with the crime.*

Further, when we nominalize *charged* we can get *charges of murder*, but *charged of murder* is usually unacceptable. Also, (3) gives an analogous three-way preposition variation following nouns.

(3) a. *They proposed a ban on tea.*
b. *They proposed a request for tea.*
c. *They proposed an alternative to tea.*

We argue that in these cases, a preceding word completely determines the preposition selected and that no further meaning is conveyed. In fact, we might say that the prepositions in this case serve analogously to morphological case marking in languages more heavily inflected than English. Freidin (1992) makes a proposal along these lines. The prescriptive rules that dictate "correct" and "incorrect" prepositions associated with certain verbs, nouns, and adjectives, as well as our robust ability to understand these sentences with the prepositions omitted, strongly suggest that this selection is idiosyncratic and cannot be derived from deeper principles.

The extreme case is phrasal verbs, for which it is problematic to posit the existence of a PP because the object can occur before or after the "preposition." As shown in (4d), this is not acceptable for standard prepositions.

(4) a. *He ran up the bill.*
b. *He ran the bill up.*
c. *He ran up the hill.*
d. * *He ran the hill up.*

For these, we say that there is one lexical entry for the transitive verb plus the particle (preposition without an object), as in *to run up*, and an optional operation reverses the order of the object of the phrasal verb and its particle.

Usual paraphrase tests, such as those described in Nakov and Hearst (2005), often do not lead to consistent conclusions about the proper attachment site for these lexically-specified prepositions. Further, two separate governors do not appear to be plausible. Therefore, these constructions probably do not belong as data points in the PP-attachment task. However, if they must conform to the task, the most reasonable attachment decision is likely to be the word that determined the preposition. Therefore, the PPs in (2) are verb-attach and those in (3) are noun-attach. This treatment of lexically-specified prepositions accounts for light verb constructions because the N_1 in those constructions dictates the preposition.

3.2 The special case of *of*

PPs with the preposition *of* attach to nouns with very few exceptions. In fact, 99.1% of the quadruples with *of* in our training set are noun-attach. The other 0.9% were misclassifications and quadruples with verbs that lexically specify *of*, such as *accuse*. The behavior of *of*-PPs has been widely studied. We take the acceptability of (5a) and not (5b) as evidence that *of*-PPs introduce argument-like descriptions of their governors.

(5) a. *a game of cards with incalculable odds*
b. * *a game with incalculable odds of cards*

The extremely high proportion of noun-attachments within *of*-PPs leads some to exclude *of*-PPs altogether from attachment disambiguation corpora. In our data, excluding this most commonly used English preposition shifts the most frequent attachment decision from noun-attach to verb-attach. This is unfortunate for systems aiming to mimic human processing, since Late Closure (Frazier, 1979) suggests a preference for noun-attach as the default or elsewhere case.

4 Methods

Our PP attachment disambiguation system is most closely related to Zhao and Lin (2004). We experimented with several similarity measures on a slightly preprocessed version of the Ratnaparkhi et al. (1994) dataset.

4.1 Training data

Because humans only perform 0.1% better than Stetina and Nagao's (1997) system when given the quadruples but not the full sentences (although technically on different datasets), we found it important to locate the full sentences in the Penn Treebank. So, we carefully searched for the quadruples in the raw version of the corpus. We ensured that the corpus would be searched sequentially, i.e. search for the current quadruple would begin on the previous matched sentence and then proceed forward. By inspection, we could tell that the sentences were roughly in order, so this choice increased performance and accuracy. However, we had to adapt the program to be flexible so that some truncated tokens in the quadruples, such as incorrectly segmented contractions, would be matched to their counterparts.

Next, we created some modified versions of the training corpus. We explored the effect of excluding quadruples with lexically-specified prepositions (usually tagged `PP-CLR` in WSJ), removing sentences in which there was no actual V, N_1, P, N_2 string found, manually removing encountered misclassifications, and reimplementing data sparsity modifications from Collins and Brooks (1995) and Stetina and Nagao (1997). In particular, we used the WordNet lemmatizer in NLTK to lemmatize the verbs in the corpus (Bird, Loper, and Klein 2009). However, for direct comparison with Zhao and Lin (2004), we decided to use in our final experiment a version of the corpus with all words lemmatized and all numbers replaced by `@`, but no other modifications.

4.2 Knowledge base

In order to compute quadruple similarity measures that take context information into account, we adopted the vector space model implemented by Dinu and Thater (2012). This model constructs distributional word vectors from the GigaWord corpus. We used a "filtered" model, meaning that the context for each occurrence is composed of words that are linked to that occurrence in a dependency parse. Therefore, the model is similar to a bag of words model, but does contain some syntactic weighting. To contextualize a vector, the model weights the components of the uncontextualized vector with the components of the context vector, using the formula

$$v(w,c) = \sum_{w' \in W} \alpha(c, w') f(w, w') \vec{e}_{w'}$$

where w is the target word, c is the context, W is the set of words, α is the cosine similarity of c and w', f is a co-occurrence function, and $\vec{e}_{w'}$ is a basis vector. Positive pmi-weighting was also applied to the vectors.

4.3 Implementation

We adopted the four-step classification procedure from Zhao and Lin (2004). At each step for each test quadruple, the training examples are sorted by a different vector composition method, a set of best examples is considered, and if these examples cast equal votes for noun-attach and verb-attach, the algorithm moves to the next step. Otherwise, the class with the greatest number of votes is assigned to the test quadruple.

1. Consider only the training examples for which all four words are equal to those in the test quadruple.

2. Consider the k highest (k experimentally determined) scoring examples, with the same preposition as the test quadruple, using the composition function

   $$sim(q_1, q_2) = vn_1 + vn_2 + n_1 n_2$$

   where v, n_1, and n_2 are the vector similarities of the V, N_1, and N_2 pairs.

3. Same as (2), except using the function

   $$sim(q_1, q_2) = v + n_1 + n_2$$

4. Assign default class for the preposition (last resort), or noun-attach if there is no default class.

4.4 Similarity measures

We implemented four similarity measures. (1) abs: absolute word similarity, which gives 1 if the tokens are identical, 0 otherwise. (2) $noctxt$: cosine similarity using uncontextualized word vectors. (3) $ctxt_{quad}$: cosine similarity using word vectors contextualized by the quadruple words. (4) $ctxt_{sent}$: cosine similarity using word vectors contextualized by words from the full sentence.

5 Experimentation

We set the k values by using five-fold cross-validation on the training quadruples. Then, for intermediate numerical checks, we tested the systems on the development quadruples. The figures in the next section are the result of a single run of the final trained systems on the test quadruples.

6 Results

Table 1 presents results from our binary classifier using the different similarity measures. Table 2 compares our best binary classifier accuracy (using $ctxt_{quad}$) to other systems. Table 3 shows the number, percentage, and accuracy of decisions by step in the classification procedure for the $ctxt_{quad}$ run.

Similarity measure	k value	Accuracy
abs	3	80.2%
$noctxt$	11	86.6%
$ctxt_{quad}$	10	**88.4%**
$ctxt_{sent}$	8	81.9%

Table 1: Similarity measure performance comparison.

Method	Sense handling	Accuracy
BR1994	All senses equal	81.8%
PL2000	Global frequency	84.3%
ZL2004	Global frequency	86.5%
SN1997	Full WSD	88.1%
Our system	Context weighting	**88.4%**
G2013	Full WSD	89.0%

Table 2: Leading PP-attachment disambiguation systems.

Step	Coverage	Coverage %	Accuracy
1	244	7.88%	91.8%
2	2849	91.99%	88.1%
3	0	0.00%	N/A
4	4	0.13%	100.0%

Table 3: Coverage and accuracy for classification procedure steps, using $ctxt_{quad}$.

7 Discussion

The results above show that contextualizing the word vectors, which is meant to implicitly represent sense information, can statistically-significantly boost performance on PP-attachment disambiguation by 1.8% ($\chi^2 = 4.31, p < 0.04$) on an already quite accurate system. We can see that using the full sentence as context, while helpful for human judgment, is not effective in this system because there are not enough examples in the knowledge base for reliable statistics. It seems as though too much context obscures generalizations otherwise captured by the system.

Nominal increases in accuracy aside, this system uses only a knowledge base that is not specific to the task of PP-attachment disambiguation. We obtained highly accurate results without utilizing task-specific resources, such as sense inventories, or performing labor-intensive modifications to training data. Since systems with full WSD modules would likely require both of these, this implicit handling of sense information seems more elegant.

8 Conclusion

This paper describes a PP-attachment disambiguation system that owes its high performance to capturing sense information in contextualized distributional data. We see that this implicit handling is preferable to having no sense handling and also to having a full WSD module as part of a pipeline.

In future work, we would like to investigate how to systematically extract contexts beyond the quadruple, such as sentences or full documents, while maintaining the information captured in less contextualized vectors. Perhaps there are certain particularly informative positions whose words would positively affect the vectors. Given that words tend to maintain the same sense within a document, it is a particularly well-suited context to consider. However, care must be taken to minimize unwanted sense mixing, combat data sparsity, and restrict the number of similarity comparisons for efficiency.

Acknowledgments

We owe sincerest thanks to Prof. Dr. Manfred Pinkal and Dr. Stefan Thater for initial direction and providing the vector space model used in our system. Also, we thank Google for travel and conference support.

References

Steven Abney, Robert E. Schapire and Yoram Singer. 1999. Boosting Applied to Tagging and PP-attachment. In *Proceedings of the Joint SIGDAT Conference on Empirical Methods in Natural Language Processing and Very Large Corpora, EMNLP-VLC*, College Park, MD. pp. 38–45.

Steven Bird, Edward Loper and Ewan Klein. 2009. *Natural Language Processing with Python*. O'Reilly Media, Inc.

Eric Brill and Philip Resnik. 1994. A rule-based approach to prepositional phrase attachment disambiguation. In *5th International Conference on Computational Linguistics (COLING94)*, Kyoto, Japan.

Michael Collins and James Brooks. 1995. Prepositional Attachment through a Backed-off Model. In David Yarovsky and Kenneth Church (ed.), *Proceedings of the Third Workshop on Very Large Corpora*, Somerset, New Jersey, Association for Computational Linguistics. pp. 27–38.

Georgiana Dinu and Stefan Thater. 2012. Saarland: vector-based models of semantic textual similarity. In *First Joint Conference on Lexical and Computational Semantics (*SEM)*, Montréal. pp. 603–607.

Christiane Fellbaum (ed.) 1998. *WordNet: An Electronic Lexical Database*. MIT Press.

Lyn Frazier. 1979. *On Comprehending Sentences: Syntactic Parsing Techniques*. Unpublished doctoral dissertation, University of Connecticut.

Robert Freidin. 1992. *Foundations of generative syntax*. MIT Press.

Clayton Greenberg. 2013. *Disambiguating prepositional phrase attachment sites with graded semantic data or, how to rule out elephants in pajamas*. Unpublished undergraduate thesis, Princeton University.

Donald Hindle and Mats Rooth. 1993. Structural Ambiguity and Lexical Relations. In *Meeting of the Association for Computational Linguistics*. pp. 229–236.

Kailash Nadh and Christian Huyck. 2012. A neuro-computational approach to prepositional phrase attachment ambiguity resolution. *Neural Computation*, 24(7): pp. 1906–1925.

Preslav Nakov and Marti Hearst. 2005. Using the Web as an Implicit Training Set: Application to Structural Ambiguity Resolution. In *Proceedings of HLT-NAACL*.

Patrick Pantel and Dekang Lin. 2000. An unsupervised approach to prepositional phrase attachment using contextually similar words. In *Proceedings of the 38th Annual Meeting of the Association for Computational Linguistics*. pp. 101–108.

Adwait Ratnaparkhi, Jeff Reynar and Salim Roukos. 1994. A Maximum Entropy Model for Prepositional Phrase Attachment. In *Proceedings of the ARPA Human Language Technology Workshop*, Plainsboro, NJ. pp. 250–255.

Jiri Stetina and Makoto Nagao. 1997. Corpus Based PP Attachment Ambiguity Resolution with a Semantic Dictionary. In *Proceedings of the Fifth Workshop on Very Large Corpora*, Beijing and Hong Kong. pp. 66–80.

Shaojun Zhao Dekang Lin. 2004. Corpus Based PP Attachment Ambiguity Resolution with a Semantic Dictionary. In *Proceedings of the First International Joint Conference on Natural Language Processing*, Sanya, China.

Open Information Extraction for Spanish Language based on Syntactic Constraints

Alisa Zhila
Centro de Investigación
en Computación,
Instituto Politécnico Nacional,
07738, Mexico City, Mexico
alisa.zhila@gmail.com

Alexander Gelbukh
Centro de Investigación
en Computación,
Instituto Politécnico Nacional,
07738, Mexico City, Mexico
gelbukh@gelbukh.com

Abstract

Open Information Extraction (Open IE) serves for the analysis of vast amounts of texts by extraction of assertions, or relations, in the form of tuples ⟨*argument 1*; *relation*; *argument 2*⟩. Various approaches to Open IE have been designed to perform in a fast, unsupervised manner. All of them require language specific information for their implementation. In this work, we introduce an approach to Open IE based on syntactic constraints over POS tag sequences targeted at Spanish language. We describe the rules specific for Spanish language constructions and their implementation in EXTRHECH, an Open IE system for Spanish. We also discuss language-specific issues of implementation. We compare EXTRHECH's performance with that of REVERB, a similar Open IE system for English, on a parallel dataset and show that these systems perform at a very similar level. We also compare EXTRHECH's performance on a dataset of grammatically correct sentences against its performance on a dataset of random texts extracted from the Web, drastically different in their quality from the first dataset. The latter experiment shows robustness of EXTRHECH on texts from the Web.

1 Introduction

Open IE is a rapidly developing area in text processing, with its own applications and approaches that are different from traditional IE (Etzioni et al., 2008; Banko and Etzioni, 2008; Etzioni, 2011). Unlike traditional IE, where systems are targeted at extraction of instances of particular relations with arguments restricted to certain semantic classes, e.g., *to_be_born_in(HUMAN; LOCATION)*, Open IE serves for extraction of all possible relations with arbitrary arguments. For example, in "*Woman who drove van full of kids is charged with attempted murder*" two relations can be identified: ⟨*Woman*; *drove*; *van full of kids*⟩ and ⟨*Woman*; *is charged with*; *attempted murder*⟩.

The ability to extract arbitrary relations from text allows applications of Open IE that are not possible in the frame of traditional IE. Among them are fact extraction at sentence level (e.g., ⟨*Mozart*; *was born in*; *Salzburg*⟩), new perspective on search as question answering (e.g., *Where was Mozart born?*) (Etzioni, 2011), or assessment of the quality of text documents at Web scale (Horn et al., 2013). Additionally, the output of Open IE systems can serve for ontology population (Soderland et al., 2010) and acquisition of common sense knowledge (Lin et al., 2010).

Although all Open IE systems are targeted at the extraction of arbitrary relations, the approaches to this task vary significantly. The pilot approach suggested by Banko et al. (2007) is based on semi-supervised learning of general relation patterns that then serve for extraction of arbitrary relations. However, the output of such systems contains many incoherent and inconsistent extractions, and the training stage is quite computationally complex. Fader et al. (2011) suggested another approach where syntactic and lexical constraints were applied over POS-tagged input. This approach has proven to be robust and fast enough for relation extraction at Web scale.

Although Open IE is targeted at extraction of arbitrary relations without any semantic restrictions, all approaches have strong language dependent restrictions and require language specific information to be introduced in the corresponding systems. For Spanish language, the apporach based on rules over dependency trees has been implemented both using full parsing

Proceedings of the ACL 2014 Student Research Workshop, pages 78–85,
Baltimore, Maryland USA, June 22-27 2014. ©2014 Association for Computational Linguistics

(Aguilar-Galicia, 2012) and using shallow dependency parsing (Gamallo et al., 2012). The former work shows that this approach is too computationally costly and is not always robust even on grammatically correct texts. The latter work does not report any results for Spanish language or discusses any details specific to implementations for languages other than English. Further, we are not aware of any existing research on whether the approach based on syntactic constraints over POS tags can be generalized to other languages. Additionally, although Open IE is claimed to be useful for information extraction from the Web, we are not aware of any research on its applicability to texts randomly extracted from the Internet, i.e., those that have not been verified for grammatical correctness by peers or editors.

In this paper we discuss Open IE based on syntactic constraints over POS tag sequences, aimed at Spanish language. We describe its implementation and introduce EXTRHECH, an Open IE system for Spanish. We also compare its performance with that of REVERB (Fader et al., 2011) on a parallel dataset. Additionally, we evaluate performance of our system over a dataset of texts randomly extracted from the Internet and discuss the issues that arise when processing random Internet texts. We also give a brief analysis of errors.

The paper is organized as follows. Related work is reviewed in Section 2. Section 3 presents our approach to Open IE for Spanish and describes the EXTRHECH system. Section 4 describes the experiments for a parallel English-Spanish dataset and for a Spanish dataset of texts randomly extracted from the Internet. In Section 5, a brief analysis of errors is presented. Section 6 draws the conclusions and outlines future work.

2 Related Work

There exist several approaches to Open IE.

Chronologically the first one was introduced in the pilot works on Open IE by Banko et al. (2007) and Etzioni et al. (2008). Their approach is based on semi-supervised machine learning principles and includes three main steps: (1) manual labeling of a training corpus for seed relation phrases and features; (2) further semi-supervised learning of relations; (3) automatic extractions of relations and their arguments. This approach is implemented in TEXTRUNNER (Banko and Etzioni, 2008), WOE^{pos}, and $\text{WOE}^{\text{parse}}$, both (Wu and Weld, 2010). In these systems, the detection of a relation triple starts from the potential arguments expressed as noun phrases, i.e., before the connecting relation phrase is detected. Once detected, neither the argument phrases nor the relation phrase can be backtracked, which makes the approach prone to incoherent and uninformative extractions. For example, in "*to make a deal with*", *deal* can be erroneously extracted as an argument, although it is a part of the relation phrase.

The group of rule-based approaches includes systems based on rules applied over linguistically annotated texts. FES-2012 system (Aguilar-Galicia, 2012) applies rules to the fully parsed sentences. However, in the same work the authors show that this approach is too slow to be scaled to a Web-sized corpus and that it is not robust. Another system implementing rule-based approach is DEPOE (Gamallo et al., 2012). In this system, the rules are applied to the output of shallow dependency parsing. In REVERB system (Fader et al., 2011), syntactic constraints are applied over POS tags and syntactic chunks. The last two systems show better results in terms of precision/recall and speed, and, consequently, scalability to a Web-sized corpus.

Finally, the approach based on the deep automatic linguistic analysis is implemented in OLLIE (Mausam et al., 2012). This system combines various approaches: it uses output of a rule-based Open IE system to bootstrap learning of the relation patterns and then additionally applies lexical and semantic patterns to extract relations that are not expessed through verb phrases. Such a complex approach leads to high-precision results with a high yield. However, there is a tradeoff between accuracy of the output and cost of implementation and computation and complexity of the training stage.

All these approaches require language-dependent information for their implementation. The third approach directly uses lexical information for the context analysis. The other two approaches employ language-specific morphological and syntactic information. Of the described systems, only two have been implemented for languages other than English. FES-2012 system is implemented for Spanish language; however, its use of the full syntactic parsing does not scale to a Web-sized corpus. DEPOE system, based on rules over shallow dependency parsing, is claimed to have its variants for Spanish, Portuguese, and Galician languages (Gamallo et al., 2012). However, the authors do not report any experimental results on languages other than English or any language-specific details.

The approach based on syntactic constraints over POS tags has not been applied to languages other than English, in spite of that this method can be easily adapted to other languages because it only requires a reliable POS tagger. The basic algorithm for relation extraction, according to Fader et al. (2011), is as follows:

- First, search for a verb-containing relation phrase in a sentence;
- If detected, search for a noun phrase to the left of the relation phrase;
- If a noun phrase detected, search for another noun phrase to the right of the relation phrase.

Additionally, the experiments for Open IE systems have been conducted only on texts that came from verified sources, i.e., Wikipedia, news, or textbooks (Banko and Etzioni, 2008; Fader et al., 2011; Mausam et al., 2012). However, Open IE is meant to work with Web text data that may come from any source including those that have not been edited or verified for grammar errors.

3 System Description

In this section we introduce ExtrHech,[1] a system for Open IE in Spanish. It takes a POS-tagged text as input, applies syntactic constraints over sequences of POS-tags, and returns a list of extracted relations as triples ⟨*argument 1*; *relation*; *argument 2*⟩ that correspond to each sentence.

3.1 Basic Processing

The system takes as input a POS-tagged text. In our experiemnts, we used a morphological analyzer from Freeling-2.2 (Padró et al., 2010). For Spanish language, it returns POS tags accoridng to EAGLES POS tag set (Leech and Wilson, 1999). Consequently, our system is designed to work with this POS tag set.

Spanish uses a number of non-ASCII characters, such as *á, é, ñ*, etc. These characters can come in different encodings. To be able to correctly analyze text with these characters, Freeling analyzer should receive the input in ISO encoding. Thus, the input text needs an additional preprocessing stage to be converted into this encoding. Though this might look as a minor technical issue, guessing the original encoding becomes a significant problem when working with texts from arbitrary sources on the Web. We discuss encoding related issues in Section 4.2.

After the text has been properly POS-tagged, we feed it into ExtrHech system, which applies the fact extraction algorithm described in Section 2 to each sentence, one sentence at a time. We use the same basic algorithm as in (Fader et al., 2011) but with different triple matching rules as appropriate for Spanish grammar.

The original POS-tag sequences for English would produce nonsense results on Spanish input due to substantial difference in grammars: infinitives are not preceded by "*to*", adjectives usually follow nouns, and oblique case pronouns precede verbs instead of following them, just to name a few peculiarities of Spanish.

First, the system looks for a verb-containing phrase in a sentence by matching it against the following expression:

$$\text{VREL} \rightarrow (\text{V W* P}) \mid (\text{V}),$$

where V stands either for a single verb optionally preceded by a reflexive pronoun (*se realizaron*, "*were carried out*"), or a participle (*calificado*, "*qualified*"). V W* P matches a verb with dependent words, where W stands for either a noun, an adjective, an adverb, a pronoun, or an article, and P stands either for a preposition optionally immediately followed by an infinitive, or for a gerund (*sigue siendo*, "*continues to be*"). The symbol * denotes zero or more matches. Here and further, the whole match is referred to as *verb phrase* (though it is not a verb phrase in linguistic sense).

After detecting a verb phrase, ExtrHech looks for a noun phrase to the left from the beginning of the verb phrase. This noun phrase is a potential first argument of the relation. If a match is found, then the system looks for another noun phrase to the right from the end of the verb phrase. The noun on the right side is treated as the second argument.

Noun phrases are searched for with the following regular expression:

$$\text{NP} \rightarrow \text{Np (PREP Np)?},$$

where Np matches a noun optionally preceded by either an article (*la dinámica*, "*the dynamics*"),

[1]All materials are available on the page `http://www.gelbukh.com/resources/spanish-open-fact-extraction`.

an adjective, an ordinal number (*los primeros ganadores*, "*the first winners*"), a number (*3 casas*, "*3 houses*"), or their combination, and optionally followed by either a single adjective (*un esfuerzo criminal*, "*a criminal effort*"), a single participle, or both (*los documentos escritos antiguos*, "*the ancient written documents*"). The whole expression matched by Np can be preceded by an indefinite determinant construction, e.g., *uno de*, "*one of*". PREP matches a single preposition. Hence, an entire noun phrase is either a single noun with optional modifiers or a noun with optional modifiers followed by a prepositional phrase that is a preposition and another noun with its corresponding optional modifiers (*una larga lista de problemas actuales*, "*a long list of current problems*"). The symbol ? denotes 0 or 1 matches.

If noun phrases are matched on both sides of the verb phrase, all three components are considered to represent a relation and are extracted in the form of a triple.

As an output unit, EXTRHECH returns a triple consisting of ⟨*argument 1*; *relation*; *argument 2*⟩, where *argument 1* semantically is, e.g., an agent or experiencer of the relation and *argument 2* is a general object or circumstance of the relation.

3.2 Additional Processing

Above we described the core rules and the basic sequence for relation extraction. In addition to them, we also implemented several optional rules for processing of certain language constructions that can be turned on and off with the input parameters.

First, participle clauses that follow a noun can be searched for a relational triple if they terminate with a noun. For example, from a phrase

Precios del café suministrados por la OIC

("Coffee prices provided by International Coffee Organization")

EXTRHECH returns the relation:

⟨*Precios del café*; *suministrados por*; *la OIC*⟩.

Second, EXTRHECH also approaches resolution of coordinating conjunctions between verb phrases and between noun phrases into corresponding separate relations. Here follows the example of a sentence with a coordinating conjunction between verb phrases:

El cerebro almacena enormes cantidades de información y realiza millones de actividades todos los días

("The brain stores vast amounts of information and performs millions of activities every day")

. Two facts are detected:

⟨*El cerebro*; *almacena enormes cantidades de*; *información*⟩

and

⟨*El cerebro*; *realiza millones de*; *actividades todos los días*⟩.

Third, relative clauses introduced by single relative pronouns (e.g., *que* ("*that*", "*who*"), *cual* ("*which*")) as in *las partes que conforman un trabajo de investigación* ("*parts that make up a research work*") are also searched for relations. However, relative pronoun phrases with prepositions, e.g. *en el cual* ("*in which*") are not taken into consideration for relation extraction due to their coreferential complexity.

3.3 Limitations

The implementation of basic processing performed by EXTRHECH system follows the algorithm introduced in (Fader et al., 2011). This means that extracted facts are limited to the relations expressed through a verb phrase. This limitation is discussed in the cited paper.

In our apporach to Open IE in Spanish, we do not allow pronouns to be potential arguments of a relation. It was mainly done because of a wide use of a neutral pronoun *lo* ("*this*", "*which*", or no direct translation) as a head of relative clauses in Spanish language, e.g., *lo que dio valor al poder judicial* ("*__ that gave value to the judiciary*"). Including pronouns for potential argument matches would return a lot of uninformative relations as ⟨*lo*; *dio valor a*; *el poder judicial*⟩. This issue can be solved only by introducing anaphora resolution techniques which involves processing on a super-sentence level. Although seemingly feasible, this modification will necessarily slow down the extraction speed which is critical while working with large scale corpora. As mentioned in Section 2, high speed performance is one of the main advantages of the approach to Open IE based on syntactis constraints compared to the others. Hence, any modifications that would affect its speed should be considered with caution.

Another language dependent limitation is related to the order of the processing. As earlier described in Section 3.1, an extracted triple is expected to correspond semantically to ⟨*agent/experiencer*; *relation*; *general object/circumstance*⟩. This is expected to be correct for a direct word order, i.e., Subject – Verb – (Indirect) Object, which is a dominant word order for Spanish. Yet the inverted word order, i.e.

(Indirect) Object – Verb – Subject (e.g., *De la médula espinal nacen los nervios periféricos*, i.e., literally *"*From the spinal cord arise peripheral nerves*"), also occasionally takes place in grammatically correct and stylistically neutral Spanish texts. However, the occurence of this construction is less then 10% according to (Clements, 2006).

4 Experiments and Evaluation

In this section we describe the experiments conducted with EXTRHECH system.

4.1 Experiment on parallel news dataset

We compare EXTRHECH's performance with that of REVERB, an Open IE system for English based on the same algorithm (Fader et al., 2011). Since these systems are designed for different languages, we ran our experiment on a parallel dataset.[1]

We took 300 parallel sentences from the English-Spanish part of News Commentary Corpus (Callison-Burch et al., 2011). Then, we ran the extractors over the corresponding languages. After that, two human annotators labeled each extraction as correct or incorrect. For the Spanish part of the dataset, the annotators agreed on 80% of extractions (Cohen's kappa $\kappa = 0.60$), whereas for the English part they agreed on 85% of extractions with $\kappa = 0.68$. For both datasets their respective κ coefficients indicate substantial agreement between the annotators.

Precision was calculated as a fraction of correct extractions among all returned extractions. We calculated *Recall* as a fraction of all returned correct extractions among all possible (i.e., expected) correct extractions. By manual revision of the sentences in the datasets, we made a list of all expected correct extractions. Their number was used to estimate the recall.

In contrast to REVERB, our system does not have a confidence score mechnaism at this point. To make the comparison between the systems appropriate, we ran REVERB extractor with the confidence score level set to 0 that means that the system returns all relations that match the rules, i.e., in the same way as EXTRHECH does. Hence, the systems were in equivalent conditions. The results of the experiment are shown in Table 1.

As we see, on a parallel dataset of texts from News Commentary Corpus, both systems show a very similar performance. Based on this observation, we can conclude that the algorithm suggested in (Fader et al., 2011) can be easily adopted for other languages with dominating SVO word order and an available POS-tagger.

System	Precision	Recall	Correct Extractions	Returned Extractions
EXTRHECH	0.59	0.48	218	368
REVERB	0.56	0.44	201	358

Table 1: Performance comparison of REVERB and EXTRHECH systems over a parallel dataset.

4.2 Experiment on Raw Web dataset

One of the most important goals of Open IE systems is to be able to process large amounts of texts directly from the Web. This requires high performance speed and robustness on texts that often lack grammatical and orthographical correctness or coherence. The study showing the approach's advantage in speed was already presented in (Fader et al., 2011). In this work we focused on robustness. We evaluated the performance of our system on a dataset of sentences extracted from the Internet "as is". For this dataset, we took 200 random data chunks detected by a sentence splitter from CommonCrawl 2012 corpus (Kirkpatrick, 2011), which is a collection of web texts crawled from over 5 billion web pages. However, 41 from those 200 chunks were not samples of textual information in human language but rather pieces of programming codes or numbers. We took out these chunks because they are not relevant for our research. In a real life scenario they could be easily detected and eliminated from the Web data stream. After this, our dataset consisted of 159 sentences written in human language. We will refer to this dataset as Raw Web text dataset.[1] Of 159 sentences of the dataset, 36 sentences (22% of the dataset) were grammatically incorrect or incoherent, as evaluated by a professional linguist.

We ran EXTRHECH system over this dataset and asked two human judges to label extractions as correct or incorrect. The annotators agreed on 70% of extractions with Cohen's $\kappa = 0.40$, which indicates the lower bound of moderate agreement between judges.

Precision and *Recall* were calculated in the same manner as described in Section 4.1. We compare these numbers to the results obtained for the dataset of grammatically correct sentences from News Commentary Corpus in Table 2.

We can observe that system's performence has

Dataset	Precision	Recall
News Commentary	0.59	0.48
Raw Web	0.55	0.49

Table 2: Performance of ExtrHech on the grammatically correct dataset and the dataset of noisy sentences extracted from the Web

not lowered significantly when processing "noisy" texts compared to edited newspaper texts. An interesting observation is that texts from the Internet are poorer in facts than the news texts. The number of expected extractions was manually evaluated by a human expert for both datasets. The ratio of extractions to sentences for the news dataset was 1.5:1, while for the Raw Web dataset it was only 1.03:1.

Now we will briefly discuss the issue arising due to various encoding standards used for non-ASCII characters, e.g., of *á, é, ñ*, etc. While applying Freeling morphological analyzer to the dataset, we encountered an issue that the sentences came in various encodings. As we mentioned in Section 3, Freeling-2.2 analyzer works properly only with ISO encoded input. Therefore, we had to convert each sentence from the dataset into ISO encoding. While most of the sentences were in UTF-8 encoding and were converted in a single pass, the encoding of about 3% of the sentences was initially corrupted, therefore, they were not processed correctly by the POS-tagger. Although the issue is manageable at the scale of a small dataset, it might affect the speed and quality of fact extraction when working at Web scale.

5 Error Analysis

After running ExtrHech on the datasets, we analyzied the errors in the output. We followed the classifications of the types of errors and their causes suggested in (Zhila and Gelbukh, 2014). The distribution of the errors in ExtrHech's output over the types of errors is shown in Table 3. The data about error types was gathered over extractions from Raw Web dataset. When errors are present both in the arguments and in the relation phrase, they are likely to have the same cause.

Based on the analysis of the outputs over Raw Web dataset, the following causes for errors have been observed:

- Underspecified noun phrase
- Overspecified verb phrase
- Non-contiguous verb phrase

Type of errors	Percentage
Incorrect relation phrase	21%
Incorrect argument(s)	45%
of them, with also incorrect relation	19%
Incorrect argument order	6%

Table 3: Distribution of errors in output by the basic error types in relation extraction for ExtrHech system run over Raw Web dataset

- N-ary relation or preposition (e.g., *entre*, "*between*")
- Conditional subordinate clause
- Incorrectly resolved relative clause
- Incorrectly resolved conjunction
- Inverse word order
- Incorrect POS-tagging
- Grammatical errors in original sentences

Inverse word order is one of the main causes for the incorrect order of arguments in extracted relations. However, as it can be seen in Table 3, this is the least common type of errors, which is in accordance to the low frecuency of the inverse word order (Clements, 2006). A more detailed analysis of the issues that cause the errors can be found in (Zhila and Gelbukh, 2014).

6 Conclusions

We have introduced an approach to Open IE based on syntactic constraints over POS tag sequences targeted at Spanish language. We described the rules for relation phrases and their arguments in Spanish and their implementation in ExtrHech system. Further, we presented a series of experiments with ExtrHech and showed (1) that the performance of this approach to Open IE is similar for English and Spanish, and (2) that ExtrHech's performance is robust on texts of varying quality. We also gave a brief classification of errors by their types and causes.

Our future plans include implementation of shallow parsing and syntactic n-grams (Sidorov et al., 2012; Sidorov et al., 2013; Sidorov et al., 2014; Sidorov, 2013a; Sidorov, 2013b), as well as learning techniques, and analysis of their influence on the system's performance.

Acknowledgments

The work was partially supported by the Government of Mexico: SIP-IPN 20144534 and 20144274, PIFI-IPN, and SNI. We thank Yahoo! for travel and conference support for this paper.

References

Honorato Aguilar-Galicia. 2012. Extracción automática de información semántica basada en estructuras sintácticas. Master's thesis, Center for Computing Research, Instituto Politécnico Nacional, Mexico City, D.F., Mexico.

Michele Banko and Oren Etzioni. 2008. The tradeoffs between open and traditional relation extraction. In *Proceedings of ACL-08: HLT*, pages 28–36. Association for Computational Linguistics, June.

Michele Banko, Michael J. Cafarella, Stephen Soderland, Matt Broadhead, and Oren Etzioni. 2007. Open information extraction from the web. In *IJCAI*, pages 2670–2676.

Chris Callison-Burch, Philipp Koehn, Christof Monz, and Omar Zaidan. 2011. Findings of the 2011 workshop on statistical machine translation. In *Proceedings of the Sixth Workshop on Statistical Machine Translation*, pages 22–64, Edinburgh, Scotland, July. Association for Computational Linguistics.

Joseph Clancy Clements. 2006. Primary and secondary object marking in Spanish. In J. Clancy Clements and Jiyoung Yoon, editors, *Functional approaches to Spanish syntax: Lexical semantics, discourse, and trasitivity*, pages 115–133. London: Palgrave MacMillan.

Oren Etzioni, Michele Banko, Stephen Soderland, and Daniel S. Weld. 2008. Open information extraction from the web. *Commun. ACM*, 51(12):68–74, December.

Oren Etzioni. 2011. Search Needs a Shake-Up. *Nature*, 476(7358):25–26, August.

Anthony Fader, Stephen Soderland, and Oren Etzioni. 2011. Identifying relations for open information extraction. In *Proceedings of the Conference on Empirical Methods in Natural Language Processing*, EMNLP '11, pages 1535–1545, Stroudsburg, PA, USA. Association for Computational Linguistics.

Pablo Gamallo, Marcos Garcia, and Santiago Fernández-Lanza. 2012. Dependency-based open information extraction. In *Proceedings of the Joint Workshop on Unsupervised and Semi-Supervised Learning in NLP*, ROBUS-UNSUP '12, pages 10–18, Stroudsburg, PA, USA. Association for Computational Linguistics.

Christopher Horn, Alisa Zhila, Alexander Gelbukh, Roman Kern, and Elisabeth Lex. 2013. Using factual density to measure informativeness of web documents. In *Proceedings of the 19th Nordic Conference on Computational Linguistics*, NoDaLiDa.

Marshall Kirkpatrick. 2011. New 5 billion page web index with page rank now available for free from common crawl foundation. `http://readwrite.com/2011/11/07/common_crawl_foundation_announces_5_billion_page_w`, November. [last visited on 25/01/2013].

Geoffrey Leech and Andrew Wilson. 1999. Standards for tagsets. In *Syntactic Wordclass Tagging*, pages 55–80. Springer Netherlands.

Thomas Lin, Mausam, and Oren Etzioni. 2010. Identifying functional relations in web text. In *Proceedings of the 2010 Conference on Empirical Methods in Natural Language Processing*, pages 1266–1276. Association for Computational Linguistics, October.

Mausam, Michael Schmitz, Stephen Soderland, Robert Bart, and Oren Etzioni. 2012. Open language learning for information extraction. In *EMNLP-CoNLL*, pages 523–534. ACL.

Lluís Padró, Samuel Reese, Eneko Agirre, and Aitor Soroa. 2010. Semantic services in freeling 2.1: Wordnet and ukb. In Pushpak Bhattacharyya, Christiane Fellbaum, and Piek Vossen, editors, *Principles, Construction, and Application of Multilingual Wordnets*, pages 99–105, Mumbai, India, February. Global Wordnet Conference 2010, Narosa Publishing House.

Grigori Sidorov, Francisco Velasquez, Efstathios Stamatatos, Alexander Gelbukh, and Liliana Chanona-Hernández. 2012. Syntactic dependency-based n-grams as classification features. In M. González-Mendoza and I. Batyrshin, editors, *Advances in Computational Intelligence. Proceedings of MICAI 2012*, volume 7630 of *Lecture Notes in Artificial Intelligence*, pages 1–11. Springer.

Grigori Sidorov, Francisco Velasquez, Efstathios Stamatatos, Alexander Gelbukh, and Liliana Chanona-Hernández. 2013. Syntactic dependency-based n-grams: More evidence of usefulness in classification. In Alexander Gelbukh, editor, *Computational Linguistics and Intelligent Text Processing. Proceedings of International Conference on Intelligent Text Processing and Computational Linguistics, CICLing 2013*, volume 7816 of *Lecture Notes in Artificial Intelligence*, pages 13–24. Springer.

Grigori Sidorov, Francisco Velasquez, Efstathios Stamatatos, Alexander Gelbukh, and Liliana Chanona-Hernández. 2014. Syntactic n-grams as machine learning features for natural language processing. *Expert Systems with Applications*, 41(3):853–860.

Grigori Sidorov. 2013a. Non-continuous syntactic n-grams. *Polibits*, 48:67–75.

Grigori Sidorov. 2013b. Syntactic dependency based n-grams in rule based automatic english as second language grammar correction. *International Journal of Computational Linguistics and Applications*, 4(2):169–188.

Stephen Soderland, Brendan Roof, Bo Qin, Shi Xu, Mausam, and Oren Etzioni. 2010. Adapting open information extraction to domain-specific relations. *AI Magazine*, 31(3):93–102.

Fei Wu and Daniel S. Weld. 2010. Open information extraction using wikipedia. In *Proceedings of the 48th Annual Meeting of the Association for Computational Linguistics*, ACL '10, pages 118–127, Stroudsburg, PA, USA. Association for Computational Linguistics.

Alisa Zhila and Alexander Gelbukh. 2014. Automatic identification of facts in real internet texts in Spanish using lightweight syntactic constraints: Problems, their causes, and ways for improvement. *Submitted.*

Improving Text Normalization via Unsupervised Model and Discriminative Reranking

Chen Li and **Yang Liu**
The University of Texas at Dallas
Computer Science Department
chenli,yangl@hlt.utdallas.edu

Abstract

Various models have been developed for normalizing informal text. In this paper, we propose two methods to improve normalization performance. First is an unsupervised approach that automatically identifies pairs of a non-standard token and proper word from a large unlabeled corpus. We use semantic similarity based on continuous word vector representation, together with other surface similarity measurement. Second we propose a reranking strategy to combine the results from different systems. This allows us to incorporate information that is hard to model in individual systems as well as consider multiple systems to generate a final rank for a test case. Both word- and sentence-level optimization schemes are explored in this study. We evaluate our approach on data sets used in prior studies, and demonstrate that our proposed methods perform better than the state-of-the-art systems.

1 Introduction

There has been a lot of research efforts recently on analysis of social media text (e.g., from Twitter and Facebook) (Ritter et al., 2011; Owoputi et al., 2013; Liu et al., 2012b). One challenge in processing social media text is how to deal with the frequently occurring non-standard words, such as bday (meaning birthday), snd (meaning sound) and gl (meaning girl) . Normalizing informal text (changing non-standard words to standard ones) will ease subsequent language processing modules.

Text normalization has been an important topic for the text-to-speech field. See (Sproat et al., 2001) for a good report of this problem. Recently, much research on normalization has been done for social text domain, which has many abbreviations or non-standard tokens. A simple approach for normalization would be applying traditional spell checking model, which is usually based on edit distance (Damerau, 1964; Levenshtein, 1966). However, this model can not well handle the non-standard words in social media text due to the large variation in generating them.

Another line of work in normalization adopts a noisy channel model. For a non-standard token A, this method finds the most possible standard word $\hat{S}$ based on the Bayes rule: $\hat{S} = argmaxP(S|A) = argmaxP(A|S) * P(S)$. Different methods have been used to compute $P(A|S)$. Pennell and Liu (2010) used a CRF sequence modeling approach for deletion-based abbreviations. Liu et al. (2011) further extended this work by considering more types of non-standard words without explicit pre-categorization for non-standard tokens.

In addition, the noisy channel model has also been utilized on the sentence level. Choudhury et al. (2007) used a hidden Markov model to simulate SMS message generation, considering the non-standard tokens in the input sentence as emission states in HMM and labeling results as possible candidates. Cook and Stevenson (2009) extended work by adding several more subsystems in this error model according to the most common non-standard token's formation process.

Machine translation (MT) is another commonly chosen method for text normalization. It is also used on both the token and the sentence level. Aw et al. (2006) treated SMS as another language, and used MT methods to translate this 'foreign language' to regular English. Contractor et al. (2010) used an MT model as well but the focus of their work is to utilize an unsupervised method to clean noisy text. Pennell and Liu (2011) firstly introduced an MT method at the token level which translates an unnormalized token to a possible cor-

Proceedings of the ACL 2014 Student Research Workshop, pages 86–93,
Baltimore, Maryland USA, June 22-27 2014.

rect word.

Recently, a new line of work surges relying on the analysis of huge amount of twitter data, often in an unsupervised fashion. By using context information from a large corpus, Han et al. (2012) generated possible variant and normalization pairs, and constructed a dictionary of lexical variants of known words, which are further ranked by string similarity. This dictionary can facilitate lexical normalization via simple string substitution. Hassan and Menezes (2013) proposed an approach based on the random walk algorithm on a contextual similarity bipartite graph, constructed from n-gram sequences on a large unlabeled text corpus. Yang and Eisenstein (2013) presented a unified unsupervised statistical model for text normalization.

2 Previous Normalization Methods Used in Reranking

In this work we adopt several normalization methods developed in previous studies. The following briefly describes these previous approaches. Next section will introduce our proposed methods using unsupervised learning and discriminative reranking for system combination.

2.1 Character-block level MT

Pennell and Liu (2011) proposed to use a character-level MT model for text normalization. The idea is similar to traditional translation, except that the translation unit is characters, not words. Formally, for a non-standard word $A = a_1a_2...a_n$, the MT method finds the most likely standard word $S = s_1s_2...s_m$ (a_i and s_i are the characters in the words): $S = argmaxP(S|A) = argmaxP(A|S)P(S) = argmaxP(a_1a_2...a_n|s_1s_2...s_m)P(s_1s_2...s_m)$ where $P(a_1a_2...a_n|s_1s_2...s_m)$ is from a character-level translation model, and $P(s_1s_2...s_m)$ is from a character-level language model. (Li and Liu, 2012a) modified this approach to perform the translation at the character-block level in order to generate better alignment between characters (analogous to the word vs. phrase based alignment in traditional MT). This system generates one ranked list of word candidates.

2.2 Character-level Two-step MT

Li and Liu (2012b) extended the character-level MT model by incorporating the pronunciation information. They first translate non-standard words to possible pronunciations, which are then translated to standard words in the second step. This method has been shown to yield high coverage (high accuracy in its n-best hypotheses). There are two candidate lists generated by this two-step MT method. The first one is based on the pronunciation list produced in the first step (some phonetic sequences directly correspond to standard words). The second list is generated from the second translation step.

2.3 Character-Block level Sequence Labeling

Pennell and Liu (2010) used sequence labeling model (CRF) for normalizing deletion-based abbreviation at the character-level. The model labels every character in a standard word as 'Y' or 'N' to represent whether it appears or not in a possible abbreviation token. The features used for the classification task represent the character's position, pronunciation and context information. Using the sequence labeling model, a standard word can generate many possible non-standard words. A reverse look-up table is used to store the corresponding possible standard words for the non-standard words for reverse lookup during testing. Liu et al. (2011) extended the above model to handle other types of non-standard words. (Li and Liu, 2012a) used character-blocks (same ones as that in the character-block MT method above) as the units in this sequence labeling framework. There is one list of word candidates from this method.

2.4 Spell Checker

The forth normalization subsystem is the Jazzy Spell Checker[1], which is based on edit distance and integrates a phonetic matching algorithm as well. This provides one list of hypotheses.

3 Proposed Method

All the above models except the Spell Checker are supervised methods that need labeled data consisting of pairs of non-standard words and proper words. In this paper we propose an unsupervised method to create the lookup table of the non-standard words and their corresponding proper words offline. We further propose to use different discriminative reranking approaches to combine multiple individual systems.

[1] http://jazzy.sourceforge.net

3.1 Unsupervised Corpus-based Similarity for Normalization

Previous work has shown that unlabeled text can be used to induce unsupervised word clusters that can improve performance of many supervised NLP tasks (Koo et al., 2008; Turian et al., 2010; Täckström et al., 2012). We investigate using a large unlabeled Twitter corpus to automatically identify pairs of non-standard words and their corresponding standard words.

We use the Edinburgh Twitter corpus (Petrovic et al., 2010), and a dictionary obtained from http://ciba.iciba.com/ to identify all the in-vocabulary and out-of-vocabulary (OOV) words in the corpus. The task is then to automatically find the corresponding OOV words (if any) for each dictionary word, and the likelihood of each pair. The key question is how to compute this likelihood or similarity.

We propose to use an unsupervised method based on the large corpus to induce dense real-valued low-dimension word embedding and then use the inner product as a measure of semantic similarity. We use the continuous bag-of-words model that is similar to the feedforward neural network language model to compute vector representations of words. This model was first introduced by (Mikolov et al., 2013). We use the tool word2vec[2] to implement this model. Two constraints are used in order to eliminate unlikely word pairs: (I) OOV words need to begin with the same letter as the dictionary standard word; (II) OOV words can only consist of English letter and digits.

In addition to considering the above semantic similarity, for the normalization task, we use other information including the surface character level similarity based on longest common sequence between the two tokens, and the frequency of the token. The final score between a dictionary word w and an OOV word t is:

$$\begin{aligned} sim(w,t) &= \frac{longest\_common\_string(w,t)}{length(t)} \\ &* log(TermFreq(t)) \\ &* inner\_product(vec(w),vec(t)) \\ &* \frac{longest\_common\_seq(w,t)}{length(t)} \end{aligned} \quad (1)$$

The first and second term share the same property of visual prime value used in (Liu et al., 2012a). The third term is the vector-based semantic similarity of the two words, calculated by our proposed model. The last term is the length of longest common sequence between the two words divided by the length of the OOV word.

Using this method, we can identify all the possible OOV words for each dictionary word based on an unlabeled large corpus. Each pair has a similarity score. Then a reverse lookup table is created to store the corresponding possible standard words for each non-standard word, which is used during testing. This framework is similar to the sequence labeling method described in Section 2.3 in the sense of creating the mapping table between the OOV and dictionary words. However, the difference is that this is an unsupervised method whereas the sequence labeling uses supervised learning to generate possible candidates.

3.2 Reranking for System Combination

3.2.1 Word Level Reranking

Each of the above systems has its own strength and weakness. The MT model and the sequence labeling models have better precision, the two-step MT model has a broader coverage of candidates, and the spell checker has a high confidence for simple non-standard words. Therefore combining these systems is expected to yield better overall results. We propose to use a supervised maximum entropy reranking model to combine our proposed unsupervised method with those described in Section 2 (4 systems that have 5 candidate lists). The features we used in the normalization reranking model are shown in Table 1. This maxent reranking method has shown success in many previous work such as (Charniak and Johnson, 2005; Ji et al., 2006).

Features:
1.Boolean value to indicate whether a candidate is on the list of each system. There are 6 lists and thus 6 such features.
2.A concatenation of the 6 boolean features above.
3.The position of this candidate in each candidate list. If this candidate is not on a list, the value of this feature is -1 for that list.
4.The unigram language model probability of the candidate.
5.Boolean value to indicate whether the first character of the candidate and non-standard word is the same.
6.Boolean value to indicate whether the last character of the candidate and non-standard word is the same.

Table 1: Features for Reranking.

The first three features are related to the indi-

[2]https://code.google.com/p/word2vec/

vidual systems, and the last three features compare the candidate with the non-standard word. It is computationally expensive to include information represented in the last three features in the individual systems since they need to consider more candidates in the normalization step; whereas in reranking, only a small set of word candidates are evaluated, thus it is more feasible to use such global features in the reranking model. We also tried some other lexical features such as the length difference of the non-standard word and the candidate, whether non-standard word contains numbers, etc. But they did not obtain performance gain. Another advantage of the reranker is that we can use information about multiple systems, such as the first three features.

3.2.2 Sentence Level Reranking and Decoding

In the above reranking method, we only use information about the individual words. When contextual words are available (in sentences or Tweets), we can use that information. If a sentence containing OOV words is given during testing, we can perform standard sentence level Viterbi decoding to combine information from the normalization candidates and language model scores.

Furthermore, if sentences are available during training (not just isolated word pairs as used in all the previous supervised individual systems and the Maxent reranking above), we can also use contextual information for training the reranker. This can be achieved in two different ways. First, we add the Language Model score from context words as features in the reranker. In this work, in addition to the features in Table 1, we add a trigram probability to represent the context information. For every candidate of a non-standard word, we use trigram probability from the language model. The trigram consists of this candidate, and the previous and the following token of the non-standard word. If the previous/following word is also a non-standard token, then we calculate the trigram using all of their candidates and then take the average. After adding the additional LM probability feature, the same Maxent reranking method as above is used, which optimizes the word level accuracy.

The second method is to change the training objective and perform the optimization at the sentence level. The feature set can be the same as the word level reranker, or with the additional contextual LM score features. To train the model (feature weights), we perform sentence level Viterbi decoding on the training set to find the best hypothesis for each non-standard word. If the hypothesis is incorrect, we update the feature weight using structured perceptron strategy (Collins, 2002). We will explore these different feature and training configurations for reranking in the following experiments.

4 Experiments

4.1 Experimental Setup

The following data sets are used in our experiments. We use Data 1 and Data 2 as test data, and Data 3 as training data for all the supervised models.

- Data 1: 558 pairs of non-standard tokens and standard words collected from 549 tweets in 2010 by (Han and Baldwin, 2011).
- Data 2: 3,962 pairs of non-standard tokens and standard words collected from 6,160 tweets between 2009 and 2010 by (Liu et al., 2011).
- Data 3: 2,333 unique pairs of non-standard tokens and standard words, collected from 2,577 Twitter messages (selected from the Edinburgh Twitter corpus) used in (Pennell and Liu, 2011). We made some changes on this data, removing the pairs that have more than one proper words, and sentences that only contain such pairs.[3]
- Data 4: About 10 million twitter messages selected from the the Edinburgh Twitter corpus mentioned above, consisting of 3 million unique tokens. This data is used by the unsupervised method to create the mapping table, and also for building the word-based language model needed in sentence level normalization.

The dictionary we used is obtained from http://ciba.iciba.com/, which includes 75,262 English word entries and their corresponding phonetic symbols (IPA symbols). This is used in various modules in the normalization systems. The number of the final standard words used to create the look-up table is 10,105 because we only use the words that have the same number of character-block segments and phones. These 10,105 words

[3] http://www.hlt.utdallas.edu/~chenli/normalization

cover 90.77% and 93.74% standard words in Data set 1 and Data set 2 respectively. For the non-standard words created in the CRF model, they cover 80.47% and 86.47% non-standard words in Data set1 and Data set 2. This coverage using the non-standard words identified by the new unsupervised model is 91.99% and 92.32% for the two data sets, higher than that by the CRF model.

During experiments, we use CRF++ toolkit [4] for our sequence labeling model, SRILM toolkit (Stolcke, 2002) to build all the language models, Giza++ (Och and Ney, 2003) for automatic word alignment, and Moses (Koehn et al., 2007) for translation decoding in three MT systems.

4.2 Isolated Word Normalization Experiments

Table 2 shows the isolated word normalization results on the two test data sets for various systems. The performance metrics include the accuracy for the top-1 candidate and other top-N candidates. Coverage means how many test cases correct answers can be obtained in the final list regardless of its positions. The top part presents the results on Data Set 1 and the bottom shows the results on Data Set 2. We can see that our proposed unsupervised corpus similarity model achieves better top-1 accuracy than the other individual systems described in Section 2. Its top-n coverage is not always the best – the 2-step MT method has advantages in its coverage. The results in the table also show that reranking improves system performance over any of the used individual systems, which is expected. After reranking, on Data set 1, our system yields better performance than previously reported ones. On Data set 2, it has better top-1 accuracy than (Liu et al., 2012a), but slightly worse top-N coverage. However, the method in (Liu et al., 2012a) has higher computational cost because of the calculation of the prime visual values for each non-standard word on the fly during testing. In addition, they also used more training data than ours.

System	Accuracy %				
	Top1	Top3	Top10	Top20	Cover
Data 1					
MT	61.81	73.53	78.50	79.57	80.00
MT21	39.61	52.93	63.59	65.36	65.72
MT22	53.64	68.56	77.44	80.46	88.10
SL	53.29	61.99	69.09	71.92	75.85
SC	50.27	56.31	56.84	57.02	57.02
UCS	61.81	69.98	74.60	76.55	82.17
Rerank	**77.14**	**86.96**	**93.04**	**94.82**	**95.90**
Sys1	75.69	n/a	n/a	n/a	n/a
Sys2	73	81.9	86.7	89.2	94.2
Data 2					
MT	55.02	63.3	66.99	67.77	68.00
MT21	35.64	47.65	54.67	56.01	56.4
MT22	49.02	62.49	70.99	74.86	80.07
SL	46.52	55.05	61.21	62.97	66.21
SC	51.16	55.48	55.88	55.88	55.88
UCS	57.29	65.75	70.55	72.64	80.84
Rerank	**74.44**	**84.57**	90.25	92.37	93.5
Sys1	69.81	82.51	**92.24**	**93.79**	**95.71**
Sys2	62.6	75.1	84	87.5	90.7
Sys3	73.04	n/a	n/a	n/a	n/a

Table 2: MT: Character-block Level MT; MT21&MT22: First&Second step in Character-level Two-step MT; SL: Sequence Labeling system; SC: Spell Checker; UCS: Unsupervised Corpus Similarity Model; Sys1 is from (Liu et al., 2012a); Sys2 is from (Li and Liu, 2012a); Sys3 is from (Yang and Eisenstein, 2013).

4.3 Sentence Level Normalization Results

We have already seen that after reranking we obtain better word-level normalization performance, for both top-1 and other top-N candidates. One follow-up question is whether this improved performance carries over to sentence level normalization when context information is used via the incorporation of a language model. Since detecting which tokens need normalization in the first place is a hard task itself in social media text and is an open question currently, similar to some previous work, we assume that we already know the non-standard words that need to be normalized for a given sentence. Then the sentence-level normalization task is just to find which candidate from the n-best lists for each of those already 'detected' non-standard words is the best one. We use the tweets in the Data set 1 described above because Data set 2 only has token pairs but not sentences.

Table 3 shows the sentence level normalization results using different reranking configurations with respect to the features used in the reranker and the training process. Regarding features, reranker 1 and 3 use the features described

[4] http://crfpp.googlecode.com/

in Section 3.2.1, i.e., features based on the words only, without the additional trigram LM probability feature; reranker 2 and 4 use the additional LM probability feature. About training, reranker 1 and 2 use the Maxent reranking that is trained and optimized for the word level; reranker 3 and 4 use structure perceptron training at the sentence level. Note that all of the systems perform Viterbi decoding during testing to determine the final top one candidate for each non-standard word in the sentence. The scores from the reranked normalization output and the LM probabilities are combined in decoding. From the results, we can see that adding contextual information (LM probabilities) as features in the reranker is useful. When this feature is not used, using sentence-level training objective benefits (reranker 3 outperforms 1); however, when this feature is used, performing sentence-level training via structure perceptron is not useful (reranker 2 outperforms 4), partly because the contextual information is incorporated in the features already and using it in sentence-level decoding for training is redundant and does not bring additional gain. Finally compared to the previously report results, our system performs the best.

System	Acc %	System	Acc %
Reranker1	84.30	Reranker2	**86.91**
Reranker3	85.03	Reranker4	85.37
Sys1	84.13	Sys2	82.23

Table 3: Sentence level normalization results on Data Set 1 using different reranking setups. Sys1 is from (Liu et al., 2012a); Sys2 is from (Yang and Eisenstein, 2013). Acc % is the top one accuracy.

4.4 Impact of Unsupervised Corpus Similarity Model

Our last question is regarding unsupervised model importance in the reranking system and contributions of its different similarity measure components. We conduct the following two experiments: First, we removed the new model and just use the other remaining models in reranking (five candidate lists). Second, we kept this new model but changed the corpus similarity measure (removed the third item in Eq(1) that represents the semantic similarity). This way we can evaluate the impact of the semantic similarity measure based on the continuous word vector representation.

Table 4 shows the word level and sentence results on Data set 1 and 2 using these different setups. Because of space limit, we only present the top one accuracy. The other top-n results have similar patterns. Sentence level normalization uses the Reranker 2 described above. We can see that there is a degradation in both of the new setups, suggesting that the unsupervised method itself is beneficial, and in particular the word vector based semantic similarity component is crucial to the system performance.

System	Word Level		Sent Level
	Data1	Data2	Data1
system-A	73.75	70.33	84.51
system-B	74.77	70.83	86.22
system-C	**77.14**	**74.44**	**86.91**

Table 4: Word level and Sentence level normalization results (top-1 accuracy in %) after reranking on Data Set 1 and 2. System-A is without using the unsupervised model, system-B is without its semantic similarity measure, and system-C is our proposed system.

5 Conclusions

In this paper, we proposed a novel normalization system by using unsupervised methods in a large corpus to identify non-standard words and their corresponding proper words. We further combine it with several previously developed normalization systems by a reranking strategy. In addition, we explored different sentence level reranking methods to evaluate the impact of context information. Our experiments show that the reranking system not only significantly improves the word level normalization accuracy, but also helps the sentence level decoding. In the future work, we plan to explore more useful features and also leverage pairwise and link reranking strategy.

Acknowledgments

We thank the NSF for travel and conference support for this paper. The work is also partially supported by DARPA Contract No. FA8750-13-2-0041. Any opinions, findings, and conclusions or recommendations expressed are those of the author and do not necessarily reflect the views of the funding agencies.

References

Aiti Aw, Min Zhang, Juan Xiao, Jian Su, and Jian Su. 2006. A phrase-based statistical model for sms text normalization. In *Processing of COLING/ACL*.

Eugene Charniak and Mark Johnson. 2005. Coarse-to-fine n-best parsing and maxent discriminative reranking. In *Proceedings of the 43rd ACL*.

Monojit Choudhury, Rahul Saraf, Vijit Jain, Animesh Mukherjee, Sudeshna Sarkar, and Anupam Basu. 2007. Investigation and modeling of the structure of texting language. *IJDAR*.

Michael Collins. 2002. Discriminative training methods for hidden markov models: Theory and experiments with perceptron algorithms. In *Proceedings of EMNLP*.

Danish Contractor, Tanveer A. Faruquie, L. Venkata Subramaniam, and L. Venkata Subramaniam. 2010. Unsupervised cleansing of noisy text. In *Proceedings of COLING*.

Paul Cook and Suzanne Stevenson. 2009. An unsupervised model for text message normalization. In *Proceedings of NAACL*.

Fred J Damerau. 1964. A technique for computer detection and correction of spelling errors. *Communications of the ACM*, 7(3):171–176.

Bo Han and Timothy Baldwin. 2011. Lexical normalisation of short text messages: Makn sens a #twitter. In *Proceeding of 49th ACL*.

Bo Han, Paul Cook, and Timothy Baldwin. 2012. Automatically constructing a normalisation dictionary for microblogs. In *Proceedings of the 2012 EMNLP*.

Hany Hassan and Arul Menezes. 2013. Social text normalization using contextual graph random walks. In *Proceedings of ACL*.

Heng Ji, Cynthia Rudin, and Ralph Grishman. 2006. Re-ranking algorithms for name tagging. In *Proceedings of the Workshop on Computationally Hard Problems and Joint Inference in Speech and Language Processing*.

Philipp Koehn, Hieu Hoang, Alexandra Birch, Chris Callison-Burch, Marcello Federico, Nicola Bertoldi, Brooke Cowan, Wade Shen, Christine Moran, Richard Zens, Chris Dyer, Ondrej Bojar, Alexandra Constantin, Evan Herbst, and Evan Herbst. 2007. Moses: Open source toolkit for statistical machine translation. In *Proceedings of ACL*.

Terry Koo, Xavier Carreras, and Michael Collins. 2008. Simple semi-supervised dependency parsing. In *Proceedings of ACL*.

Vladimir I Levenshtein. 1966. Binary codes capable of correcting deletions, insertions and reversals. In *Soviet physics doklady*, volume 10, page 707.

Chen Li and Yang Liu. 2012a. Improving text normalization using character-blocks based models and system combination. In *Proceedings of COLING 2012*.

Chen Li and Yang Liu. 2012b. Normalization of text messages using character- and phone-based machine translation approaches. In *Proceedings of 13th Interspeech*.

Fei Liu, Fuliang Weng, Bingqing Wang, and Yang Liu. 2011. Insertion, deletion, or substitution?: normalizing text messages without pre-categorization nor supervision. In *Proceedings of the 49th ACL: short papers*.

Fei Liu, Fuliang Weng, and Xiao Jiang. 2012a. A broad-coverage normalization system for social media language. In *Proceedings of the 50th ACL*.

Xiaohua Liu, Ming Zhou, Xiangyang Zhou, Zhongyang Fu, and Furu Wei. 2012b. Joint inference of named entity recognition and normalization for tweets. In *Proceedings of ACL*.

Tomas Mikolov, Kai Chen, Greg Corrado, and Jeffrey Dean. 2013. Efficient estimation of word representations in vector space. *Proceedings of Workshop at ICLR*.

Franz Josef Och and Hermann Ney. 2003. A systematic comparison of various statistical alignment models. *Computational Linguistics*, 29(1):19–51.

Olutobi Owoputi, Brendan O'Connor, Chris Dyer, Kevin Gimpel, Nathan Schneider, and Noah A. Smith. 2013. Improved part-of-speech tagging for online conversational text with word clusters. In *Proceedings of NAACL*.

Deana Pennell and Yang Liu. 2010. Normalization of text messages for text-to-speech. In *ICASSP*.

Deana Pennell and Yang Liu. 2011. A character-level machine translation approach for normalization of sms abbreviations. In *Proceedings of 5th IJCNLP*.

Sasa Petrovic, Miles Osborne, and Victor Lavrenko. 2010. The edinburgh twitter corpus. In *Proceedings of NAACL*.

Alan Ritter, Sam Clark, Oren Etzioni, et al. 2011. Named entity recognition in tweets: an experimental study. In *Proceedings of EMNLP*.

Richard Sproat, Alan W. Black, Stanley F. Chen, Shankar Kumar, Mari Ostendorf, and Christopher Richards. 2001. Normalization of non-standard words. *Computer Speech & Language*, 15(3):287–333.

Andreas Stolcke. 2002. SRILM-an extensible language modeling toolkit. In *Proceedings of International Conference on Spoken Language Processing*.

Oscar Täckström, Ryan McDonald, and Jakob Uszkoreit. 2012. Cross-lingual word clusters for direct transfer of linguistic structure. In *Proceedings of NAACL*.

Joseph Turian, Lev-Arie Ratinov, and Yoshua Bengio. 2010. Word representations: A simple and general method for semi-supervised learning. In *Proceedings of ACL*.

Yi Yang and Jacob Eisenstein. 2013. A log-linear model for unsupervised text normalization. In *Proceedings of EMNLP*.

Semi-Automatic Development of KurdNet, The Kurdish WordNet

Purya Aliabadi
SRBIAU
Sanandaj, Iran
puryait@gmail.com

Abstract

Recently, we reported on our efforts to build the first prototype of KurdNet. In this proposal, we highlight the shortcomings of the current prototype and put forward a detailed plan to transform this prototype to a full-fledged lexical database for the Kurdish language.

1 Introduction

WordNet (Fellbaum, 2010) has been used in numerous natural language processing tasks such as word sense disambiguation and information extraction with considerable success. Motivated by this success, many projects have been undertaken to build similar lexical databases for other languages. Among the large-scale projects are EuroWordNet (Vossen, 1998) and BalkaNet (Tufis et al., 2004) for European languages and IndoWordNet (Bhattacharyya, 2010) for Indian languages.

Kurdish belongs to the Indo-European family of languages and is spoken in Kurdistan, a large geographical region spanning the intersections of Iran, Iraq, Turkey, and Syria (as showed in Figure 1). Kurdish is a less-resourced language for which, among other resources, no wordnet has been built yet.

Despite having a large number (20 to 30 millions) of native speakers (Hassanpour et al., 2012; Haig and Matras, 2002), Kurdish is among the less-resourced languages for which the only linguistic resource available on the Web is raw text (Walther and Sagot, 2010). In order to address this resource-scarceness problem, the Kurdish language processing project (KLPP[1]) has been recently launched at University of Kurdistan. Among the the major linguistic resources that KLPP has been trying to develop is KurdNet, a

[1]http://eng.uok.ac.ir/esmaili/research/klpp/en/main.htm

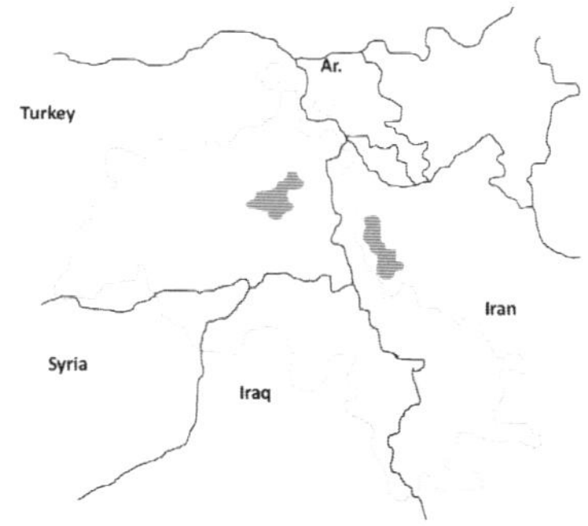

Figure 1: Geographical Distribution of Kurdish Speakers

WordNet-like lexical database for the Kurdish language. Earlier this year, we reported (Aliabadi et al., 2014) on our effort to build the first prototype of KurdNet. In this paper, we propose a plan to transform this preliminary version into a full-fledged and functional lexical database.

The rest of this paper is organized as follows. We first (in Section 2) give a brief overview of the current state of KurdNet. Then after highlighting the main shortcomings of the current prototype in Section 3, we present our plan to transform this prototype to a full-blown lexical database for the Kurdish language in Section 4. We conclude the paper in Section 5.

2 KurdNet: State-of-the-Art

In our previous work (Aliabadi et al., 2014), we described the steps that we have taken to build the first prototype of KurdNet. There, we

1. highlighted the main challenges in building a wordnet for the Kurdish language (including its inherent diversity and morphological complexity),

2. built the first prototype of KurdNet, the Kurdish WordNet (see a summary below), and

Proceedings of the ACL 2014 Student Research Workshop, pages 94–99,
Baltimore, Maryland USA, June 22-27 2014.

3. conducted a set of experiments to evaluate the impact of KurdNet on Kurdish information retrieval.

In the following, we first define the scope of our first prototype, then after justifying our choice of construction model, we describe KurdNet's individual elements.

2.1 Scope

Kurdish has two main dialects (Esmaili and Salavati, 2013): Sorani and Kurmanji. In the first prototype of KurdNet we focus only on the Sorani dialect. This is mainly due to lack of an available and reliable Kurmanji-to-English dictionary. Moreover, processing Sorani is in general more challenging than Kurmanji (Esmaili et al., 2013a).

2.2 Methodology

There are two well-known models for building wordnets for a language (Vossen, 1998):

- **Expand**: in this model, the synsets are built in correspondence with the WordNet synsets and the semantic relations are directly imported. It has been used for Italian in MultiWordNet and for Spanish in EuroWordNet.
- **Merge**: in this model, the synsets and relations are first built independently and then they are aligned with WordNet's. It has been the dominant model in building BalkaNet and EuroWordNet.

The expand model seems less complex and guarantees the highest degree of compatibility across different wordnets. But it also has potential drawbacks. The most serious risk is that of forcing an excessive dependency on the lexical and conceptual structure of one of the languages involved, as pointed out in (Vossen, 1996).

In our project, we follow the Expand model, since it can be partly automated and therefore would be faster. More precisely, we aim at creating a Kurdish translation/alignment for the Base Concepts (Vossen et al., 1998) which is a set of 5,000 essential concepts (i.e. synsets) that play a major role in the wordnets. Base Concepts (BC) is available on the Global WordNet Association (GWA)'s Web page[2]. The Entity-Relationship (ER) model for the data represented in Base Concept is shown in Figure 2. A sample synset is depicted in Figure 3.

[2]http://globalwordnet.org/

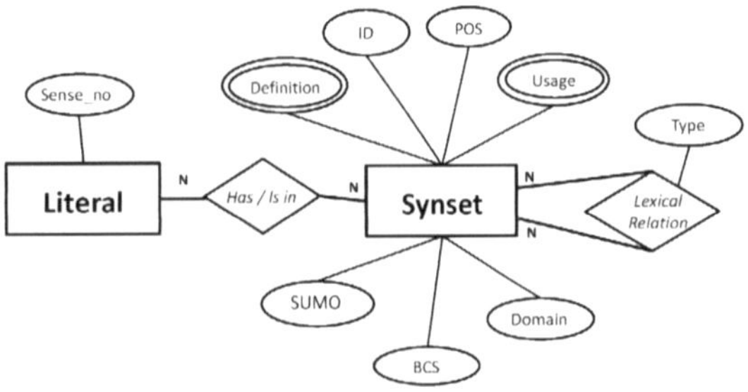

Figure 2: Base Concepts' ER Model (Aliabadi et al., 2014)

```
<SYNSET>
    <ID>ENG20-00008853-v</ID>
    <POS>v</POS>
    <SYNONYM>
        <LITERAL>shed<SENSE>4</SENSE></LITERAL>
        <LITERAL>molt<SENSE>1</SENSE></LITERAL>
            <LITERAL>exuviate<SENSE>1</SENSE></LITERAL>
        <LITERAL>moult<SENSE>1</SENSE></LITERAL>
        <LITERAL>slough<SENSE>1</SENSE></LITERAL>
        </SYNONYM>
    <ILR><TYPE>hypernym</TYPE>ENG20-01471089-v</ILR>
    <ILR><TYPE>eng_derivative</TYPE>ENG20-01245451-n</ILR>
    <ILR><TYPE>eng_derivative</TYPE>ENG20-08844332-n</ILR>
    <ILR><TYPE>eng_derivative</TYPE>ENG20-12753095-n</ILR>
    <ILR><TYPE>eng_derivative</TYPE>ENG20-12791455-n</ILR>
    <DEF>cast off hair, skin, horn, or feathers</DEF>
    <USAGE>out dog sheds every Spring</USAGE>
    <BCS>2</BCS>
        <DOMAIN>zoology</DOMAIN>
    <SUMO>Removing<TYPE>+</TYPE></SUMO>
</SYNSET>
```

Figure 3: A WordNet verb synset in XML (Vossen et al., 1998)

2.3 Elements

Since KurdNet follows the Expand model, it inherits most of Base Concepts' structural properties, including: synsets and the lexical relations among them, POS, Domain, BCS, and SUMO. KurdNet's language-specific aspects, on the other hand, have been built using a semi-automatic approach. Below, we elaborate on the details of construction the remaining three elements.

Synset Alignments: for each synset in BC, its counterpart in KurdNet is defined semi-automatically. We first use Dictio (a Sorani-English dictionary, see Section 4.2) to translate its literals (words). Having compiled the translation lists, we combine them in two different ways: (i) a maximal alignment (abbr. **max**) which is a *superset* of all lists, and (ii) a minimal alignment (abbr. **min**) which is a *subset* of non-empty lists. Figure 4 shows an illustration of these two combination variants. In future, we plan to apply

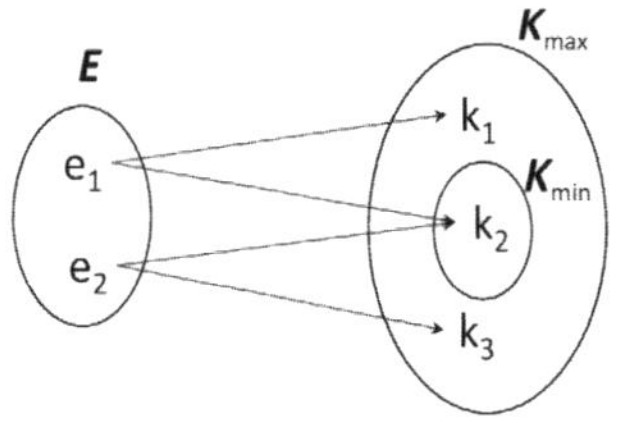

Figure 4: An Illustration of a Synset in Base Concepts and its Maximal and Minimal Alignment Variants in KurdNet (Aliabadi et al., 2014)

	Base Concepts	KurdNet (max)	KurdNet (min)
Synset No.	*4,689*	*3,801*	*2,145*
Literal No.	*11,171*	*17,990*	*6,248*
Usage No.	*2,645*	*89,950*	*31,240*

Table 1: The Main Statistical Properties of Base Concepts and its Alignment in KurdNet (Aliabadi et al., 2014)

more advanced techniques, similar to the graph algorithms described in (Flati and Navigli, 2012).

Usage Examples: we have taken a corpus-assisted approach to speed-up the process of providing usage examples for each aligned synset. To this end, we: (i) extract all sentences (820,203) of the Pewan corpus (Esmaili and Salavati, 2013), (ii) lemmatize the corpus to extract all the lemmas (278,873), and (iii) construct a lemma-to-sentence inverted index. In the current version of KurdNet, for each synset we build a pool of sentences by fetching the first 5 sentences of each of its literals from the inverted list. These pools will later be assessed by lexicographers to filter out non-relevant instances. In future, more sophisticated approaches can be applied (e.g., exploiting contextual information).

Definitions: due to lack of proper translation tools, this element was aligned manually. We built a graphical user interface to facilitate the lexicographers' task.

Table 1 shows a summary of KurdNet's statistical properties along with those of Base Concepts.

The latest snapshot of KurdNet's prototype is freely accessible and can be obtained from (KLPP, 2013).

Noun	Verb	Adjective	Adverb
Antonym	*Antonym*	*Antonym*	*Antonym*
Hyponym	*Troponym*	*Similar*	*Derived*
Hypernym	*Hypernym*	*Relational Adj*	
Meronym	*Entailment*	*Also See*	
Holonym	*Cause*	*Attribute*	

Table 2: WordNet Relational (Beckwith et al., 1993)

3 KurdNet: Shortcomings

The current version of KurdNet is quite basic and therefore its applicability is very limited. In order to expand the usability of KurdNet, the following shortcomings must be overcome:

3.1 Incomplete Coverage of Kurdish Vocabulary

KurdNet has been built as an alignment for Base Concepts and since Base Concepts contains only a small subset of English vocabulary, KurdNet's coverage is inevitably small. Furthermore, as it can be seen in Table 1, due to the limitations of the dictionaries used, not all English words in the Base Concepts (Vossen et al., 1998) have an equivalent in KurdNet. Hence the current mapping between WordNet and KurdNet is only partial. Finally, the lexical idiosyncrasies between Kurdish and English should be identified and included in KurdNet.

3.2 Refinement of Automatically-Generated Content

Each synset must contain a comprehensive definition and a practical example. While KurdNet definitions are provided manually and therefore enjoy high quality, the actual words in each synset as well as the usage examples have been produced manually. In order to increase the reliability and correctness of KurdNets, there need to be mechanisms to refine the existing machine-generated components.

3.3 Limited Support for Semantic Relation Types

As shown in Table 2, there are several WordNet semantic relations for each syntactic categories. Each syntactic categories are organized to component files (Miller et al., 1993). The most important semantic relation in WordNet is Hyponymy and this relation is the only one support in KurdNet (Aliabadi et al., 2014).

3.4 Absence of Kurmanji Synsets

Kurdish is considered a *bi-standard*[3] language (Gautier, 1998; Hassanpour et al., 2012): the **Sorani** dialect written in an Arabic-based alphabet and the **Kurmanji** dialect written in a Latin-based alphabet. The linguistics features distinguishing these two dialects are phonological, lexical, and morphological. The important morphological differences that concern the construction of KurdNet are (MacKenzie, 1961; Haig and Matras, 2002): (i) in contrast to Sorani, Kurmanji has retained both gender (feminine v. masculine) and case opposition (absolute v. oblique) for nouns and pronouns, and (ii) while is Kurmanji passive voice is constructed using the helper verb "hatin", in Sorani it is created via verb morphology. As explained in Section 2, the current KurdNet prototype only covers the Sorani dialect and therefore it should be extended to include the Kurmanji dialect as well. This would require not only using similar resources to those reported in this paper, but also building a mapping system between the Sorani and Kurmanji dialects.

3.5 Dictionary Imperfections

Dictio, the dictionary that was used for building KurdNet, is relatively small. We have recently discovered new linguistics resources that can improve the quality of automatic translation of English words and sentences into Kurdish and vice versa (see Section 4.2).

4 KurdNet: Extension Plan

4.1 Goals and Envisioned Outcomes

The main objectives and expected artefacts for this proposals are the following:

- to refine the current prototype, through use of intelligent algorithms and/or manual assistance.

- to winden the scope (i.e., including Kurmanji synsets), the coverage (i.e., going beyond Base Concepts) , and richness (supporting additional semantic relations) of the current version.

- to produce tool kits for users (e.g. graphical interfaces), developers (e.g., drivers and programming interfaces), and contributors (e.g., navigation/edition tools).

- to design and conduct experiments in order to assess the effectiveness of KurdNet in NLP and IR applications.

- to publish the innovative aspects as research papers.

4.2 Available Resources

Below are the Kurdish language resources that can be potentially used throughout this project:

- **KLPP Resources**
  – *the Pewan corpus* (Esmaili and Salavati, 2013): for both Sorani and Kurmanji dialects. Its basic statistics are shown in Table 3
  – *the Renoos lemmatizer* (Salavati et al., 2013): it is the result of a major revision of Jedar, a Kurdish stemmer whose outputs are stems.
  – *the Pewan test collection* (Esmaili et al., 2013b): is a test collection for both Sorani and Kurmanji.

- **Online Dictionaries:**
  – *Dictio*: an English-to-Sorani dictionary with more than 13,000 headwords. It employs a collaborative mechanism for enrichment.
  – *Ferheng*: a collection of dictionaries for the Kurmanji dialect with sizes ranging from medium (around 25,000 entries, for German and Turkish) to small (around 4,500, for English).
  – *Inkurdish*[4]: a new and high-quality translation between Sorani Kurdish and English.
  – *English Kurdish Translation*[5]: especially can translate words in Kurmanji and English together.
  – *Freelang*[6]:supports 4000 words in kurmanji.
  – *Glosbe*[7]: is a multilingual dictionary, that includes Soranii, Kurmanj, and English .
  – *Globalglossary*[8] is a Kurdish-English dictionary.

[3]Within KLPP, our focus has been on Sorani and Kurmanji which are the two most widely-spoken and closely-related dialects (Haig and Matras, 2002; Walther and Sagot, 2010).

[4]http://www.inkurdish.com
[5]http://www.englishkurdishtranslation.com/
[6]http://www.freelang.net/online/kurdish.php
[7]http://glosbe.com/en/ku/
[8]http://www.globalglossary.org/en/en/kmr/

	Sorani	Kurmanji
Articles No.	*115,340*	*25,572*
Words No. (dist.)	*501,054*	*127,272*
Words No. (all)	*18,110,723*	*4,120,027*

Table 3: The Pewan Corpus' Basic Statistics (Esmaili and Salavati, 2013)

- **Wikipedia**
  It currently has more than 12,000 Sorani[9] and 20,000 Kurmanji[10] articles. One useful application of these entries is to build a parallel collection of named entities across both dialects.

4.3 Methodology

As mentioned in Section 2, we have adopted the Expand model to build KurdNet. According to (Vossen, 1996), the MultiWordNet (MWN[11]) model (Expand model) seems less complex and guarantees the highest degree of compatibility across different wordnets. The MWN model also has potential drawbacks. The most serious risk is that of forcing an excessive dependency on the lexical and conceptual structure of one of the languages involved, as (Vossen, 1996) points out. This risk can be considerably reduced by allowing the new wordnet to diverge, when necessary, from the PWN.

Another important advantage of the MWN model is that automatic procedures can be devised to speed up both the construction of corresponding synsets and the detection of divergences between PWN and the wordnet being built. According to the Expand model, the aim is to build, whenever possible, Kurdish synsets which are synonymous (semantically correspondent) with the PWN synsets. The second strategy is based on Kurdish-to-English translations. For each sense of a Kurdish word K, we look for a PWN synset S including at least one English translation of K and a link between K and S is established (Pianta et al., 2002).

For the correct alignment of Sorani and Kurmanji synsets, we propose to use three complementary approaches:

- use of English (here, Base Concepts) synsets as reference points between both dictionary-translated synsets of Sorani and Kurmanji.

[9]http://ckb.wikipedia.org/
[10]http://ku.wikipedia.org/
[11]http://multiwordnet.fbk.eu/

English	Sorani	Kurmanji
word1	*S-translation1*	*K-translation1*
word2	*S-translation2*	*K-translation2*
word3		*K-translation3*
word4	*S-translation4*	
word5		

Table 4: English-Sorani and English-Kurmanji dictionaries structure

  The results would be structured as shown in Table 4.

- development of a transliteration/translation engine between Sorani and Kurmanji, that is capable of matching closely-related words and synstes.

- For the cases in which, more than one or no mapping has been found, manual filtering or insertion will be used.

4.4 Timing and Logistics

Based on our estimates, we plan to carry out the research highlighted in this paper in the course of one-and-an-half to two years. To this end, a timeline has been prepared (see Figure 5). We believe that since the preliminary work on KurdNet (e.g., literature review, development of the first prototype) has already been completed, most of our resources will be dedicated to designing new algorithms and system building.

Moreover, in terms of technical logistics, we are hopeful to receive full IT and library systems support from the Science and Research Branch Islamic Azad University(SRBIAU[12]) and University of Kurdistan(UoK[13]).

5 Summary

In this paper, we underlined the major shortcomings in the current KurdNet prototype and proposed a concrete plan to enrich the current prototype, so that it can be used in development of Kurdish language processing systems.

Acknowledgment

The authors would like to express their gratitude to `Yahoo!` and `Baidu` for their generous travel and conference support for this paper.

[12]http://krd.srbiau.ac.ir/
[13]http://www.uok.ac.ir/

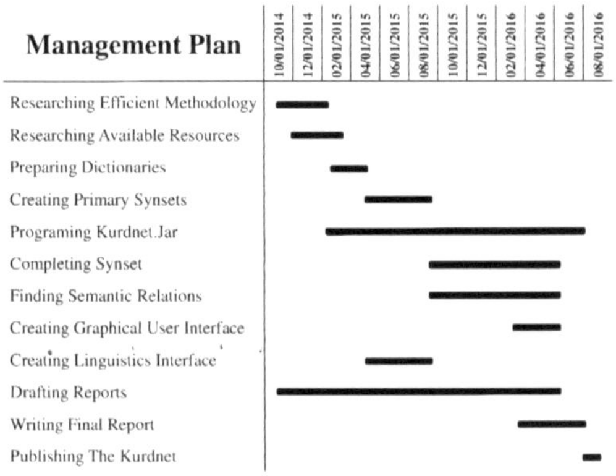

Figure 5: Management Plan

References

Purya Aliabadi, Mohammad Sina Ahmadi, Shahin Salavati, and Kyumars Sheykh Esmaili. 2014. Towards Building KurdNet, the Kurdish WordNet. In *Proceedings of the 7th Global WordNet Conference (GWC'14)*, pages 1–6.

Richard Beckwith, George A. Miller, and Randee Tengi. 1993. Design and Implementation of the WordNet Lexical Database and Searching Software. In Christiane Fellbaum, editor, *WordNet: An Electronic Lexical Database*. MIT Press.

Pushpak Bhattacharyya. 2010. IndoWordNet. In *Proceedings of the 7th International Conference on Language Resources and Evaluation (LREC'10)*.

Kyumars Sheykh Esmaili and Shahin Salavati. 2013. Sorani Kurdish versus Kurmanji Kurdish: An Empirical Comparison. In *Proceedings of the 51st Annual Meeting of the Association for Computational Linguistics (ACL'13)*, pages 300–305.

Kyumars Sheykh Esmaili, Shahin Salavati, and Anwitaman Datta. 2013a. Towards Kurdish Information Retrieval. *ACM Transactions on Asian Language Information Processing (TALIP)*, To Appear.

Kyumars Sheykh Esmaili, Shahin Salavati, Somayeh Yosefi, Donya Eliassi, Purya Aliabadi, Shownem Hakimi, and Asrin Mohammadi. 2013b. Building a Test Collection for Sorani Kurdish. In *Proceedings of the 10th IEEE/ACS International Conference on Computer Systems and Applications (AICCSA '13)*.

Christiane Fellbaum. 2010. *WordNet*. Springer.

Tiziano Flati and Roberto Navigli. 2012. The CQC Algorithm: Cycling in Graphs to Semantically Enrich and Enhance a Bilingual Dictionary. *Journal of Artificial Intelligence Research*, 43(1):135–171.

Gérard Gautier. 1998. Building a Kurdish Language Corpus: An Overview of the Technical Problems. In *Proceedings of ICEMCO*.

Goeffrey Haig and Yaron Matras. 2002. Kurdish Linguistics: A Brief Overview. *Language Typology and Universals*, 55(1).

Amir Hassanpour, Jaffer Sheyholislami, and Tove Skutnabb-Kangas. 2012. Introduction. Kurdish: Linguicide, Resistance and Hope. *International Journal of the Sociology of Language*, 217:1–8.

KLPP. 2013. KurdNet's Download Page. Available at: `https://github.com/klpp/kurdnet`.

David N. MacKenzie. 1961. *Kurdish Dialect Studies*. Oxford University Press.

George A. Miller, Richard Beckwith, Christiane Fellbaum, Derek Gross, and Katherine Miller. 1993. Introduction to WordNet: An On-line Lexical Database. In Christiane Fellbaum, editor, *WordNet: An Electronic Lexical Database*. MIT Press.

Emanuele Pianta, Luisa Bentivogli, and Christian Girardi. 2002. Developing an Aligned Multilingual Database. In *Proceedings of the 1st Conference on Global WordNet (GWC'02)*.

Shahin Salavati, Kyumars Sheykh Esmaili, and Fardin Akhlaghian. 2013. Stemming for Kurdish Information Retrieval. In *The Proceeding (to appear) of the 9th Asian Information Retrieval Societies Conference (AIRS 2013)*.

Dan Tufis, Dan Cristea, and Sofia Stamou. 2004. BalkaNet: Aims, Methods, Results and Perspectives. A General Overview. *Romanian Journal of Information science and technology*, 7(1-2):9–43.

Piek Vossen, Laura Bloksma, Horacio Rodriguez, Salvador Climent, Nicoletta Calzolari, Adriana Roventini, Francesca Bertagna, Antonietta Alonge, and Wim Peters. 1998. The EuroWordNet Base Concepts and Top Ontology. *Deliverable D017 D*, 34:D036.

Piek Vossen. 1996. Right or Wrong: Combining Lexical Resources in the EuroWordNet Project. In *EURALEX*, volume 96, pages 715–728.

Piek Vossen. 1998. Introduction to EuroWordNet. *Computers and the Humanities*, 32(2-3):73–89.

Géraldine Walther and Benoît Sagot. 2010. Developing a Large-scale Lexicon for a Less-Resourced Language. In *SaLTMiL's Workshop on Less-*

Author Index

Aliabadi, Purya, 94
Attokurov, Ulukbek, 64

Bayazit, Ulug, 64
Beck, Daniel, 1

Gelbukh, Alexander, 78
Greenberg, Clayton, 71

Illouz, Gabriel, 34
Ilvovsky, Dmitry, 56

Letard, Vincent, 34
Li, Chen, 86
Li, Dongchen, 48
Liu, Yang, 86

Mirza, Paramita, 10

Rosset, Sophie, 34

Schütze, Hinrich, 41

Wu, Xihong, 48

Yin, Wenpeng, 41
Yung, Frances, 18

Zhang, Xiantao, 48
Zhila, Alisa, 78
Zirn, Cäcilia, 26